HEALING
THE
ASTROLOGER'S
WORLD

JACOB DAVIDSSON

HEALING
THE ASTROLOGER´S
WORLD

Contact information author;

www.astrojacob.com

e-mail: info@astrojacob.com

Copyright © 2017 Jacob Davidsson

Illustration: BooksOnDemand

Photos: Amanda Davidsson, Jacob Davidsson, Alexander Rosengren & Pia Stengard

Additional Participants: Tina Lundberg

Supervising editor: William L. Shaffer

Publishers: BoD – Books On Demand, Stockholm, Sweden

Printed: BoD – Books On Demand, Norderstedt, Germany

ISBN: 978-91-7699-756-7

CONTENTS

Foreword by Tina

Gothenburg 9th of january 2017

I remember it well, the first day, sitting in the livingroom, after I had finished listening to the tape.

I was shaken.

It was a beautiful day. Beams of light shimmering against the sky and not a cloud in sight. I went outside on the balcony and breathed the fresh air whilst gazing at the sea. The feeling that filled me was a deep sense of confidence. That finely tuned sensitive feeling that I could feel when I was deeply moved came back. I just stood there, I can´t remember for how long, until questions surfaced in my consciousness.

I went back inside and replayed the cassette.

As I finished listening a second time I noticed the tears. A gentle gratitude of tears came over me. I felt seen deep inside.

Then my intellect began to understand. Intellectually, my prejudices and my questioning were aroused. How could this be possible? How come? How could this astrologer pinpoint me as a person just by "some calculations of stars, houses and planets"?

Later that night I listened to the cassette for a third time.

As I sat there listening, I looked into the flames that burned so beautifully from the candelabra. I realized that my prejudices came from fear of what was unknown and beyond my own knowledge and needs of inner discipline. With this insight, I landed safely in a space of acceptance. I had no idea how astrology worked with Jacob's calculation of "all stars, houses and planets". On the other hand, I found it to work. Jacob had succeeded in the art of capturing me and my person exactly. He also gave me wise advice that was up to me to take if I wanted to.

That night, I realized that there were many ways to consider and explain who we are and the reality of the world in which we live and work. Jacob's astrology was one way. He had in a very humble and extremely respectful way revealed the nuances and differences about me that no one had previously succeeded in. I was moved, touched and even impressed.

It has now been 20 years since then.

To Jacob, I have returned when I have had questions in the hope of further clarity. His reflections and interpretations have offered me concrete tools that I have been well served by during the journey of life. He has seen and understood. And still today he continues to do so.

The book you hold in your hands is so much Jacob. A well-researched document that he gives off all of himself, his thoughts and experiences. Jacob describes the keys of astrology in a colorful fabric of humor, seriousness, wisdom and so much care and love.

Jacob, you give wisdom as an astrologer. The words you said on your first tape became a guiding star: a metaphor I have followed to make something really important to me. Thank you.

True Women's Power

As beautiful as the butterfly
Like sore and shine

It endures all
It forgives all
Does not create barriers
No walls build around their essence
Always choose the highest purpose
The noblest motive
Does not judge
Never seeks revenge

True women's power spreads caution
As well as limits required for their own sake
as well as allowing other spirits finding their Butterfly

Thinking, it´s not strange that the King´s mathematicians, scientists, astronomers and astrologers since ancient times around the world have placed horoscopes for their masters when they have faced any crucial or decisive decision. We can follow the astrology back to Jesus' birth and further, beginning in Babylon as well as finding it in ancient Greece to name an example. To me it is no wonder that our dear C.G Jung, 1875-1961, Swiss psychiatrist, psychologist and writer took the astrological knowledge very serious just like me.

Obviously, today's interdisciplinary science has so far missed something significant; To put astrology cn the map as a very important piece of the puzzle in understanding our inner being.

A warm good luck to you Jacob. Your knowledge as an astrologer is a gift to humans.

Your friend

Tina Lundberg

Foreword by Jacob

The end comes closer. Not my own, but the insight that the power and the energy of writing begin to decline. Today, 60 years young, I can look back on a long walk on my own country road. Today, I want to clarify the concept of astrology and try to explain in a simple and understandable way, for anyone to share. As a good friend said, I think it was Johnny in Gamlestaden, Gothenburg, in the 80's: "But then the purpose of astrology is not to need astrology?" Astrology's basic rules are simple and can be understood by the youngest children. For example, use a palette of colors. If you mix them they create new colors. The variants are endless. My simple ambition is to demystify the subject and provide a range of examples from life and the world today. Celebrities, politicians and historical people.

The need is not for my own sake. Possibly there may be some satisfaction in the background or a feeling of leaving something behind. I often ask others an ironic question: What have you achieved for humanity or your fellow human beings? - What have you built or produced that benefit other people? Not just your own children and relatives. Poor are those who only think of themselves. I have saved a quote upon my wall for more than thirty years: "You can never be happy if you do not engage in something that is good for other people."

I have tried to "save the world" in my own way, one person at a time, so to speak. Early I felt that helpfulness gave more joy. As far as ethical standards are concerned, my religious or philosophical curiosity came to be my carrot. I already studied in my teens many dogmas, religious communities, sects, spiritual teachers and approaches to life.

Nevertheless, I never felt really satisfied. Everyone seemed isolated and self-absorbed in their own little selfish perfection. "My truth is the only truth" went as a red thread. The only "teacher" who illuminated an overall view of life and the world was the Danish mystic Rolf Martinus. He is one of the few writers I can actually recommend. His books were called "*The Third Testament*".

I want to try to describe the big contrasts in life. Good against evil. Darkness and light. Negative and positive. Fear and joy. Love and hatred. Do not think you can understand one without understanding the other. Therefore, this book will not only be a relaxing and interesting read. I want to awaken, provoke, challenge, question and ask difficult questions. I think it is important with both political awareness as well as an empathetic understanding of all people's different living conditions and individual karma.

I'm spontaneously referring to books, music, movies and day-to-day people in the world and you will find a source list at the back of the book. For example, I'm currently listening to the Wishbone Ash group from the 1970s and the song *So Many Things to Say.* It was really the song *Everybody Needs to Have a Friend* I wanted to hear. This song gives sweet memories of a romantic decade with love and an idealistic vision of Love. I will also spontaneously mention many people I met, but only use the first name for reasons of their integrity.

I have already written some articles online, which are on my website today, but they are mostly about astrology and you can share them in order to immerse yourself. Most of them I am relatively satisfied with. This "first" book will not be published online for free, but will be published for anyone to share and buy. I have no prerequisites to "work for free" and therefore have to charge for it. Today, we live in a world where much is "free" (illegal downloads) which affects poor poets, musicians and film workers. I have also received a request for an English edition and have already contacted a translator for this purpose. It will be exciting to see what effects this process will have.

Maybe even you get something to bring along as you can spread on. As my youngest daughter, when I mentioned that I was going to write a book, said: "But then it will not be just about astrology?" I was at first surprised, but then realized that she actually thought I could write about something else in my life? This gave me a grateful mindset and inspired me to deepen this need to carry on my own life experience.

I hope you enjoy this book and feel it makes you stronger and more convinced that we humans must change our way of thinking and acting before it's too late.

I want to try to pull my straw to the stack. This time around I became an astrologer. Apparently, according to various mediums, I have worked many times as teachers and tried to help others through my own insights. Now I hope to give something back to all those I have met and worked with in this incarnation. You are welcome to join me in an exciting, a little worrying, but hopefully inspiring journey on my own "road of life", a quote many of you are told at the end of my analysis.

"Love and Light I send today from Anebo".

For You

The idea of writing this book has been around for many years. In the beginning maybe out of pure vanity. You might want to become more famous or just be published. Other astrologers wrote books. But time was never enough. Later came the self-criticism and the doubts. Why write another book about astrology? There are already so many. Astrology's language with all its grammar is already available and the interpretations are universal, regardless of language, so you can not really write anything *new* about astrology.

During my more than 35 years as a professional astrologer, I've met over 2 300 clients and always endeavored to do my best. However, it happened several times that afterwards I discovered a sense of lack or incompleteness after completion of the process, or after a meeting with a client. I soon realized that some things were forgotten or that I should have stressed. I felt I would like to complete or continue the process and it was never quite enough even with the follow-up feedback call. In addition, I did not meet all the clients either. Perhaps a maximum of 25%.

The majority of clients have been over the years by telephone or by letter, although in the 80's and 90's it was common for personal visits both in my own home and sometimes in the clients' homes. I did a home-time visit, which was exciting, but at the same time it held a lot of unknown factors. I also remember that a couple of people who, due to their various disabilities, were grateful for my visit anyway.

During the 2000s, personal visits have decreased and it was a conscious strategy from my side. It takes a lot of energy to prepare and be with a client for two to three hours and some of these visits were not so successful. Sometimes I had to shower before, maybe dust the house, and be sure I was both relaxed and happy when the visitor arrived. Often the client talked more than I did, and it became funny.

With the Internet, things were both happier and harder at the same time. In addition, it was difficult and stressful with the technology if the client wanted to record the sessions. Now people communicate via email and gladly have a website that attract new customers. This can not only be complicated, but it can take a lot of time and effort. Nor is it free.

The driving force and motivation to write this book is simply to give you a little more. You as at some time have received an analysis, or maybe attended my courses, heard some of my presentations or just have been talking to me on the phone. My ambition is to give you a bigger picture of the astrologer himself while giving you more tools to use if you want to move on. My homepage today may meet several of these criteria, but it can both end or change form, so a book is more carved in stone, so to speak. You do not even need to have a good signal on your mobile or wifi to bring the book wherever you want.

The decisive decision grew in 2013 when I was unexpectedly asked to help with the editing of a book about my father's life. Jan-Erik and Gunvor in Alsjöholm had helped dad compile his diaries and old photographs from his long career as a cook steward on all the world's seas. I slipped in and suddenly got a chance to relive much of my own childhood and upbringing and this was obviously the start of my own process.

My hope is that this book will give you a little more perspective on both astrology as well as on life as a whole and the role of astrology today. At the same time, I hope to give that little extra of myself that I never had the time to when we met. I hope you can take the bad with the good in this book and feel that you get that little extra.

TIP: It's good if you have your own resources available when you read this book that offer you a definition or explanation of the different astrological terms and symbols because I can not go into every place and explain all these various astrological words and meanings. If you do not have such resources, you will still get an explanation in the chapter dealing exclusively with Astrology.

PS. Those of you who have ordered an E-book edition can also use lots of direct links to websites, music, Youtube, etc. These links are visible in the printed edition underlined with light gray or blue-colored text. This, of course, does not apply to the printed book.DS.

Love

"If I speak the language of both people and angels, but missing Love, I'm just an echoing bronze, a scary cymbal.

And if I have a prophetic gift and know all the secrets and have all the knowledge, and if I have every faith so that I can move mountains, but missing Love, I am nothing.

And if I divide everything I own and if I let myself burn on fire, but missing Love, I have not won anything.

Love is patient and good. Love is not fierce, not proud and not inflated. It is not challenging, not selfish, it does not mess up, it wants to do no harm. It does not find joy in injustice but is pleased with the truth. It carries everything, it believes everything, it hopes everything, it endures everything.

Love never ceases. The prophetic gift, it shall perish. Speaking in tongues shall be silenced. Knowledge, it shall pass away. For our knowledge is limited, and the prophetic gift is limited. But when the perfect comes, the limited will perish.

When I was a child, I spoke as a child, understood as a child and thought like a child. But since I became an adult, I have removed that childhood. We still see a mysterious mirror image, then we'll see face to face. Yet my knowledge is limited; then it will be complete as God's knowledge of me.

But now faith, hope and love consist, and the greatest of them is Love."

(First Corinthians: Chapter 13, New Testament)

" All you need is Love"?

One of the most difficult aspects of writing this book was how to put the different chapters in a logical order. If you ask the question, "what is important in life?", you can get many different answers. "Love" is not always the most common answer. Other possible answers include to have a purpose or objective in life, to be healthy. Interestingly, money was almost never listed as the most important. Yet if I remember correctly, employment was actually quite often in the top of the list. Not just having a job, but having a meaningful task. I've nevertheless had the request to begin writing about Love. It is, after all, the dominant energy we all aspire to and want to achieve. So, let's start with what almost everyone asks when they contact me as an astrologer.

So what do I feel is the most difficult and important topic today? Love. Love can be easy to give but sometimes so hard to receive and appreciate. Although I was lucky enough to both love and be loved many times, often the feelings of sadness and some sort of personal lack always slams under the surface. I have read lots of books about love, sex and relationship problems, but I rarely experienced any complete insight and explanation. "Wonderful is short," you say and I have experienced a lot of endorphins. Unfortunately, you just seem to get a glimpse of happiness in a short moment. As a soulful orgasm, it's quickly over and you really wake up again.

Encounters in life

However, there are people you've met that mean what they say. Others may have an attitude of well-being, but more like a protection against attack. If you just smile, others do not feel threatened, right? But a relaxed attitude is hard to find. I must admit that my own attitude varied over the years. I have tried the "tags outwards", which was good if you want to be alone. One of my favorites is the "Clown." I understood early in school that you got attention if you were witty or behaved playfully. My Ascendant in Sagittarius harvested many successes, and I quickly gained popularity among the girls. "Wrinkles in the forehead" can give respect but also be rejective. I have only tested "Sad puppy "but never enjoyed it. Nobody loves a loser. It's all about signals we send out.

Childhood

If you analyze the concept of Love, then one has to look at the psychological factors that characterize people early in life. You have probably seen a lot of examples of this. "Children do not do what you say, they do as you do". Already as an infant, Love is taken for granted. You feel warmth, closeness and security in someone's arms. If you feel uncomfortable you are screaming and getting help. (There are many adults still using this strategy). How the process progresses is primarily up to the respective parent. If you ignore the child early then you create consequences. Overprotecting leads to completely other consequences. What I mean is that whatever you do, you create consequences that the child takes with him or her throughout life. Teaching your child *Love* is not the main objective. Security is probably more important for the growing child. Do not get me wrong now. The child requires through their signals a confirmation of their need to feel safe. Failing this early creates inevitably consequences that later on can be difficult to adjust. Here, negative experiences can quickly escalate into years of insecurity and create lifelong traumas, especially in cases of abuse.

I would like to reveal a conservative setting that might upset someone. I belong to those who consider the child fares far better during a longer period of basic security - the longer the better.

It's much better to grow up in family safety until you get curious about the big world. It's much healthier to slowly adapt among peers and get to learn cooperation, respect and community, without the parents' protective "help". Today, unfortunately, many parents often believe they must get back to work quickly, otherwise this will affect the household economy. Many single people have no other choice today. Already here I think a lot of insecurity in the child begins. You can sometimes also hear from others that 'it´s good for the child to be separated from the parent."

As a young person, one learns not only to "behave", but also to respect the opinions or wishes of others, which is not always easy if you get used to always getting your way. One must accept one´s role in the group and learn that everyone is different. Some people tend to be more quiet while others are dominant and loud. Already in school, new and unfamiliar behaviors are experienced. One will realize that one must either claim or disappear in the crowd. If you deviate too clearly, you may risk being chopped or bullied.

Teens

When you get into your teens and discover your sexuality, it gets even more complicated. One seeks *Love* but becomes misunderstood. Guys in their teens can be hugely childish and emotionally immature but at the same time sexually curious, which of course complicates the search for *Love*. The difference between *Love* and *Sex* is probably more difficult for boys than girls to understand. Believe girls are more naturally and spontaneously emotional, and here we find more examples of "unhappy love". The teens are probably the "worst" period in life for most, because you often experience the very worst "rollercoasters" in the heart. Today, the phenomenon of "sex" has had a completely different impact, which imposes unreasonable demands on ignorant seekers who only want to experience Love and proximity. I personally believe that many people bring their experiences from childhood and teens into adult life relationships. Either you get burned and suspicious, or you can easily understand separations and failures. Regardless, I think the phenomenon is about human need to feel loved and feel that love affirmed. Here comes an ancient truth to use: "He who does not give will not get anything back in return." So you have to do or give something to get something back? Here you can reflect on the difference between egoism and altruism. In the end, it is clear that those who can not give love have a harder time to receive. This may seem like pretty simple maths.

Families today

Now, maybe someone thinks I'm not entitled to come with pointers. I who had married three times and failed. At least I have tried in several ways and always learned from my mistakes. I was married both "too young" and "too old". *"Love is blind"* and reality changes while living together. Sometimes you grow apart and sometimes you find things about your partner which are harder to live with. There are a lot of examples of how a relationship can break and cease: abuse, infidelity, lies, violence, insecurity, inability to give love or to show appreciation, bad sex life, poor economy and constant disappointments on themselves or their partners. Unfortunately, the list can be made infinite. Diligence in the nuclear family seems to be an endangered species, and today you will all too often find families do not have many children but the children have many families.

Love in the horoscope

Purely astrologically, it is a cauldron of different phenomena. Both Saturn and Neptune can occur, but usual y more involved during a love crisis. As a starting point, the most important trends may be seen through the Moon's position, because this shows our instincts and our basic needs and thus also our ability to just "show feelings" towards our partner. Venus's location is clearly overrated and certainly shows our values but also our own ability to experience love in different situations. You can both show and experience love in many ways. To your children, your partner, your parents, siblings, friends or colleagues.

As a rule, you always return to the question of basic security. If you do not receive love as a child, you do not learn to give or show respect yourself. If, on the other hand, you are "spoiled" and getting everything you're pointing to, there is the risk of becoming self-sufficient and demanding in your adult relationship. Overprotection can be as destructive as emotional rejection. Unfortunately, I have met several adults who do not meet the very least demands of loving parents. One of the worst is the parent who has "obedient" and carefree children, according to themselves. Here we can talk about future visits to the child psychologists. In fact, children need both liberation and to train their own will to mature as independent individuals. The umbilical cord may be tough sometimes ...

For me, I think *Love* is a hard work. My own experiences have nevertheless taught me something. If you are "young and stupid", you can not be expected to succeed in everything you do and resistance and demands are, of course, more difficult to master. As a little older, you may still struggle and stand a little longer with worries and problems, but if the relationship does not work whatsoever, perhaps you may realize its limit to the end. I have nevertheless never lost my faith in *Love*. Today I'm still an innocent or hopeless romantic and open to once again experience romance and love, even if, with the right of age, you have of course other priorities and needs. As I said, in my world, love is still a matter of a "hard" work. You must be alert and especially to signals from the partner. One must be responsive, able to listen, show your support, advice, encourage, inspire and show your appreciation with both praise and hugs. But one must also dare to question and set demands without threat of reprisals or revenge. I think it is as important to understand as how one´s sex life works. Unfortunately, I think just sex can be one of several reasons why relationships deteriorate.

However, perhaps the biggest reason why a relationship is deteriorating is that you can not talk to or understand each other. Read an investigation already in the 80's where it was found that the inability to speak to one another was the biggest reason for relationship breakups - larger than bad economy, infidelity or bad sex life. Talking about "being able to talk" with each other, I remember a comic comment about sex. "I would like to have sex with her, but what should we talk about afterwards?"

I do not want to say I know what *Love* is, but through my own experiences, and through many books I have read, I have learned at least that whoever does not give does not gain either. One could say that the degree of generosity and honesty determines your ability to give and gain. Stingy, demanding people neither get nor give. (*"Rulers make bad lovers."* from *"Gold dust woman "* by Fleetwood Mac). Venus combination with both the Moon and Jupiter is often a hint of a high moral and a good heart. As of course, the Moon's own location and aspects show your ability.

Unfortunately, unrequited Love is perhaps the most painful and most common of phenomena, especially to suffer from longing for confirmation of love or of one's lovability. (*Love Hurts* – Nazareth 1976). That he or she will only see me or understand that I am there. Not daring or being able to show love is not only depressing and frustrating without even a cause for both mental as well as physical vigilance. The location of the moon in your natal chart can illuminate this pattern in your life. But it can also be a transient process that can lead to unnecessary suffering. The dreamy illusion of Neptune has to be studied both in the birth chart and in the ongoing process.

Knowing that you have a sensitive Moon with some contact with Neptune, Saturn or Uranus, is the risk, the more you can become sad and hurt (for example, through a mistake of judgment or perception). You may imagine something that makes you behave differently than if you saw or understood the situation in another way.

My experience is that especially Neptune's contact with Venus, both in the birth chart and during a transient process, can trigger a lot of suffering, bringing tears, loneliness and self-damaging illusions.

Neptune both fools us and gives us false hopes because it shows the ideal state of your experience, and when reality catches up, the glow drops and the dust is seen everywhere. That is, the "bad" sides of the object that you never saw under the Neptune veil. ("*I´m not in love*" – 10cc 1975)

I must also point out that just the contact between Venus and Neptune can lead to a celestial sweet experience based on both spirit and empathy. If this is confirmed, one can achieve an optimal Love. Unfortunately, when the opposing party does not live up to this ideal, the disappointment will unfortunately increase. I often call this effect the "Cinderella Syndrome". This higher octave of Love occurs very often in the charts of musicians and composers. (Pavarotti, Leonard Cohen, Ulf Lundell).

Relationships

Why doesn´t my relationship work? Is it my fault or my partner? These are some of the most common questions I have received. Here you must not only take great care, but also try to bring all the puzzle pieces into the relationship. Some of these puzzle pieces include economy, practical family situations, your own as well as your partner's children in the family, possible illnesses or other responsibilities within the family. Earlier disease history may also be important to know as well as "tragic childhood" histories and more.

I can be very strict and careful to ask similar difficult questions before I want to comment on the emerging situation. Then there is a big difference in comparing two natal charts (Synastri) and to note that it is only a temporary phase for either party.

Astrologically, it may be a little tricky to get out if problems arise from one or both parties. If nothing is found in their respective charts, there may be problems that may arise and that can be found in a process that will pass (during a Transit or Prognosis). Should it be a temporary state, this process can be described more easily and people can take advice by focusing on alternatives to solutions. The best thing about astrology is that you can see a kind of cosmic timetable over the phenomenon and therefore perhaps more easily have indulgence and be more patient.

Sun signs

Another prejudice I want to address is the vulgar platitudes of weekly magazine or "Sun signs" interpretations. For example "Are you a Libra, you should avoid Aries, and Cancer can never marry Capricorns". Yes, you hear how wrong it can be. Got to figure out these mistakes when I found out that I not only had my Moon in Scorpio, even though I was a Leo, but also the sensitive Venus in Cancer and my Mars in Pisces. That is, there are many different aspects to consider and you should preferably have two complete maps to compare them objectively.

However, there are a number of points that could inhibit or frustrate a relationship and there are unfortunately no perfect relations. For example, if you have your Moon or Venus in contact with your partners Mars, Saturn or Uranus, you may experience some discomfort in some situations. Uranus's contact with the partner's Venus is also a perfect indicator of amorous excitement and it can mean a strong attraction, but the risk is that it will pass quicker. It takes some stability and reason for this combination to last.

A rule of thumb in relation analysis is otherwise to see how many common denominations you have, that is, how many planets or aspects are tangent points in the partner's map. Dare to say that there must be at least one pair of contacts to trigger a magnetic attraction. Missing these, you may have been attracted to external attributes, such as the body, the face, or even worse, the social status(The person is rich or successful). Another perhaps neglected rule of thumb is also the previously mentioned ability or inability to communicate. A difficult or completely unaspected Mercury may mean that you can not express yourself or simply do not speak the same language

A combination that you may not think of directly is the purely physical interaction. Here, attention is paid mainly to the contacts of the Sun but also to the delicate Mars. This can also be perceived as pure sexual attraction, which may not be the most important at the beginning of a relationship.

Kim Ung-yong

One or more contacts with the partner's Mars may admittedly show sexual attraction but incorrectly channeled even on the tendency to conflict or disagreement. A comical effect seems to be that the more combinations between the persons, the more fruitful they appear to be.

I read many years ago an article about a couple from South Korea who got in touch via a third person. They happened to be born the same day and they had many children, but it was fascinating that one of the sons was extremely talented. Kim Ung-yong was a child with over 210 in IQ at the age of 4. He could read and speak several languages already in school age and be ready with the university in the 10's, if I remember correctly. You can read about him on *wikipedia*. He solved quantum physics in his teens and finally realized that once he had learned everything, there was only one difficult challenge left. Writing poems ...

Sex

Yes, everything connects. Love, sex, pregnancy, childbirth and death.

Purely astrologically there is lots to analyze. It's not enough to have Mars in Scorpio for a strong sexuality. Feelings must be included in the picture and mutual sympathy or attraction. To produce children is, of course, nice, otherwise nobody would have sex. The problem is perhaps more today that many people use sexuality in many different ways, such as manipulation, attraction or to enjoy benefits. You can say a little cynically that sex is a product you can negotiate with. Sexual abuse has become a new kind of "disease" today. This may or may not be typical for the times we are living.

Pornography

The pure pornographic part of sexuality is a tragic piece of art. Certainly, single, disabled, or inhibited people may be entitled to sex, and there is a supply that today is gigantic, namely via the Internet. But especially the exploitation of women and children today is not only tragic but degrading. Low morality succumbs to making money, and even in TV humans degrade themselves to create interest and attract viewers. I can´t help but comment on, for example, "Paradise Hotel" which, in my opinion, is on the verge of a degenerative display of banal stereotypes and caricatures. The men must have sixpack abdomens, well-developed biceps and be sunburnt with Pepsodent-smiles and look like pure sex machines. While the female bimbos have to have *Big Tits*, minimal swimsuits and be tanned and also be able to manipulate, lie or gain benefits by being smart, (ie winning the competition.) Just imagine how many insecure teenagers feel ugly in comparison. I accidentally happened to see a section in an obscure channel many years ago and was most annoyed by the fact that this was on the best broadcast time for children and adolescents. It must have been between (5:00-7:00 PM). I thought spontaneously about all the young children and teens who might have thought that this is the case today, otherwise you have no chance. Don´t misunderstand me. I love sex and have enjoyed both my own and my partner´s needs my entire life. It has not only been the spice in my relationships, but more a kind of drug to enjoy, even if everything else in life goes to hell. What I am today facing and staggering over is the huge online net of pure porn. Yes, I have seen lots and educated myself to have an opinion. You don´t even have to pay to find all sorts of tastes today. Throughout, I have to say that it is most tragic. Both women and men pretend to enjoy each other. Again, I think of the risks that young people "learn" about sex through these channels. How many parents are watching their children's surfing habits or what they are exposed to? Here there are both animal sex and pedophiles, young and single-minded ones who humiliate themselves.

I saw a documentary about Linda Lovelace, who became world famous by the movie *Deep Throat* and it was a tragic story of abuse, beatings and humiliation. I have seen her chart and she was a fragile soul who tragically passed away too early in a car accident, just 53 years old. She was born January 10, 1949, a Capricorn with the Moon in Taurus (represents the throat). Yes, of course, I have seen this infamous movie and it was no elevation. Pure crap actually. Ed Wood made better movies. It was a phenomenon when it came to theaters in the US in 1972 and many celebrities just "had to" see this crappy movie.

Another phenomenon I want to mention is Viagra. Discovered by chance in research on cardiac medicine, I think, when it was discovered that patients got an erection, and of course it became the rescue of many impotents. Unfortunately, the popularity led to Viagra making normal people abuse the product just to enhance sex. And of course, it was exploited simply to make more money.

Sex is not just our need to reproduce and thus carry on our genes, but also it is an important essence in our most serious relationships. I am very aware that there are gray zones, ie, love without sex and sex without love, but living in a relationship today can be difficult regardless of the quality of sexuality.

LGBT or GLBT (LGB & T)

As for LGBT, I can not speak astrologically. I simply do not have that much experience with clients with different orientation to see some typical astrological trends. Also, I do not want to "reveal" any special codes that would suggest a certain position. However, you can easily find out if a man or woman likes the masculine (the sun) or the feminine (moon) side and that could indicate the spontaneous orientation. Indeed, there are actually masculine women as well as feminine men. However, I note that the transparency of LGBT has radically improved over the past 50 years. Sean Penn made an amazing interpretation of the real pioneer, the gay Harvey Milk in California. Harvey was Gemini, born May 22, 1930, and had the Moon in Pisces.

To "get out of the closet" today has almost become a bit comical. "Everyone does it" and celebrities reveal themselves on a regular basis. Sorry about my weird sense of humor. Obviously, it takes a huge courage to openly dare to declare one´s sexual orientation, even today. Historically, there are many tragedies given that not so long ago, it was illegal to be gay.

In historical terms, I also mention Edward D. Wood Jr., who was already known as probably the "world's worst director" in Hollywood in the early 1950s. He, however, made a brave and pioneering film about a guy who wanted to change sex and gladly walked around in women's clothes. The film is called *Glen or Glenda* and came in 1953. The film is wonderfully naive, innocent and humorous, despite the serious message.

Ed Wood was born a Libra on October 10, 1924 with the Moon in conjunction Uranus in Pisces (change gender?). Johnny Depp later performed the role of Mr. Wood in the movie *Ed Wood* from 1994. A quote from Hollywood: "When it came to making bad movies, Ed Wood was the best."

Another great movie is *Transamerica,* from 2005, highlighting a transgender's battle to change sex. The film was honest, serious and even comical, and it received two Oscar nominations.

The Pride festivals today have a lot of their roots in the 60's. Combined with an increased interest in meditation and Eastern mysticism, which many saw as a clear threat to the nuclear family, during the 70's when

Pluto passed through Libra, and divorces increased dramatically. As a subculture, pornography also exploded and many became rich overnight by exploiting mainly young naive women. Also stereotype, naive men of course. If you were unemployed or without school grades you could always be a prostitute or sell your big breasts to photographers or directors. The number of porn papers and porn movies increased and the censorship of course received moral panic. Prostitution is one of the world's oldest "occupations", but everything became "clearer" and more commercial, and many utilized these energies for their own gain. One example of this is the founder of the Playboy magazine, Hugh Hefner, an Aries with the Moon in Pisces.

Internet and Sex in the Film Industry

In line with computerization in the 1990s, the sexual exploiters found new ways on the Internet and new phenomena emerged. The number of porn pages online today is immeasureable, and the defenders point out that this is good for lonely and disabled people. But the question is what it "does" with young people with this increased fixation on the body and their view of sex. Today there are payment services where young people are forced to expose themselves inadvertently. Tragic is just the first name. The movie *Disconnect* (2012) addresses this in a good way.

Another terrible side is human trafficking. Have seen several unpleasant movies about this. Lukas Moodysson recorded this in the movie *Lilja 4-ever* in 2002. The 2007 *Trade* film is another very unpleasant example of how young girls are kidnapped and sold as sex slaves. Also, the commercial success *Taken* with Liam Neeson from 2008 addresses the subject. Today, we have seen several examples of perverse channeling after several disclosures about abductions, such as Josef Fritzl, born April 9, 1935, Aries with the Moon in Twins / Cancer (insecure Time). Even the newly-featured *Room* film from 2015 addresses this phenomenon.

Today, we have sex advisors and puzzles in all kinds of publications, and the newspapers also want to attract readers with "the best sex tips in the holiday".

A little odd example in the world of music: In 1969 in February, a lion strike was released as a bomb. In the song *Je t'aime ... moi non plus,* by Serge Gainsbourg, an Aries April 2, 1928 and singer Jane Birkin, a Sagittarius born December 14, 1946, it sounds like they are having sex during the song. "Absolutely not," Serge said afterwards, "then it would have been an LP, not a single."

Love & Sex in the Horoscope

Purely astrologically, this is fascinating. Although I have written some cookbook interpretations on my website, I would like to address a couple of typical examples. However, these must definitely not be read as stand alone features but must be seen in relation to all other aspects of your chart.

The Sun - the body

Body functions and how we use the body are usually seen from the characteristics of the Sun. A strong Mars increases both the ability and the desire while Neptune can both weaken and sometimes even eliminate the sexual energy. Neptune aspects to the Sun also provide an interesting link between drugs and sexuality, such as the possibility that certain aspects may increase lust but reduce ability.

The Sun's contact with the Moon sometimes shows which gender a person may be most attracted to. A balance can mean the popularity of both sexes, while a conflict can be traced to any gender if there is an imbalance between these.

The Sun's contact with Venus provides a softer setting and can be positive for both sex and emotions.

The Sun's contact with Jupiter may be a pure rollercoaster, for example, indicating a sexually sloppy or immoral attidue, or sometimes they take too easily what they want for themselves. Positively, however, Jupiter can illustrate a generous attitude to his or her partner's needs.

The Sun's contacts with Saturn can be frustrating. Here comes the demands and expectations into the bedside room and these people are more skeptical and suspicious of the partner. They really do not trust themselves or their partners and can develop a sort of control mania, most often caused by a lack of se f-confidence.

The Sun's contact with Uranus is extremely complicated. These people always want an escape route and are difficult to bind traditionally. Freedom needs do not have to mean worse sex, but emotionally they have difficulty compromising. Between two partners, a purely rebel side can emerge and strong upset occurs if either tries to manipulate or control. *"One night stand"* often becomes their the only solution.

The Sun's contact with Neptune has several effects. Sexually loyal or light-headed, because they may be weak for flirting and illusions, but emotionally very empathetic and self-sacrificing.

The Sun's contact with Pluto can be difficult to interpret. Often the person experiences that he or she has no control, but things are done without resolving the situation. Sexuality can be strong and a little dangerous, certainly challenging, with elements of threats, violence and abuse. These people can just as easily be manipulated as manipulate.

Moon – Feelings

The Moon's position and aspects to the other planets reveal both your needs as well as your spontaneous reactions. A weakened or passive Moon can lead to both inconvenience and fear of sexuality. An active Moon with strong energy can at the same time imply both indecent and irresponsible sex. Influence from the other planets usually reveals what is hidden underneath the surface.

Moon's contact with Mars can give an impatient and explosive sex drive. Irritation can flare up and disturb the enjoyment. Sexual experience can be reminiscent of compulsive overeating.

Jupiter's influence on the Moon may mean a generous setting, while pointing out a relaxed attitude with nonchalance and risk taking, such as taking on the attitude "who cares?"

Saturn to the Moon can mean fear for both women and their own feelings. These people tend to feel safer in the physical aspects than the purely emotional ones.

Uranus influence upon the Moon, on the other hand, produces a highly dramatic effect. These people ignite without thinking and spontaneity have no limits. The extreme curiosity and spontaneity can lead to both a promiscuous and light-footed attitude, as well as self-absorbed lust. Here we find the type "I do what I want, with whom I want." As for the more emotional love bit, this is an intense energy, but restlessness and sudden mood swings make a calm relationship virtually impossible.

Neptune's influence over the Moon is complicated as a daydream. Neptune, indeed, affects our imagination and inspiration, but the scratch of reality is too often led to broken illusions. Neptune People are perhaps very generous and considerate sexually, but they do not get as much of the enjoyment themselves. Assimilar to the Christian complex, where they consider that "it is more blessed to give than to receive". This influence obviously created the phenomenon "Broken hearts". Neptune people are not uninterested by sex but clearly have their ideals in other places than in the bedroom.

A completely different and unpleasant connection to Neptune is bacilli, infections and diseases. Even lack of hygiene may occur. Given that in 2016 there are about 37 million people in the world infected with HIV / AIDS, the link is clear. Here you can thus track how vulnerable or susceptible to infection the person is and also temporarily by a forecast see when you can be in the danger zone. These phenomena may exist at Moon's all contacts with Neptune.

Pluto's presence is not always so clear but often leads to confusion. Pluto's contacts with the Moon can give both phobias and irrational fear but also make the person both manic and obsessed with sexuality. Here we have sex junkies or sex addicts. The reason for these irrational behaviors often lies deep within personality, perhaps even on an unconscious level. There may be unpleasant experiences from childhood. When Pluto has control needs, jealousy and infidelity are other possible effects. Manipulative sexuality occurs as well as exploitation for own gain.

The perfect relationship?

In conclusion, there are no so-called perfect relationships, nor the perfect sex experience / partner. Nobody is perfect and we have all our faults and flaws. The astrological points may still point to what we should look into, and also to take into account our partner's needs and behavior. These thoughts were intended to give a greater and more tolerant attitude to both how you work and a better understanding of how your partner works.

Jacob's astro history

Everything started in 1972. In the summer I worked on a tankboat and the mate showed me late one night the planet Jupiter with its three biggest Moons in a binoculars. Inconceivable but breathtaking. That same fall, I began by impulse on a beginners course in yoga under the direction of pioneer Bert Yoga Jonson, later called Bert Yogson. After a yoga class, he started talking about different zodiac signs and guessed that I was Sagittarius. I said no. 'Then you must be a Leo," he said, and thus my interest was rooted, because he impressed guessfully on the second attempt.

A few years later I managed to figure out my own chart and discovered that I had my so-called Ascendant in Sagittarius, the sign that Bert first guessed. The Ascendant represents our externalized signals and all other external behavior. Bert thus had double the right.

Throughout the 70's, I searched for books on the subject. There was hardly any Swedish literature, but you could borrow a huge book at the library in Danish, in English called *The Great Astrology Book* by Derek and Julia Parker. It remained for many years my own little (thick) bible. The book was translated in 1974 in Swedish, and a new improved edition came out in 1991.

There were some Swedish books, including Ulla Sallert's Sun sign books, but it remained badly with Swedish books. If you wanted to learn more, you could always go to Näckrosen's bookstore in Gothenburg and take in the atmosphere. There you found a lot of books, mostly in English. In Gothenburg there were already several astrologers in the 70s, Roland Skogkvist and Roger Algehov, who were very helpful during my first years. Roland also started an astrology association that I participated in until 1984 when I moved to Småland.

At a seminar with the Gothenburg astrologers in September 1984, they had invited several famous names: Robert Hand, Donna Cunningham and Michael Lutin, et al. Donna has written a lot of stuff today, and I have read several of her books. Robert Hand has also written many books, of which "Planets in Transit" was a constant reference book for many years.

For most of the 80's I was also a member of S.A.R. - Sveriges Astrologers Riksförbund, which was a major forum for astrologers, where we met and shared experiences. I can happily remember Per and Karin Dahlin, Ivan Wilhelm and several others. If I recall right, the association dissolved in the 90's. However, there are many cassette tapes in my private collection left from several lectures in the 80's.

Ironically, I was not exposed in mass media until after moving to Småland in 1984, which reminded me of the expression "nobody becomes a prophet in his own hometown". The end of the 80's was intensive, with both courses for beginners, many lectures around Småland and almost daily clients. In addition, I read all night everything I came across.

The 90's became intense with lectures, many courses, invited guest several times in Radio Kalmar and in TV 4 where I was lucky enough to meet *Peter Jihde and Rikard Sjöberg*, who both later made a career in television.

After moving to Simrishamn, I tried to establish myself as an astrologer, but it was not easy. However, I met again at an event Bert Yogson, when he held a lecture in Simrishamn. Even my friend and medium Pia Palm from Kalmar gave a presentation one evening. I was also several times an invited guest in Radio Active in Ystad and met medium Carina Jeppson from Oxie.

Back to Anebo in 2002 I consciously spent a few years taking time off and now the web was about to become important. The new technology was difficult and I struggled with some different websites and began to communicate via email, something that I personally thought impaired the dialogue between myself and the client. Also, I began to avoid visitis here at home because it took a lot more energy and time.

Today, I sometimes feel lucky that most people do not know what they're missing. Astrology is a superb and unbeatable tool and had more people trusted their intuition or just been the least curious, I would not have always been overworked with jobs.

As for my situation today, 2017, when this book became available, I'm still fully up. But with five grown children, six grandchildren and both my parents still alive, I've had to adjust my life with a little less time for astrology than before. My family today with five cats and my old father on the same farm takes most of the time. The garden is my paradise but requires care all year round. Still feeling lucky, living in the countryside with my cats, 61 years old and will publish my first book. There will be more. You can take that as a promise. I can easily admit that I got a blooded tooth. I already have several books ready in my mind, one of which will focus on movie stars, musicians, writers and famous historical people with their respective horoscopes. The working title is already done; *Stars of the Stars* with the subtitle *Who are they really?* In addition, I plan to write more books on astrology and more focused on the future and different areas where astrology can be applied.

Hopefully, both an English edition of this first book, as well as an audiobook, will be available as soon as possible.

The future can look both intimidating and inspiring. For the part of the astrologer, it will probably be more of dialogue via the network, Twitter account for my "faithful" disciples, webcam and maybe even a daily updated blog, as well as a forum where you can enter and participate and "see me" live with a camera. Also planned are uploads on Youtube with my own lectures or astrological lessons. Well met in the new age!

Part 1 ASTROLOGY

ABC of Astrology

This part should not be seen as a textbook but more like a kind of dictionary of all the puzzle pieces.

Signs

Aries	21 March – 20 April
Taurus	21 April – 21 May
Gemini	22 May – 21 June
Cancer	22 June – 22 July
Leo	23 July – 23 August
Virgo	24 August – 22 September
Libra	23 September – 23 October
Scorpio	24 October – 22 November
Sagittarius	23 November - 21 December
Capricorn	22 December – 20 January
Aquarius	21 January – 18 February
Pisces	19 February – 20 March

As for your zodiac sign, it's the position of the Sun the day you were born. Sometimes you can get close to the line between two signs. Then it may be a mix, but with a little more emphasis on the sign the Sun enters. Sometimes even the day can vary from year to year, mostly due to the leap year when everything is progressing one day after February 29th. If you have your birthday after 29th of February, you will be having your "astrological" Solar Return birthday "really" one day sooner than usual.

If there is something I want to emphasize, do not put too much weight on the birth sign. Unnecessary prejudices can give wrong perceptions and you may have several other important points in other signs. The position of the Sun and aspects to the other planets is more about inner or spiritual beliefs and also describes more the physical body, and thus also the health. Psychologically, you also see the person's attitude to the male sex. The position of the Moon shows the opposite, that is, relation to women.

Here is a brief symbolic description of the twelve signs with emphasis on physical resources. Those of you who know that you have the Moon or Ascendant in their respective signs might probably recognize the descriptions as well.

Aries: With impatient force, they love challenges and efforts. Here we find many athletes but also police, military and doctors. The physical body is at the center and is often used as a tool.

Taurus: Tough and strong but not too interested in effort if it does not pay off. Sensual life connoisseurs and wise investors give a trick to business and all basic needs, such as food, clothes, art and entertainment. The body sometimes tends to swell the less they use it and this is often the target group for all diet tips.

Gemini: Like a butterfly on a flower bed, they flutter freely between both life-mates, occupations and homes. Physically, they are often on the move, but tend to tear apart and stress unnecessarily unless discipline exists. They may seem superficial but think more than they show. The mental talent makes them curious and social but they love to vary and can have some difficulties in completing all they start. The are the typical multi-task players.

Cancer: The person who is constantly seeking security, and a steady living can be a strain if they commit too much. Cancer people need routines and fixed income, otherwise life causes them stomach upsets and sleep disorders. They can show tremendous physical strength despite a sometimes unstable psyche.

Leo: Leos can seem both self-worthy and arrogant, but they want to take responsibility and plan for others. The driving force to decide gives responsibility and they are most comfortable as managers. Physically, they can burn out because of excessiveness and overconfidence. The symbol of authority sometimes has back pain and the heart may fail if they do not lower their ambitions. They are the born entrepreneur.

Virgo: These people can appear shy, but they often possess both a good heart and capacity to work behind the scenes. Physically, often both body and soul hygiene are important. Physically, Virgos tend to not be so active and can suffer from both digestive problems and internal diseases due to stress and anxiety. They are the most constant in highly detailed and refined work.

Libra: Librans are the diplomats in the company who love everyone and just wants peace. Physically, they tend to have problems with their weight if they are too passive. They should avoid drugs because the kidneys can be fragile. Obscurity is their worst enemy, but they are also highly productive and high when they finally make a clear decision. Librans will often win other people's appreciation. Loneliness is their Achilles heel. They represent the artist's soul.

Scorpio: Here we burst boundaries and obsessions where projects sometimes lead to extreme success both on the psychological and physical levels. Actually, they stretch on the limits of their ability and here are all activities that require courage and an ability to surpass others. Physically, they easily burn their candle at both ends and they do not meet the wall but rather pass through it. Scorpio is the survivor who easily gets remarried and is not afraid to start over again, with love, work or themselves. For good or bad, they become the expert in their chosen fields due to their obsessions.

Sagittarius: Here we have the visionary who lives to spread his or her insights but also wanders around the world to continually increase their experiences. Physically, they carry a large, basic capacity, although both overweightness and a nonchalant attitude can impair health. Hips and back need to be in focus when overloaded. The clown's heavy mind can occur in adversities in life, but optimism makes them last longer than many others. They are known as the entertainer on the stage of life.

Capricorn: Long-term projects can succeed if necessary discipline is accepted. As builders, designers and architects, they always have the ability to be both concrete and productive. The realist among us may seem stubborn but Capricorns have an inherent loyalty and solidarity that gives them both a good reputation and respect over time. Physically, they are very persistent and rarely waste energy on unnecessary activities that do not produce results. Knees and bones become fragile when overloaded. High goals can give high social status.

Aquarius: These are the reasons that everything in life changes. Aquarians never look back but rather look too far ahead and sigh over all resistance to change. They are always a little ahead of their time and constantly offer new options and opportunities for man to develop. Here we find both eccentric egotrippers as well as the barricade-revolutionaries we see nowadays in the many protests against the world's injustice. Physically, they are a little extreme and can live very spartanly. The body is really uninteresting to them; therefore, paradoxically, they are rarely ill. It's the thought that counts. Cramp states may, however, occur as well as various side effects of over effort.

Pisces: Pisceans are the dreamers and idealists who often lives in their own bubble but are always ready to sacrifice and forfeit everything for the sake of others. Martyrs sometimes, but often deep insights into life beyond and they love to create beauty based on their inspiration, with music, words or art. Physically, they are a little oversensitive and susceptible to infections and bacilli, and all forms of drugs and stimuli should be avoided or taken with great caution. The feet and the subconscious can be affected positively or negatively; therefore, they sometimes doubt and are often restlessness in adversities. They are known as the good samaritan or deep sea scientist.

The Planets and the Sun and Moon

The three basic symbols **Semi-Circle**, **Circle** and **Cross** form in various combinations to symbolize the planets.

Semi-circle or **half moon** - symbol of the Soul and feelings. The earthly personality.

The circle - symbol of the spiritual principle. The ultimate infinity.

The cross - symbol of matter and the physical body.

The Planets

The Sun: This heavenly body mobilizes our physical body: the heart, thymus gland, spine, cells and circulatory system. Psychologically, the Sun also represents the masculine principle, i.e., self-awareness, parenthood, the father, authority and organisation. Time-wise, the Sun represents life from the the age of approximately 20 onwards. It also symbolizes leadership, the ability to produce or create any kind of results, morality, ethics and spirituality-- the "God" within you. If the Sun is the body and your temple, then the Moon is your soul living in the temple. The Sun represents games, leisures, entertainment, hobbies, and sexuality. It also symbolises the right eye of the man and the left eye of the woman (in case of injury or vision problems). The Sun rules both Leo and the fifth house as well as the metal Gold.

Occupations ruled by the Sun include supervisors and managers, being your own entrepreneur, actors, artists, writers, musicians, dancers, youth leaders, astrologers, entertainers, celebrities, priests and public relations in television, movies and media.

Moon: The Moon symbolizes both the child (childhood up to school age and everything in the past – including our past lives) and the woman and the feminine energies as well as our feelings, instincts and drives, our needs and habits, our memory and the past. The Moon also represents our family trees. Sociologically, the Moon reveals "the people" in a country's horoscope. Also under the influence of the Moon are childbirth, menstruation, pregnancy. rituals and obligatory needs. In the physical body, the Moon symbolizes the cerebellum, the lymphatic blood, the left eye of the man, the right eye of the woman, the chest, lymph nodes, stomach, digestion, body fluids, ovaries and sympathetic nervous system. The Moon rules the sign Cancer and the fourth house. Its symbolic metal is silver.

Occupations ruled by the Moon include everything in care and daycare, school, old age home, hotel owner, hostels, nursing, fishing, boat building, sailors, antique dealers, museum directors, historians. The restaurant trade, body care, psychologists, therapists, the travel industry, archaeologists and midwives.

Mercury: This planet oversees thoughts and communication, siblings and neighbors, school time. intelligence, knowledge and intellect, the ability to learn and to pass on information. Mercury is called "the winged messenger". Today the planet is connected to all forms of communication, computers, cells and phones, daily shorter trips and transportation in general. Mercury wields its strongest influence in the three air signs, Gemini, Libra and Aquarius because they spread information. Mercury is physically linked to the arms, hands, fingers, nervous system, lungs, brain and intestinal tract. Mercury rules both Gemini and Virgo and the third and sixth houses. Its symbolic metal is Mercury.

The occupations under Mercury's influence include all professions in schools and education, newspapers, media, journalism, writers, shorter trips (taxi, bus, train) and transportation, politics, commentators, all aspects of teaching, lecturing, writing, secretaries, analysts, craftsmen, drivers, business assistants, telephonists, mailmen and speakers, bloggers, news brokers, webpages. Mercury is known for the desire to be free and independent, shunning anything that is sedentary.

Venus: The planet Venus influences beauty and balance, multi-level cooperation, partnerships, marriages, colleagues, coalitions, associations, aesthetics, fashion, art and creativity enjoyment, fun, money, values and morals, love and passion, rich and poor, luck and bad luck, teens and puberty. Physically, Venus rules the kidneys, the hormone system, arthritis, thyroid glands, ovaries, and ear-nose and throat. Venus rules both Taurus and Libra and the second and seventh houses. The symbolic metal is copper.

Occupations ruled by Venus include all businesses, economics, banks, insurance companies, basic needs (food, restaurants, clothes), hairdressers, beauty care, cosmetologists, seamstresses, receptionists, agriculture, gardening, flowers, builders, architects, sculptors, inspectors, jewelers, chambers, brokers, art dealers, bank directors, modeling, celebrities, diplomats and all public occupations with social status or attention.

Mars: The red planet influences physical energy and power sources, initiative ability, ability to work, sexual activity, struggle, sport, competition instinct, war, violence, threats and accidents. In the physical body, Mars rules the head, face, muscles, ovaries, testicles, adrenaline, red blood cells, kidneys, cuts and burns, weapons, sharp tools, fire, and the adult's optimal time of ages 20 to 50 years. Mars rules Aries, the first house and traditionally Scorpio. (before Pluto was discovered in 1930). Its metal is iron.

Occupations represented by Mars include pioneers, athletes, policemen, firefighters, physicians, psychologists, psychiatrists, butchers, the military, dentists, metal workers, engineers, industrial workers and trade unionists.

Jupiter: The largest planet in our solar system rules expansion, magnification, prosperity or success, optimism, visions, the willingness to spread knowledge, learning, philosophy, higher education, language, and travel abroad. Physically, Jupiter rules the back and hips, the liver, the mucous membranes, the brain bifurcation and glands that regulate hormone production. Jupiter rules Sagittarius, the ninth house and traditionally Pisces and the twelfth house. (Before Neptune was discovered in 1846). Its metal is tin.

Occupations under the influence of Jupiter include teaching, professorships, lecturing, philosophers, lawyers, interpreters, veterinaries, publishers, authors, librarians, bookstores, educators, politicians, reporters, media, priests, travel leaders and entertainment.

Saturn: The first of the ringed planets represents reality, limitation, concentration, time, aging, difficulties and crises in life, high status by patience, discipline, endurance, trustworthiness, ambition, responsibility and success after a long effort. Physically, Saturn rules the gallbladder, spleen, skin, knees, teeth, joint diseases and bone. Saturn rules Capricorn, the tenth house and traditionally also Aquarius and the eleventh house. (Before Uranus was discovered in 1781). Its metal is lead.

Occupations under the influence of Saturn include scientists, researchers, analysts, statistics, controllers, architects, archaeologists, lawyers, attorneys, public service officers, the publically employed, mathematicians, politicians, engineers, farmers, minerals, builders, administrators, all responsibilities in any field, directors, chiefs, organizers, ruling monarchy and presidents. Saturn people often achieve fame in their chosen goals.

Uranus: Discovered in 1781, Uranus is the first of the outer planets to operate partly subconsciously and partly on the collective plane. Uranus influences all change, development, progressive activity, modern science, technology, computers, the Internet, New Age, aviation, radio and mass media, spacecrafts, science fiction, the future, genius consciousness, odd and deviant behavior, originality, eccentricity and perversions. Physically, Uranus rules the circulatory system, the glands and the pelvic gland, the calves, the ankles, convulsions, paralysis, sudden nerve collapse and electric shock. Uranus rules Aquarius and the eleventh house. Its metal is uranium.

Occupations under Uranus' influence include inventors, scientists, sociologists, public relations, astrologers, astronomers, archeologists, UN workers, adventurers, globetrotters, loners, freelancers, all new technology, computers, communication, media, mass media and political revolutionaries. Uranus is known as the world enhancer and also influences Amnesty International and Greenpeace.

Neptune: Discovered in 1846 and known as King Poseidon in Roman mythology, Neptune rules the dim, invisible and abstract in existence, everything beyond the horizon and in the subconscious, dreams, imagination, inspiration, creativity, spiritually, physically caring, empathy, sacrifice, identification with the weak as well as animals, religiousity, interest in the mysterious and spiritual, institutions, hospitals, prisons, separation, isolation, all chemical impact on the brain because it controls the center of vision-hearing-smell-taste, drugs, medicines, alternative healing, abuse, the socially vulnerable, desperation, enlightenment, spiritual suffering, loneliness, spiritual strength, medial ability, meditation, yoga and spiritual talent with healing. Neptune rules Pisces and the twelfth house. Its metal is platinum.

Occupations under Neptune's influence include all occupations in the care industry as well as within the church, shipping, long journeys, acting, poetry, writing, nursing, hypnotists, illusionists, photography, artistic professions, dancers, musicians, film, theater, artists, entertainers, dream interpreters and sleep study scientists.

Pluto: Discovered in 1930 and also known by the Greek name Hades, lord of the underworld and son of Chronos (Saturn). Pluo rules the psyche, all bodily eliminations, blockages, congestion, the invisible or hidden, the symbol of death and the regenerating energy (both psychologically and physically), rehab, rebuilding, renovating, transforming, sexuality, reproduction, manic obsessions, extreme effort (both bodily and mental), curiosity, analytical, criticizing, questioning, large-scale finance, banks, insurance companies, the stock exchange, volcanic eruptions, earthquakes, storms and "force majeure," collective mass influences, political currents, the rise of Nazism (since it was discovered in 1930), birth, maternity hospitals, funerals, cemeteries, life's beginning and end, paternity births, starting new projects and exiting old ones, crime, the underworld, mafia, forbidden activities, anything taboo, prostitution, pornography, rape, pedophiles, abductions, mentally disturbed people and mental hospitals. Pluto rules Scorpio and the eighth house. Its metal is plutonium.

Occupations under the infuence of Pluto include professional criminals, insensitive killing, banks and major finance, police, military, firefighters, pharmacists, detectives, pathologists, surgeons, doctors, dentists, psychologists, psychiatrists, gynecologists, priests, therapists, x-ray assistants, car testers, referees, lawyers, judges, prostitutes, pimps, sex therapists, family therapists, and healers.

Houses
(Or area of life / "cakes")

This is unfortunately the weakest link in the Horoscope, except perhaps from an unknown or uncertain time of birth. This depends on the complex interpretation of the place on earth at birth. Depending on whether you are born far north or south or maybe around the equator, the size of the houses will sometimes be a bit extreme and easily misleading.

There are a variety of house systems that can fit different on different latitudes. The worst may be, however, the "Equal-house system", where you completely disregard the difference between the location and the equator. Placidus, Campanus, Regiomontanus or Koch are different and more adapted to the location's "slope" towards the Zodiac and the equator. It took many years before I understood this myself, and it is difficult to visualize the differences. If you set a horoscope for a person born, in for example, the northern hemisphere, the houses may look tricky. Some may span several signs while other signs contain several house cusps. This, of course, makes it both difficult and complicated.

My recommendation is, first of all, not to emphasize the interpretation of the houses, and to be critical and flexble if a planet happens to be at the beginning or end of a house. If it is in the middle of a house, it may have some meaning.

The twelve houses are as many as the signs and also reflect the signs from 1 to 12, starting with Aries linked to house 1, etc. counter clockwise.

Actually, I do not like the term "house", as it has nothing to do with buildings. When I talk about them, I would rather use the term *life-area*. Nevertheless, for your curiosity, I will mention some of the clearest trends that the various "houses" represent.

As you may understand, all the planets can end up in all 12 houses and the combinations can be 10 x 12. = 120 pcs. And this is what you call *cookbook* interpretations. I could describe all of these 120 pcs, but it would take too many pages and also risk repeating myself. A fun idea is to try to puzzle and interpret the meaning of each planet with the different houses. It´s rather like painting with different colors.

HOUSE 1 - also the house of Aries and planet Mars

House 1 house cusp (where the house begins) is the same as the **Ascendant**. It represents our personality on the surface, what we display, our attitude, image, role, *persona* or radiance. This is sometimes described as our "shop window." The planets in this house can resemble flowers in our shop window. Health can play a certain role, such as bodily appearences, but the Ascendant and the 1st house are no concrete point but actually an abstract empty point in the sky, so I do not usually exaggerate the physical description. However, let's mention the signal system, i.e, what we send out for signals and how we receive. This house also symbolises the aura.

The 1st house is associated socially with the nation or country, war, struggle, conflicts, competitions, accidents, violent crime, fires, military, police and physicians or physiologists and professionally heavy labour.

HOUSE 2 - also the house of Taurus and planet Venus

House 2 cusp and the sign it lies in shows our material attitude or ability, economic success or failure, your own earned money (in contrast to the 8th house which shows "others money"). This house also shows our basic needs and pleasures, such as food, drink and clothes, even trade and business, as well as gardening and farming.

The 2nd house is associated socially to banks, shops, hairdressers, flower shops, fashion, food, drinks and amusements.

HOUSE 3 - also the house of Gemini and Mercury

House 3 cusp points to relationships with siblings, neighbors and colleagues. It also refers to school, education, letters, books, shorter trips and transportation. This house governs communication and the ability to express oneself in daily life.

The 3rd house connects socially to all education, media, postal services and all communications and transport within the country. This house also refers to TV, radio, phones and traffic data.

HOUSE 4 - also the house of Cancer and the Moon

House 4 cusp is also called IC (Imum Coeli) and represents our past, family ties, the bloodstream, history, archeology and "past lives." It refers to our home as a base. The influence of the mother is strong here and shows the attitude towards one's own family as well as the emotional need for privacy.

The 4th house connects socially to the "people" in a country and all care, e.g., kindergarten and preschool, agriculture, land, housing and food as a basic need, e.g., restaurants, dining and cafés or pubs.

HOUSE 5 - also the house of Leo and the Sun

House 5 cusp shows our attitude towards parenting, but also our ability to create and produce things in life. It also includes our ability or attitude to fun, procreation (breeding), leisure and private passions.

Socially, the 5th house connects to the symbols of authority, the monarchy, presidents or leaders of countries. Also included are the roles of the church as well as other corridors of power as well as public entertainment, sports and games. The gestational power can be expressed through actions or artistic activities.

HOUSE 6 - also the house of Virgo and Mercury

House 6 cusp points to the type of working methods or conditions as well as our attitudes toward our work and the conditions in which we experience them. This house can reveal our ability to cooperate with others and our willingness to take action where and when needed. Health is also important here, and latent diseases can sometimes be traced through this house.

Socially, this house illustrates the "working classes", working life and working methods, but also to the view of our health, crafts, botany and medical work.

HOUSE 7 - also the house of Libra and Venus

House 7 cusp shows all cooperation and attitude towards groups, relationships, partnerships, marriage and cohabitation as well as the ability to maintain contacts, our views on separations or divorces and also reveals our enemies or antagonists.

Socially, house 7 is connected to fun, art and entertainment, fashion trends, beauty products and diplomats. It sheds light on everything we do together with others, fame or recognition versus misperceived reputations and mismatches in society.

HOUSE 8 - also the house of Scorpio and Pluto

House 8 cusp can show circumstances about the death of our own and close relatives and our attitudes towards death itself. It also shows our base properties as house and land and relationship to other people's money, the will, inheritance, insurance companies, bank loans, shares and speculations. Even games and financial speculations have a strong impact on our subconscious. This house shows the paths our lives take from beginning to end. The 8th house includes maternity wards and cemeteries. Also under the influence in this house are the sexual activity on a subconscious level, crime, the mafia and everything considered illegal, everything underground, all that is invisible as well as that which is dangerous or socially taboo. The 8th house is linked to concepts such as control, needs, manic behavior, pro, expert and everything in psychiatry -- including regression.

Socially linked to not only death and funerals but also to mines, detectors, births, fears, cancer, diseases and all sexual drives and diseases. Financial relations between countries. Public security.

HOUSE 9 - also the house of Sagittarius and Jupiter

House 9 cusp shows our morale, perceptions of right and wrong, our view of life, the desire to learn more, train and gain insight through knowledge, longer voyages, languages, contacts with other cultures, the conscience, luck and bad luck, philosophers, researchers, teachers, writers, journalists and priests. This is also the house of visions, dreams and hopes.

Socially, the 9th house refers to all higher education, the church, judgments, laws, long journeys, press and publications, the judiciary field, and also all entertainment and vacations.

HOUSE 10 - also the house of Capricorn and Saturn

House 10 cusp is called Medium Coeli (the MC) and represents our ambitions and aspirations, what we want to achieve or perform, our way of life either professionally or privately, our dreams, expectations and hopes. It shows our attitudes toward power and social status, as well as our own attitudes toward our careers. Sometimes this house can reveal how others see us, especially our own social status or reputations.

Socially, the 10th house illustrates our perceptions and relations to heads of state, governments, power structures, politicians, architects and designers. Institutions and larger companies or associations, retirement homes and work in major organizations -- such as government or municipal employees.

HOUSE 11 - also the house of Aquarius and Uranus

House 11 cusp shows our willingness to be in groups, belonging to associations, our contacts with like-minded people, intellectual entertainment, clubs and common goals. In this house, friendship is more important than love. This house also reveals connections to classmates, teamwork, group community, unions, coworkers, capacity and areas of genius, eccentric behavior, selfishness, self-absorbed behavior, feelings of alienation, rebelliousness, possible areas of revolution, New Age, astrology, political interests, social awareness and universal idealism.

The 11th house connects socially to all political changes, parliaments, unions, political parties, special associations, clubs, special societies, energy systems such as nuclear power, global problems such as conflict in the Ukraine, "the Arab Spring", Syria, the UN, the World Health Organization (WHO), Amnesty International and Greenpeace.

HOUSE 12 - also the house of Pisces and Neptune

House 12 cusp reveals our attitudes toward loneliness, seclusion and self-denial exclusion (such as going to a monastery), rehab, retreats, ending in prison or in a hospital, service activities in church or social services, Jesus as a spiritual symbol of universal love, sacrifice and forsaking one's own needs for others, how we live this life and how we perceive or expect "the other side" to be. This house can show hidden fears and suppressed needs, how concerns of negative influence can lead to the need to escape reality through drugs or self-pity. As all these aspects can take control of our subconscious, everything that has to do with dreams and sleep is connected here. Spiritual suffering may occur and this house can reveal strong beliefs, open or hidden. Spiritual needs, strength, empathy, sacrifice and martyrdom are common issues in the 12th house. Artistic inspiration can be drawn from elements of music, dance, theater, photography or film. Meditation, self-retreat and silence are important if life is experienced too hard. Intuition is often strong and not uncommon with psychicism and a certain mediumship talent.

Socially, the 12th house is linked to all healthcare facilities, churches, monasteries, priests, hospitals, the navy, physicians, psychologists, drugs, drug abuse, scandals, chemicals, oils, art, HIV, AIDS, EBOLA, viruses, infections, bacilli and the immune system as well as those who are socially excluded or homeless and long distance travel by sea. Animals are also linked to this house.

The Moon in the different houses

Moon in House 1: Personality outwards.

Here the person wants to be at the center and get attention, either through achievements or via external attributes such as highly developed muscles, expensive clothes or surface beauty. This is the house of vanity, and these people are often emotionally vulnerable unless they are constantly *seen.* Today's Facebook phenomenon illustrates Moon in the 1st house: showing off to others parts of ourselves of what we think or feel. First house Moon people may be very spontaneous and ruthlessly explosive in their honesty. They are known to "lay the cards on the table." Self-assertion is often evident, but this can also lead to pure bloating of the ego and arrogance. They can be boastful, know-it-alls, tyrannical and despotic. In a man's chart this can sometimes mean fear of women or conflicts with the mother or other women, as this symbolically suggests contact with strong self-employed women.

Moon in House 2: Possessions and financial resources.

Here, interest may be in business or pure commerce, and in combination with our basic needs, such as food, beverages, clothing or building materials. The economy can be irregular and varied, which can sometimes lead to insecurity. However, there is a talent to save and spend a wise budget. The security of life is usually based on purely tangible assets. In case of severe impact, one can be afraid to bet, take chances or speculate if no obvious guarantees exist. If they are too careful they may also considered to be cheap.

Moon in House 3: Siblings, neighbors and coworkers.

May mean a big family with many siblings but also a great circle of friends. Interchangeable friends but sisters good for mental stimulation. Other apsects include love's shorter journeys, walks and being easy going. Studying tends to come easier, and many varied interests occur. But they are also known for splitting from a relationship at the first negative occurence. Interchangeability can stimulate rather than split.

Moon in House 4: Home environment and family.

The Moon in this house reinforces all the needs of the family, and blood ties are important. There is a great influence on 4th house Moon people from the mother. In a man's chart he might be searching for his mother instead of a wife. Maternity ties are strong, as well as the protection of their own family. A deeper interest in the past occurs, such as archeology or history. There is a tendency towards isolation because the home is important for a feeling of basic safety.

Moon in House 5: Parenting and authority.

This is a very good position for teachers and educators, stimulating a deep need for creativity and artistic activity. These individuals do not mind public attention and can be recognized for their expressive power through art, music, film or theater. They possess and express good authority towards children and are often a most generous leader. Sexuality tends to be more spontaneous and strong in both sexes.

Moon in House 6: Health and Working Conditions.

This Moon placement usually indicates very good health. There is a larger interest in both hygiene and diet, and they are highly disciplined at their workplace. They prefer a subordinate role with their own area of responsibility, since their sense of responsibility is strong. Having a job or important employment is vital to these loyal employees.

Moon in House 7: Partnership and Love.

Love is certainly important, but *all* types of cooperation are also extremely important for their emotional harmony and balance. There is a strong need for encouragement and support and a certain tendency to depend on others for important decisions.

They may sometimes be very changeable, but they detest loneliness. Therefore, many compromises are made to maintain their sense of balance.

Moon in House 8: Our subconscious and powers we can not influence.

Eighth house Moon people are often attracted to psychology, psychiatry or police activity, as well as in hidden activities or behind the scenes. They're drawn to mystery and occult as well as to crime and all things forbidden. Sexual needs are linked to safety, but fears may occur in relation to women, regardless of their own gender. Nightmares, phobias, taboos, and thoughts of death lurk under the surface, and all escapes from reality can be very destructive.

Moon in House 9: Our longing and hopes for the future.

This placement illustrates the globetrotter who likes to walk far from home. This may lead to temporarily or permanently living abroad. Perennial longings for higher education can occur as well as work that involves contact with abroad. Religion and moral importance to the person and success can occur within the legal world. Languages can attract and long journeys become a habit. Women from abroad can play an important role for the person.

Moon in House 10: Our Ambition or Aim in life.

The Moon in this house can indicate a strong link between feelings and work and emotional commitment necessary at work. They often prefer to own their business at home or live at work on a regular basis. Women are important in the career as well as to work with children. Female bosses or women with power can also hinder or endorse progress in their career. Social status varied and probably a certain reputation as being too emotional at work.

Moon in House 11: Friendship relationships and common goals

Social interaction is important with an extensive network of contacts. Emotional needs of friends usually takes preference over love relationships. Objectives in life can change but are often achieved through work in larger organizations, associations and clubs. Also, the symbol of different family forms with stepchildren, foster children or adopted. In a man's chart they may be attracted to independent and / or original women.

Moon in House 12: The hidden and subconscious.

Here there is often a strong attraction to mysticism and spiritual life, and these needs are sought by seclusion and silence. There is emotional empathy and deep understanding of life's suffering and vulnerable people. Perhaps not so spontaneous with their own feelings, but they always express through participatory actions. Fantasy, meditation and intuition are important for the spiritual stimulus. This placement may indicate periodic stays in a hospital or in prison.

OTHER PLANETS

Of course, you can make an overview of all the planets and their respective signs and houses, but it would become a *cookbook* and take too much space. (e.g., Mercury's position in all 12 signs and all 12 houses, then Venus, etc.)

I just want you to note that the Sun and Moon are the most important, and you must also take into consideration the position of all other planets and their mutual aspects or function before you can begin to interpret. You can never actually interpret a single aspect literally. Everything must be taken into account before making conclusions. For those who are still curious and do not trust their ability to "pair" the planets with their respective signs or houses, there are several books with complete *cookbook* interpretation. Look in "Books" in the Appendix at the end of this book.

What does a horoscope consist of?

I do not explain how to calculate your own chart. There is a complicated manual on my website that surely can "discourage" most. There are many online services today where you can quickly and cheaply get your own calculation in one minute. I myself sat in anguish with a ruler, calculator and various colored pencils in the early 70's. One also needed both Ephemeris (Star Tables), and the Table of houses (Longitude and Latitude) of the place where you were born. It all felt like quantum physics at Einstein's level for my high school teens, but shame on the one who gives up. I once got a book in Danish (!) from the library in Gothenburg; and with the insanity of a fool, I managed to figure out my own chart. I prefer to call it a chart instead of a horoscope as it is actually just a chart or map of the starry sky.

When this chart is complete, you get a giant puzzle with "cakes," a lot of astrological symbols and even colored with red, green or blue lines inside the circle. Now you have to familiarize yourself with the symbols.

A chart actually consists of several circles with twelve sections or signs and "houses" respectively. By the way, "house" is an idiotic expression that does not have anything to do with "buildings." Instead, I prefer to call these cakes "areas in life". The outer circle is the Zodiac or the Signs, which always goes counterclockwise, and inside lie the 12 cakes or houses. As a rule, you always place the Ascendant to the left of the map. To know the signs of the Ascendant, MC and the twelve houses, you must know both the accurate time and place of birth. If you have this information, the sign that the Ascendant is in is on the left and goes counterclockwise around the other signs. Inside the chart, the Sun, Moon and Planets are placed after a calculation of their exact positions.

If you unfortunately do not have the accurate time of birth but maybe just the location, you can still draw a chart at 12 o'clock noon and at least get an idea of the major features, the most important aspects and not least the location of the Moon. So it is possible to interpret a person even if you do not know the accurate time, or if there are no important components, such as the Ascendant, MC, the houses or the Moon's exact position. This can become complicated if you would like to make a forecast of the future. Then there can be quite a big deviation for certain times. I have frequently been asked about the need for the exact time of birth because there are actually people who do not have their accurate birth time because they were either adopted, born abroad or very old people who may have been born at home or have no birth certificate.

Once we have got the Ascendent, MC and the location of the houses, you can place the Sun, Moon and Planets in their places. The next step is now to figure out the so-called aspects. This is simply the angular distance or angular ratio in degrees between the various points on the map, and we also take into account the Ascendant and Medium Coeli, from now on abbreviated MC. This process is fun and exciting because you often find the person's most important or strong characteristics among these aspects.

As a rule of thumb, you can say that the placement of the planets in their respective signs describes how you perceive or use the respective energies, while the aspects between the planets show how the qualities or issues express themselves through your life experience. The locations inside the houses, however, indicate in which *areas* of life you focus on these energies.

For example, we can take the Moon in Gemini, which is completely different from the Moon in Scorpio. In addition, the Moon's location in the 3rd house is completely different from the Moon in the 12th house. How and in what way they are perceived or expressed are often shown by the aspects of the other symbols, both through the planets and the ASC and MC.

I usually emphasize that I prioritize the aspects since they are actually both concrete and very typical of the person. Often it does not matter what sign you've been born in (the Sun) or where your Moon is, if it turns out that one or a few strong aspects may dominate the entire chart. Then look for the strongest aspects when you start your interpretation. If an aspect is "strong" depends on how close the exact angle lies. The deviation from an exact aspect is called *Orbis*. In addition, the "red" aspects are usually called strong, as they symbolize activity or energy. The "blue" aspects are inversely called weak because they describe more of a state of mind.

The emphasis on the aspects is important because they simply show how we behave and what energies we use most often. I can say that I often sat for an hour and discussed with a person his or her strongest qualities without even mentioning what sign they were born in. That about says it all!

Since there are lots of mathematical aspects, I only pick up the most important ones and also divide them into the main aspects and less important ones.

ASPECTS

The major aspects

Conjunction: This occurs when two points (Planets or ASC or MC) are in the same place or within approximately 8 degree deviation (orbis). The orb can vary depending on which points are included. Conjunctions belong to the strong because they form a fusion or synthesis of two or more energies. Sometimes this can be interpreted as negative if it includes two symbols that may sometimes not be good together; e.g., Mars-Saturn, while others may amplify or increase the meaning of the two energies. A conjunction can also include more than two symbols, which complicates the conclusion itself. I have seen conjunctions with up to 5 symbols in almost the same place, though this is rare. The conjunction is not actually drawn on the map because it is visible to the naked eye.

Sextile: This happens when the exact angle is 60 degrees between two points, within an orbis 6 degrees. This is most often considered positive and stimulating and often shows slumbering talent. It happens often if they are two signs apart. On the chart they are drawn with the color blue (or sometimes green).

Square: This occurs when the exact angle between two points is 90 degrees within an orbis of 8 degrees, depending on the symbols. The square is considered one of the main aspects, but it also belongs to the most active. Here things happen, and energy can slum until it is activated. The interpretation can be both positive and negative depending on the symbols involved. On the chart, the square aspect is colored red.

Much *red* in the chart (several squares and oppositions) often indicate a lot of energy in different forms, including a great ability to actually achieve a lot in life. In a forecast, there must be clear *red* energies for anything to be done or "happening" at all.

Trine: Trines exist when the exact angle between two points is 120 degrees, within an orbis 8 degrees, depending on the symbols. The trine is traditionally interpreted as positive and is linked to both talent and ease. There can be a little more flow or cooperation between the implicated symbols. On the chart, the trine is drawn with the color blue.

Much *blue* can cause too little resistance or make it easier to succeed (gold bark in the mouth) but can sometimes also lead to lack of energy. However, too much passivity can for example lead to an addictive behavior of some kind.

Trines are usually considered to be for the good, but my own experience is that it is too prominent in people who do not care or strive enough, so there must be a balance or more energy (*red*) elsewhere in the chart to compensate for too much *blue*. As a prediction, it is the inverse square. That is, too much *blue* can mean eventlessness and lack of energy to perform things. Obviously, some *blue* is nice sometimes for calmness, especially if you create or work with fantasy of any kind.

Quincunx, Inconjunct or 150 degrees: This has many names, but the exact angle should be 150 degrees between the points, within an orbis of 3 degrees. This one is extremely flexible and can be interpreted both positively and negatively depending on implicated symbols, but I count it as one of the main aspects and also consider it strong. Some believe that this is part of the weaker and bias aspects, but following my own experiences with this in transit (temporary passage), I have noticed that it can be both positive and negative. It is probably due to the fact that it often occurs between different elements, e.g., Air-Earth or Air-Water.

Opposition: When the exact angle between the points is 180 degrees, (ie., they are located opposite each other in the chart). Orbis can vary, but with a maximum of 8 degrees. Considered among both the major aspects and the strong ones, oppositions are drawn in the chart in red. In general, this can also be interpreted both positively and negatively depending on the symbols involved. However, like the conjunction, it often has a strong triggering energy. Psychologically, oppositions are similar to the interpretation of Gestalt therapy.

Minor aspects

Here you can quickly get lost. There are a lot of minor aspects, but for practical reasons, they can not be drawn or interpreted unless they are included in other important contexts.

Semi-sextile: 30 degrees. Orbis 2 degrees. Blue color if you want to paint it.

Semi-quintile: 36 degrees. Orbis 2 degrees. Blue.

Semi square: 45 degrees, ie., half of 90 degrees. Orbis 2 degrees. Red. Activating.

Quintile: 72 degrees. Orbis 2 degrees. Blue.

Trisquare or "**One-and-a-half**" (90 + 45): 135 degrees. Orbis 2 degrees. Red. Activating.

Biquintile or **double quintile**: 144 degrees. Orbis 2 degrees. Blue.

For practical reasons, I do not have any pictures on these symbols because they do not exist among my keys, but it needs to be photographed and cut. You'll find them and what they look like in any astrological book or on my website.

Retrograde

Another phenomenon that sometimes appears is *retrograde*. It is usually marked slightly below to the right of the symbol of the planet with an "R" and a line over the right leg. Retrogrades are in reality an illusion. The planet that is retrograde "looks like" it´s going backwards in the sky. This is obviously not true but depends on the perspective changing because of the planets' varying distances from the sun (and Earth) and therefore the length of their orbits. Using Mercury as an example, as it is between the Sun and Earth, it can often *appear* as if it is moving backwards, depending on where it is in it´s orbit around the Sun in relation to the Earth on its orbit. This phenomenon sometimes happens with all the planets except the Moon, but they are always moving forward and never actually backwards. Interpretations may vary and are sometimes contradictory. I have even read a book that only interpreted retrograde planets from a karmic perspective.

Exceptions

* Use less orb if the aspect falls between two signs it should not normally "be" in if it was accurate. For example: A trine 120 degrees should normally be between two signs with the same element (fire - fire) if it is accurate.

* Use less orb in doubt if it falls between two slow planets, such as Uranus, Neptune, Pluto, or the Moon's nodes and if any of the involved are retrograde. (The Moon's nodes are not actually planets but slowly goes backwards - retrograde).

* When using wide orb, the aspect is "weak". Select this with a W (English weak) next to the symbol.

* If the aspect is almost exact, mark this with an E after the aspect. An aspect is exact if it is within 20 minutes from exactly. 1 degree = 60 minutes. These are called arch minutes, not time-minutes.

* There may also be points in the chart that lack aspects and others that have a lot of aspects, and here we must figure out which ones are relevant or significant for the person. An entirely unaspected planet can indicate that the person may rarely be aware of the particular talent (or a shortage of energy) represented by the unaspected point. However, even an unaspected point can be triggered or affected as soon as it is aspected through a prognosis or transit. (Transit =

temporary passage of planets after the birh and during your lifetime in relation to your birthchart).

Basic components of the horoscope

What sign you are born in is determined by the birthday. Here we have a difficult division because 365 days are divided into twelve different parts. 365: 12 = 30.4. Add to this a variation by 28, 30 and 31 days in different months. In order to struggle further, we have leap years every four years. That's why all signs sometimes begin and end at varying dates. Actually, the months should be thirteen instead of twelve because the month cycle is approximately 28.6 days, ie., exactly as long as the woman's menstrual cycle. 28 x 13 = 364.

In the calculation itself, the exact time is added, and this is usually the weak link in astrology as this is needed to know the exact position of the Ascendant, MC and the houses. An incorrect time ("Mom thought it was around 4 pm") can turn the whole interpretation upside down and both miss important pieces as well as highlight completely wrong things. Add to this your mother's (or anyone else´s) "weak" memory! If you do not have a baptismal, birth certificate or certificate from the maternity ward where you were born, you understand what I mean. It may be like with the old Indian who answered when he was born; "It was in the summertime!"

Some basic rules to take into account

"POSITIVE" or "NEGATIVE"

Every second sign is Positive, while every other sign is Negative, beginning with the first sign Aries. This is not in any psychological sense but rather in terms of electrical charge. Very simply, the positive signs are more active and expressive while the negative signs are more passive and receptive.

Positive; Aries, Gemini, Leo, Libra, Sagittarius, Aquarius.

Negative; Taurus, Cancer, Virgo, Scorpio, Capricorn, Pisces.

QUALITY

There is also a division in various so-called "Qualities", where you have either leading, solid or changing quality.

Leading are initiative, will and the creative force in the world. The **Leading** signs are also called **Cardinal** signs, which are: Aries, Cancer, Libra, Capricorn.

Solid are stable, the community's pillar of support. **Solid** signs are also called **Fixed** signs and they are: Taurus, Leo, Scorpio, Aquarius.

Mutual are customizable dualistic and versatile. The **Mutual** signs are: Gemini, Virgo, Sagittarius, Pisces.

As an example, the Sphinx is a combination of the **solid** signs: The bull's body - Taurus. Lion feet with claws - Leo. The wings of the eagle - Scorpio. Human head - Aquarius.

ELEMENTS

Then you can divide the twelve signs into elements and temperament. Here we have fire signs, earth signs, air signs and water signs.

Fire signs are lively, eager, active and choleric (from the Greek word for yellow bile or bugs). Fire sign people are dynamic, idealistic and self-conscious – but also self-confident in leading and organizing others. The **fire** signs are: Aries, Leo, Sagittarius.

Earth signs are stable, practical, cautious, materialistic, focused on earthy targets, preservering and are more focused on maintaining rather than creating something new. They are known to be somewhat strong-minded and are melancholic (from Greek word for black bile or bugs.) The **Earth** signs are: Taurus, Virgo, Capricorn.

Air signs are about communication and all kinds of associations, art and creativity. They are sanguine (from the Latin word for blood, here being used to symbolize purity and clarity.) Air signs are refined, sore, alert and idealistic. The **Air** Signs are: Gemini, Libra, Aquarius.

Water signs symbolize the changing and immutable. **Water** sign people are filled with emotions, very receptive to impressions, led by instincts, intuitive, imaginative and phlegmatic (from the Greek word meaning mucus). The **Water** signs are: Cancer, Scorpio, Pisces.

TRIVIA

The five-pointed star below is called a **Pentagram**. This is the symbol of the ancient Pythagoran concept of the perfect cosmos. The five points represent the five known planets in Pythagoras' time as Mercury, Venus, Mars, Jupiter and Saturn. Compare with the Pentagon in the United States.

The **Chaldean** star, on the other hand, has seven points and is an ancient symbol which includes the Sun, the Moon and the then known planets Mercury, Venus, Mars, Jupiter and Saturn. They also represent the weekdays. The Sun - Sunday; The Moon - Monday, Mars - Mardi (French) Tuesday, Mercury - Mercredi (French) Wednesday, Jupiter - Jeudi (French) Thursday, Venus - Vendredi (French) Friday, Saturn - Saturday.

A Child

By: Dorothy Law Holte

A child who is criticized - learns to condemn

A child who gets a stroke - learns to fight

A child who is mocked - learns shyness

A child exposed to irony - learns to have a bad conscience

but

A child who gets encouragement - learns confidence

A child who meets tolerance - learns patience

A child who gets praise - learn to appreciate

A child who experiences pure play - learns justice

A child who gets to know friendship - learns kindness

A child who experiences safety - learns faithfulness

A child who becomes popular and hugged - learns to feel love in the world

Children´s charts

The author, 2 years old, with tender mother

I have for many years been given the confidence to interpret many newborn´s charts for curious and wise parents. Surprisingly, I have to admit that I had expected more curious parents. The strange thing is that you can not get any feedback or judgment about a newborn. However, parents have listened over and over after a few years, and by listening again, they were able to recognize the major important features. Concerning older children up to the adolescents, however, it has been very grateful for parents to have been given important explanations.

It is often both exciting and fascinating to interpret a newborn individual or young person, prior to the teenage years. It is an enormous advantage and privilege to know early on how and in what ways you can be of support and better be able to have an oversight with some different or original behavior.

The role and importance of parents

As an unwritten piece of paper you see potential and future difficulties in life. Interpreting this to parents has often been a delicate balance. It has occasionally happened that I instinctively felt that one of the parents, for some incomprehensible reason, did not want the best for their child (probably a karmic issue). I have not been able to reveal this to the parents, but perhaps I tried to emphasize a bit of forebearence with behavior that would bring about negative feelings with mom or dad. Sometimes I have felt pure powerlessness and anxiety during the interpretation, possibly because I was influenced by the child's aura or karma.

There is actually no such thing as "time" in the interpretation. Everything is timeless and evolves during life. As a roadmap, you can follow the child's upbringing and conditions during school age, teens, adulthood and old age. Of course, one does not go through a newborn's entire life but instead focuses mostly on the development of the very first years, often up to school. Emphasis is placed on driving forces, impulses and instincts. Different needs are always unique. Some children need a lot of space and freedom with the body. Others are a bit slower in pace. They may develop more quickly mentally than physically. Some are more introverted while others may be outgoing. Different talents can be easily discovered through a summary. After listening, parents can also figure out what's best for the importance of any particular stimulus.

The difficulty with child interpretation is really how the parents perceive the interpretation. I see "directly" what kind of person both mom and dad are in relation to the child, ie., how the child perceives and experiences the parents. I do not want to list a lot of codes here and reveal what it means. This would do more harm than good. The person with normal imagination can look at both his own and his child's horoscope.

As a parent, you look primarily at the Moon and its location and aspects to other points in the chart. You can quickly form an idea of how the person experiences both parenthood, sexuality, pregnancy and possible childbirth. Thus, it also reveals what a child means to the person in question. The reverse applies in a child´s analysis. First of all, you look at the Moon to see the first years of life in a timely manner. But both the Moon and the Sun play a part in the relationship with both parents. It is often easy to see which of the parents has the most influence, but also what parent the child may spontaneously avoid.

If you want to know how your own childhood looked, study your Moon and / or Sun for finding out the different influences. If you want to know how your own children experience you, study your own Moon and the Child's Moon and Sun, depending on whether you are mom or dad. Here are no simple rules, neither a certain gender prejudice. There are both masculine and feminine signals that the child experiences. One could say that the children experience sex as asexual until their own puberty.

Some simple interpretations can not be harmful. However, I will only look at the Moon's significance for the respective children and parents.

The Moon of the Child and the Parent

Moon in **Aries**: These children are often impatient and energetic. A lot of will can be tough for parents. They are often brave and daring and, hence, more accident prone. Emotionally, mom can be the stronger one of the parents, but she can also cause anger or irritation. As an adult, the Aries Moon person often looks for a strong and authoritative woman. This Moon person is often chosen first at team play at school.

As a parent with Moon in **Aries**, you can be too impatient and want your child to become strong and independent quickly. They are often shockingly spontaneous and open to the child, perhaps not always so educational but always honest. The Aries Moon parent would like the child to distinguish him/herself at different stages of competition and would like to show offspring publicly ("Look what a beautiful child I have!").

Moon in **Taurus**: These children are more physical and down to earth. They love food and physical touch. They are not so much active but rather productive in their interests. There can be interest in clothes and their appearance, needing to move more than they want, they like activities with their parents and more often they are more interested in practical than theoretical subjects in school.

Parents with Moon in **Taurus** are very physical and enjoy the child's entire being. To them basic needs are important, such as food, clothing and physical security. Perhaps they worry too much about the child's social and economic conditions. There can be a tendency to spoil the child.

Moon in **Gemini**: Children with this location have more mental than physical relationships with their parents. They do not see their parents as authorities but rather as friends. These children are inquisitive and curious and do not have the same emotional needs as other children. They want to wander, look around and discover their surroundings early. Above all, they always relate to the outside world with their communication skills. Sometimes there can be a light-hearted and slightly superficial relationship with their parents, especially with the mother.

Parents with Moon in **Gemini** think it's important to be knowledgable. They prefer to teach their children pedagogically rather than "ruling" them, and often these parents are more like friends with their own children up to adulthood.

Moon in **Cancer**: Delicate and fragile, these children are often intense in their experiences, with their emotions up and down like a rollercoaster. They need to live out all their experiences and not close them. The relationship to the mother can be fragile, with a stress on a need of feeling safe. Often these children are a little too home-loving, and they do not like new environments. They are anxious and reserved in front of new people and places.

Parents with Moon in **Cancer** may be protective but need to give their children a little longer running line. They are affected too much by the child's feelings, which the child can quickly learn to manipulate. Food and financial security are vital to give to their children. There is always a certain risk of being overprotective as a Moon in Cancer parent.

Moon in **Leo**: These children quickly learn to be determined and get their will through. They may experience conflicts with both or one of the parents, but these children will adore them at the same time. Often they become confident and strong unless they are hindered or held back during childhood. Often there is a natural protection instinct against both siblings and peers. If they are spoiled, an arrogance can lead to them being disliked instead.

Parents with this Moon may have too high ambitions for their child. They can spoil them and always want their child's best, but at the same time they want them to be on their own feet early. These parents would like to show off their children and what they achieved or succeeded in. Pride is an understatement.

Moon in **Virgo**: Initially, these children are very careful and cautious, but ambitious when they understand their task. Often they become good at school but simultaneouslly avoid too much attention. They seek knowledge their whole lives but need to be encouraged to be more social. Moon in Virgo children can be a little sensitive to criticism and can over-worry if there is not enough time. They are the heavy laborer or over-precise secretary of the group.

Parents with this Virgo Moon are constantly concerned about their child's physical and practical conditions, such as clothing, food, money, times that have to be met and responsibilities that must be fulfilled. The need for care can become manic, and these parents need to give their children more freedom. There is the tendency to have a more intellectual relation to their children than emotional.

Moon in **Libra**: These children can be rays of sunshine in any group. They live to relate to others and love all group activities. They balance their diplomacy skills towards both sexes and makes friends easily. Some uncertainty may hamper them, and they need to learn to act more on their own to succeed. Often they show early creative talent that should be encouraged.

As a parent, they may have difficulty with parenting because they prefer to be friend and mate rather than the one who decides for their children. These parents refuse to bark and be angry at their children and always strive for consensus their entire lives.

Moon in **Scorpio**: These children quickly learn to manipulate their surroundings, rejecting all authority as they are likely to become an authority themselves as an adult. They are not the easiest of children to raise, and emotional outbursts can be relentlessly exaggerated. However, they have a rigorous self-discipline and may be the fastest of all signs to become independent during childhood. Their feelings, however, are deep and empathetic towards those they respect.

As parents, they give more and more to their offspring, but also feel as much as their child if they suffer. Here is a good warning: *Never* attack a child whose parent has this Moon. It can be *very* dangerous. At worst, they can be unnecessarily strict and demand high standards for their children as they quickly want them to learn how to survive.

Moon in **Sagittarius**: These children love to care for themselves and do not always take school very seriously. However, they are easily popular in any group and always spread a certain amount of humor and readiness. They love animals and travel as a child. These visionaries strive high and far and rarely give their parents any major concerns. Sometimes they may be a little too carefree.

As a parent, they love to play and play games with their children, and learning may be important, but you have to laugh first. They may sometimes appear carefree or uninterested to their children, but they always support their children in a crisis and are often very positive as educators and teachers. Hence their children are often more relaxed and harmonious.

Moon in **Capricorn**: These children may have difficulty initially without the parents' support. They experience unprecedented demands and duties much more difficult than other children and quickly learn what is important and serious in life. Precociousness sometimes occurs here. They bear much responsibility and take responsibility for everything and everyone around them, including both parents as well as siblings and friends. This may sound foolish, but these children often become very responsible and purposeful and can handle and take responsibility for life faster than other children. They gain a lot of confidence due to their attitude towards responsibility, and usually they do very well during school time. These serious children are hardest to enjoy but are always optimally loyal and wise. You can always trust them to do what they promise.

These parents at the same time take full responsibility for the best of their children. They are often prepared for great sacrifices and are prepared to do much for their children's sake. But they should learn to give their children a little more freedom and responsibility and for the children to do more for *themselves*. Deficiency symptoms may otherwise occur with time, energy, finances and emotions.

Moon in **Aquarius**: These children may feel a bit odd at times and do not always fit into any groups. This is usually because they will not follow the *status quo* as adults. Often they go their own way and are not afraid to distinguish themselves early in life. They quickly learn to choose and decide for themselves and do not need their parents as much as other children. They can also experience a superficial friendship instead of respect for their parents.

As parents, they early encourage their children to take care of themselves and to do things on their own. They are more likely to be friends rather than authorities to their children. They often end up with rather special children. I have often found this combination among both children and parents who had unusual family relationships or constellations involving adoption, family fostering, living in a collective and so on.

Moon in **Pisces**: These children may seem easiest to both raise and provide security. They live more often than other children in their own *bubble* and are often surprised by too much attention. They can be very sensitive and need a lot of tolerance and patience from both parents. With their natural feelings, they love animals and are often very physical in their experiences. Their imagination needs to be encouraged even though school is not always the best place. They do better with friends than with school requirements.

As adults with this Moon, they can sometimes be over-protective. They suffer from the difficulties of their children and cry openly in front of them. They encourage their children to dream and create their own imagination. They would like to help all other children, not just their own.

Health and Illness

"A physician without knowledge of astrology is not entitled to call himself a doctor!" (Hippocrates born about 460 BC)

In order not to mix different concepts, I will divide this into three major sections: The physical, mental and spiritual health.

Physical health

"A healthy soul in a healthy body" is everybody's goal, but with an ever increasing danger from the environment, the food, the air and the water, one has to struggle today to stay healthy.

I do not go into the subject of cancer purely astrologically, because I do not want to "create" any prejudice or reveal typical signals that could indicate cancer. It can do more harm than good, I'm afraid. However, my personal opinion is that many different sorts of cancer are a consequence of many different factors: including genetic disposition, psychological effects, longer-term accumulated toxins from the environment or food and our living behavior. With living behavior, I refer to how much you reduce your own life energy through smoking, alcohol, stress or unnecessary or toxic food, emotional status and attitude, etc.

Here you can see not least the importance of the food. If you are oblivious to you or your children, a lot of candy containing dyes, sugar and preservatives will blind you from recognizing many hidden hazards. Extreme intake of sweets and snacks can lead to unexpected consequences such as sugar shock, diabetes, abnormal hyperactivity and a variety of allergic reactions. This explains why so many children end up being ADHD.

As for the food we eat, of course, we try to eat as natural raw materials as possible. We may rather choose GMO-free or organic products. Maybe there are more than I who noticed that the organic products have increased in recent years. Now you can ask where the non-organic goods are.

You don't have to be a vegetarian or vegan to stay healthy today, even though it increases the chances of staying healthy. But I think you have to be critical of everything you eat. "You are what you eat" could account for a lot of examples of people who are more healthy by just changing their diet. I want to mention a pioneer, the Aries Are Waerland, born in 1876. As a young man suffering from severe migraines, Are decided to analyze how the body reacted when he excluded different food types. He simply removed almost everything and then ate different products for a certain amount of time to see how the migraine was affected. In the end he cured his migraine. He said for instance, "We do not have to deal with diseases, but with our way of living or eating wrongly. Abolish this and the diseases disappear by themselves." Wise words indeed.

In the horoscope you can quickly and easily assess the body's conditions and possible weaknesses. Some of us are more infection-sensitive than others, while some people can not keep impulses or muscles under control but are more easily injured. However, with regard to the physical body, there is an indication of the body parts or areas that may be in focus "when the accident is at hand." It's not enough to just look at their birth sign. All Capricorns, for example, do not hurt in their knees. No, if you look for wrongs and weaknessess in the body, it's better to look at the positions and aspects of the Moon. The Sun can indicate bodily defects or weaknesses or our "Achilles heel," but the Moon often activates our weak points through the area or body part symbolized by the sign where the Moon is located.

Thus, it is more likely to wonder about weaknesses when analyzing the location of the Moon. One can say that a combination often occurs between the effects of the Sun and the Moon.

Here follows a symbolic list of the body parts that control or rule over their respective signs. Consideration must also be given to the aspects of the Sun, and the position of the Moon may be worse or more prone. Important to consider is also the polarity; ie., weaknesses can sometimes be in the characteristics of the opposite sign. For example, Leo´s may have Aquarius´ troubles, etc. Polarity sign in parentheses.

Birth signs with ruling Planet

Aries / Mars - The head, face, bile, red blood cells, ovaries, ovary, body hair, adrenal glands.

Trends: Fever, headache, migraine, more frequent accidents rather than diseases, nasal blood, meningitis, cranial injury, gall disorder, kidney disease (Libra).

Food and Herbs for mineral deficiency: Tomatoes, bryony, ranunculus, honeysuckle, hazelnuts, rhubarb.

Taurus / Venus - Throat, neck, thyroid gland.

Trends: Weight gain due to passivity, mucous membranes, hoarseness, colds, throat diseases, abdomen, genitals (Scorpio).

Food - Herbs: Celery, arrack, beans, elder.

Gemini / Mercury - Arms, shoulders, key legs, hands, fingers, lungs, brain, nervous system and joints.

Trends: Pulmonary diseases, asthma, bronchitis, nervous disorders, calcifications, back pain (Sagittarius).

Food - Herbs: Salad, cauliflower, pineapple, carrot, fern, hare´s foot, lavender.

Cancer / Moon - Stomach, breast glands, liver, gall bladder, pancreas, eyes – the left eye for men and the right eye for women.

Trends: Psychosomatic disorders, digestion, syncope, depression, bleeding, gastric catarrh, gastric ulcer, reflux, bulimia, anorexia, rheumatism (Capricorn).

Food - Herbs: Milk, watercress, flax, lilac, quarry.

Leo / Sun - The heart, spine, back, eyes – the right eye for men and the left eye for women.

Trends: Heart failure or heart problems, back pain, vision defects, cramps (Aquarius).

Food - Herbs: Plum, peas, oranges, layers, lesser celandine, walnuts.

Virgo / Mercury - Intestinal system, abdominal cavity, intestines.

Trends: Hypochondria, bowel diseases, appendicitis, sleep disorders, intoxications (Pisces).

Food – Herbs: lemons, cumin, horehound, myrtle.

Libra / Venus - Kidneys.

Trends: Kidney failure, diabetes, fever, headaches (Aries).

Food – Herbs: strawberries, asparagus, chestnuts, daisy, cultivated mint.

Scorpio / Pluto - Genitals, ovaries, prostate, bladder, anus.

Trends: Diseases of the genitals, urinary infection, hemorrhoids, throat (Taurus).

Food – Herbs: cabbage, prunes, broom, gorse, hops, tobacco plants.

Sagittarius / Jupiter - Hips, thighs, back, blood circulation, pituitary gland, liver.

Tendencies: Jaundice, insecretory disorders, back problems, sciatica, blood and liver disease, nervous system (Gemini).

Food – Herbs: asparagus, cucumber (silicic acid), Stachys officinalis, borage, turmeric, dandelion, moss.

Capricorn / Saturn - Knees, skin, bones, teeth, gallbladder, the muscles, spleen, the hearing.

Trends: Skin disorders, indigestion (Cancer), skeletal disorders, low blood pressure, low heart rate, rheumatism, calcification, knee injuries, dental problems, orthopedic defects.

Food – Herbs: cabbage, kale, amaranth, beet, hemlock, onion.

Aquarius / Uranus - Calves, ankles, bloodstream, gonads, pituitary gland, pineal gland, the "third eye".

Tendency: Blood deficiency, paralysis, convulsions, overwork, leg and ankle fractures, sprains, varicose veins, scarring, osteosclerosis, spasms, ticks, "restless legs", heart disease (Leo).

Food – Herbs: pomegranate, pansy, hemp, loquat.

Pisces / Neptune - Feet, amniotic fluid, spinal cord.

Trends: Dropsy, drug problems, poisoning, hypersensitivity to medication, rheumatism, mental disorders, foot warts, foot sweat, intestinal problems(Virgo).

Foods – Herbs: raisins, dates, different cereals (iron phosphate), acid, fig, sage, chicory.

Mental and Spiritual Health

Mental or emotional problems are first and foremost something very individual. Unfortunately, there are still a lot of taboos and prejudices around these effects. In the name of justice, however, I must point out that none of us can live a whole life without so-called "crises", and/or serious adversities at some point. The question is more when they occur, how do we deal with them.

Disposition for ill health can often be both physical and emotional, but very often they are linked. There are some key interpretations, but it is usually a mix of several effects. Concerning the soul, it is mainly about the Moon and its location and aspects. Then one may have to take into account whether it is a congenital structure or if the ill health is temporary and thus not constant. If you know that you have one or more possible health issues, this may lead to a more careful attitude towards certain situations.

However, if the person still experiences discomfort or fear of some degree, as an astrologer you can only periodically determine the process (suffering). You should never take full responsibility for being able to "heal" or cure the client. Never forget that the person may also need to consult a doctor or psychiatrist to get professional advice and competent help. Even though I have completely wiped out medicines, tablets and temporary "patches", I've even had to take easier drugs to cope with particular crises. Some form of medication can be vital during a difficult crisis.

I have dedicated an entire chapter to the topic of "anxiety", but all variants of mental illnesses could not be listed here without getting lost, so I focus on examples instead.

Any combination between the Sun and Moon may reveal the root of any mental or emotional problem. The exception may be a trine (great harmony) that more tends to give the person a huge self-esteem and an inner balance between the symbols of men and women (or Yin and Yang) in the psyche. However, the stronger aspects (squares, oppositions, semisquares, inconjuncts and 135 degrees) can point to a slumbering or hidden inner imbalance. This can be triggered suddenly by stronger emotional experiences, already experienced in childhood. For example, the square aspect between the Sun and Moon is sometimes called the "divorce aspect," although this is somewhat excessive. However, depending on where relief and tension are located, with the Sun or Moon, you can figure out which gender the person feels is either disturbing or attracting. Even transgenders may have an element of this. However, it must be emphasized that one can not absolutely "see" any particular sexual orientation in the horoscope. There are too many aspects involved. In fact, at some times, people have become a little annoyed that I did not "see" that they were gay or lesbians.

However, it is sufficient that the basic analysis may indicate that it is either "the mother" or "the father" who was responsible for a remodeling treatment during childhood. Simply put, one can "see" if the person in question feels more confident with one or the other side of his sexual polarity, ie., from the parents different influences. I usually describe this as the fact that mom and dad often have different signaling, which can be extremely confusing for the child. (James Dean shows this ingeniously in the movie *Rebel Without a Cause*: "You say one thing and you say another -- and then you switch back.")

Should we still try to find some kind of reason, I list below the degree of probable effects.

Saturn

Saturn in the birth chart, or in a temporary prediction or transit, can be perceived as a prolonged depressive effect and associated with longer fatigue or depression. It can indicate a necessary longer stay in hospitals, and rehabilitation usually can take a long time. A transit (certain time) from Saturn does not have to be life-threatening, but it can lead to many serious decisions and conclusions, such as divorce, separation or change of residence or work. The consequence is often stronger if the person has a similar contact in the birth chart. Saturn's transit to the **Sun** reduces both the physical energy and the lust, and "time" is limited as the demands increase from the outside world.

Saturn's contact with the **Moon** may belong to the more likely triggers of mental disorders. Here, many shortcomings can occur, including shortness of time, money problems as well as strength or sexual desire issues. People born with strong aspects between them often live with various fears and phobias, avoiding more conflicts and the unknown than encountering their demons. This does not necessarily develop any diseases, but the person could attempt to withdraw from the world of reality and instead choose isolation and exclusion in order not to be exposed to the opinions and judgments of others. The newer phenomenon "Emo" resembles this experience. However, eating disorders and some temporary stomach disorders (Moon) may occur. The immune system may be or become weak.

Uranus

Uranus can contribute with both genius and mediumship, but in aspects with Moon-Saturn-combinations, this can be too much and panic arises. Saturn slows down and Uranus accelerates, similar to the acceleration and braking in a car at the same time. This can wear down the "engine" of the body and soul.

The combination between the Moon and Uranus can, without external pressure, lead to normal harmless restlessness. It could, for example leave a person never sitting still. However, if this is triggered by an unexpected experience or event, panic may lurk. The very concept of panic disorder comes from this combination. "Unusual feelings" or "quick surprises," like a physical or emotional shock, may make the most calm person stressed out. However, I need to point out that I have often found this in peoples' charts who have been both conscious and sometimes unconscious about their own mediumship talent. These energies can give the person a sixth sense, and intuition is often strong.

The **Sun's** contact with Uranus can also show a slumbering worry or anxiety. This is very common in geniuses and extremely talented people, and these people are often both eccentric and a bit odd to their disposition. This combination can definitely lead to unconscious stress, and both the heart and nervous system can be exposed to extreme tension. At worst, pure physical complications, such as a heart attack or myocardial infarction, can occur.

Mercury combinations with Uranus I spontaneously couple with several symptoms that may be classified as mental health issues. Uranus speeds up Mercury's communication and it speeds up with "all the balls in the air." If this becomes permanent or excessive, I may think of a mental meltdown in the form of psychosis or traumatic anxiety. These people are obviously very quick-witted and can be brilliant debaters, but they must learn how to focus and reduce the pace so as not to be too fragmented.

Uranus combinations with **Venus** are not associated with any actual mental health, but the person can be both promiscuous and unstable in their relationships, as well as in their values. This applies, for example, to adventurers who constantly require new excitement and constant endorphins, resulting in possible manic-depressive behavior. Ironically, they can have great luck with money, but they can never hold on to it. Hormonal disorders occur as well as irregular menstruation if the Moon is involved.

As a curiosity, it can be mentioned that this combination often occurs in so-called "celebrities" or movie stars' charts, whether with temporary fame or long term notoriety. I once found the combination of Moon-Venus-Uranus-MC in a chart belonging to a midwife. Could this mean she was suddenly meeting happy women at work?

With **Mars** combinations to Uranus, there is no real mental discomfort, except, perhaps, for explosive outbreaks similar to those shown by psychopaths. Everything from extreme restlessness to explosive aggression may sound more like a psychopath, but the effect is probably more physical. Body injuries and accidents of all varieties occur during these transits. Perhaps they also may occur amongst people who have some form of hyperactivity or ADHD, because the body's functions often is affected. But I'm not an expert and have no statistics on this, so I can only assume. It may need some Mercury influence added to this combination in this case.

Jupiter's combination with Uranus is not associated with mental illness, but linked to other more difficult aspects. These can increase other tensions, and Uranus often releases the energies of other planets. This can be seen more commonly in litigation.

Saturn combinations with Uranus is a little tricky, but no indication of mental illness unless the Sun is involved. Traditionally, they can cooperate but often go in different directions. The contrast between conservativism and new technology can lead to moral dilemmas, and I would rather see it as a lighter burden on the person's choice. They can detest change or break protest against everything old and deceased and do not care about the consequences. With the **Sun** involved, these can probably go to extremes. The conflict between authority and freedom can both isolate the individual and make him or her a ruthless rebel.

Neptune's involvement is probably the most subconscious, and a strong involvement with Uranus can lead to unpleasant dreams and anxious fantasies. In a waking state, this may seem to be splitting, even if the Sun (the body) or the Moon (the soul) is involved.

Pluto's effects are classical because they control everything in the psyche we are not aware of. The subconscious is like "The Sleeping Bear." If Pluto is activated, there may be a chaos in the psyche. When Pluto not only represents "Death" but also the "Unknown," these effects can be very unpleasant and scary. In case of active release, the person may end up in a pure psychosis or acute stress and must be treated very carefully.

I have experienced several effects myself. **Pluto's** contacts with the Sun can mean both an ending and a new birth, which is often the effect of this combination. Like shedding skins or experiencing "a brave new world," this effect can be very liberating and lead to greater awareness and thus greater freedom. Transformation is the key word, and it takes a lot of courage to dare to go down into your mental basement and analyze all the old bodies in the closet, thus healing and transforming them.

Pluto's contact with the Moon resembles this effect, but more emotional suffering occurs. Normally, carefree people often experience this as "bad luck" because things often go wrong or something interferes. In the worst case scenario, this contact may trigger an emotional shock or wake a slumbering trauma. This effect is common during regression therapy, where you can experience true depths in your mind. Also note that this contact or aspect often occurs in the charts of therapists, psychologists and psychiatrists. They are often working to delve in the depths of the soul. (Yes, I have this one as well).

Some astrological phenomena to watch out for; Transits to the Birth Map

Moon - Sun: In a strong aspect (square, opposition, etc.) sudden fatigue, drained of energy, inconstancy, indecision or distressed feelings can occur. Imbalance in the psyche can lead to or result from a separation or loss of something/someone. A sudden crisis can also lead to a break-up and separation from the other sex.

Moon - Mars: This usually indicates an emotional affect due to physical overload. A person can suddenly experience hyper-stress, uncontrollable anger, emotional lameness, physical pain, the need to withstand violence or bodily fear.

Moon - Jupiter: This occurs in all aspects, both strong and weak. Keywords here include gormande, gluttony, comfort-eating, indifference, sloppiness and an abusive addiction to junk-food. Always there is a high risk of weight problems. And there is an extra large risk if one of the planets is located in Pisces or Sagittarius, creating a double effect.

Moon - Saturn: This can occur in most aspects. "Why do I need to eat?" can become a common theme, with skipping meals rather than safe fasting, masochistic behavior, time mismanagement, economic crises, martyr behavior, refusing any food at all and allergies to certain foods. On the reverse side, there can also be extremely healthy persons with emphasis on strong principles, eg., veganism or for religious reasons. Melancholy or pessimism catalyzed by women (the Moon) can lead to depression. The symbolic projection here is of "a strict or authoritative woman," often older than the person. There can be an attempt to escape oneself by becoming "comfortably numb" (Pink Floyd).

Moon - Uranus: This occurs in the strongest trends of conjunctions, oppositions and squares. They are seen in eating disorders, bulimia, anorexia, gastric catarrh, ulcers or reflux. These patterns need the expressing and releasing of uncompromising feelings. These people want to break out of limiting routines and patterns. This can result in a strong need for certain freedoms or a strong need to revolt.

Moon - Neptune: This occurs in most aspects, often resulting in cases of colds, infections, flu or necessary medication. If Pluto is present, there is a risk of genital disorders. The risk of drug abuse is always great if you have this in your map. Take special care even with necessary medication. Comically, these people are also easier to heal by psychological influences as they are so highly susceptible for hypnosis and hypnotherapy.

Moon - Pluto: Actually this is found in all aspects, but conjunctions, squares and oppositions have the strongest effects. Here we can find the "Dr. Jekyll & Mr. Hyde" pattern. Skeletons in the closet can suddenly appear (unpleasant memories of the past). Lurking trauma comes up to the surface. Feelings become difficult to control because they are suggested or provoked by circumstances such as "bad luck," humiliation, lies, someone talked badly about you, being unfairly accused, feeling ignored, feeling overlooked and feeling spurned. All of these feelings and reactions can attract the "devil in you." This basic aspect may be most common among psychopaths, borderline schizophrenia or other hard-to-treat mental and emotional symptoms. The person can benefit from conversational therapy or mental training.

When it comes to certain mental disabilities such as ADHD, Asperger's or autism, I have no sure statistics to lean against, but they are usually like ordinary people. Some are silent, some are hyperactive and also externalising. Individuals with Asperger's often seem to have special talents and can be extremely intelligent in their special areas. I interpret this as a combination of the Moon-Mercury-Uranus. They can also easily become emotionally stressed out, like in the film *Rainman*, which is typical of a strong Uranus. Autism is a bit more complicated. There are also different degrees of autism. Most, however, seem to have in common that they prefer to live in their own little world, and that indicates a strong Neptune. Because of their behavior, they are perceived as more passive and friendly, so I guess that the Ascendant plays a certain role.

"It's not good that everything you want is fulfilled

Through illness you realize the value of health

By the evil value of goodness

Through hunger saturation

By effort the value of rest "

Herakleitos

"Wrong" Astrology

After studying horoscopes for more than 40 years, it has long been clear to me that the main features are interpreted in the wrong order. You may mention that director *Alfred Hitchcock* was Leo, but not that he had his Moon in Scorpio, which should be more correct if you look at his life with movies. He was known for the thrill in his movies, and fears are linked to Scorpio. I could give you more examples, but it's enough that you can call this "the missing link," or perhaps better "the wrong interpretation." In other words, it is not good to focus solely on the so-called Sun Sign (the birthday sign).

Of all those who applied to me over the years, there has always been a strong dominance of women, which may seem obvious because women put more trust upon their instinct (including intuition) than men, and instincts are connected to the Moon. I would guess an average of nine out of ten applicants were women, and then one should understand that women are not only ruled by the Moon. But it is also men who actually think that the usual Sun sign interpretations do not match, so it's almost comical. The traditional basic interpretation is based on the Sun Sign (your birthday), and it is the Sun's position, not the Moon. Thus, it should "attune" better when men read about their Sun signs and do not match the same to women. From a purely psychological perspective, one can see that women are more responsive to feelings and more often trust their intuition than men.

I read many years ago about an investigation where you cut out symbolic words that represented the Sun Sign and Moon Sign, and then let the person choose which characteristics they thought fit best.

The majority of women always chose the characteristics that were connected to the Moon, not the Sun. I have tested this myself many times, and there may be many who recognize my expression: "Yes, you are Pisces, but to me you are Gemini because you have your Moon in Gemini!", or "Sagittarius Moon with Sun in Capricorn, " etc.

In the 80's when we met astrologers in associations and conferences, we never asked "what sign are you?". The question was rather which Ascendant they had. This is because the Ascendant often describes our attitude and radiance, or the signals we send out. Had you instead asked "Where have you got your Moon?", then perhaps you would have been a little more curious about the SOUL you met, not the BODY (the Sun).

Here is a summary of the general basic rules:

The Sun represents a lot of our values and our view of life, but more on a spiritual level, where we find opinions, perceptions and views of life as a whole. Otherwise, the Sun represents most of the body, the physical being we are, and how we perceive and manage the qualities that are generally called masculine energies. The Sun is connected to symbols like the father, the husband, and "God", but also the concepts of productivity and procreation/conceiving. In a woman's chart I try to describe not only her attitude towards the other sex, but also her views on parenting, authority, leadership or the view of her own sexuality, as this indirectly controls child-raising and parenting. The Sun's position and aspects of the other symbols in the chart describe these characteristics for both men and women, while the Moon symbolizes the more personal or emotional instincts, such as needs, habits, moods, temperaments, rituals or unconscious reactions.

The Moon is not only the symbol of the woman but is also the child in the person's life. It symbolizes not only temporal childhood but also the relationship with your own mother and/or possible influence from other women during childhood, such as a grandmother or an aunt, as well as older or younger siblings. Whether you are male or female, the Moon's location and aspects reflect your attitude to all women. However, the effects of the Moon are many. Over the years, I have noticed that it usually controls our rituals, traditions or cycles. This would include tradition-bound rituals such as Easter, Christmas or other celebrations. Furthermore, the periodicity or cycle of the Moon is exactly as long as the woman's menstrual cycle. It also controls the seasons and really all our daily habits and routines and whether we are night owls or morning girls. The need for security is often reflected by the Moon's aspects to the other planets and can also symbolically describe our childhood in general. As an adult, the Moon aspects reflect your attitude towards your own and others' children and how your own needs and priorities change during life.

I can not recall if it was Oscar Wilde who said that if you want to get to know someone better, then you should tease or ridicule them, because then you attract the instinctive feelings that describe more about a person's Soul, rather than only the external personality with their opinions or perceptions. I totally agree.

If you compare the differences between Sun and Moon, then I hope you more easily understand what a huge difference it is. Since the traditional Sun sign interpretation can not simply "match 100%," it should be clear. Rather call it Moon interpretation. This now creates a whole new phenomenon, namely that the likelihood that a simple platitude and weekly magazine interpretion will be drastically reduced. Most women who, out of pure curiosity, read in a blink about their Sun signs, can hardly think it is 100% accurate, especially if she is not born around new Moon when the Moon is closest to the birth sign. If you might have this in your chart, you call it a "Double-Sunsign-character." Should you make it even more typical, you may also have the Ascendant in the same sign (born close to sunrise), and perhaps both Mercury and Venus. The more present in the birth sun sign, the more typical of the sign of course.

The Moon's location in the houses reflects "where" in life one usually feels safe or prefer to show their feelings. For example, in the 12th house, it is common for you to go out of the world's chaos and rather seek solitude or isolation to feel safe, unlike having the Moon in the 1st house, where you are more like an open book and most often governed by external impulses and stimuli. In that particular situation, being called an extrovert is an understatement.

If you want to get to know another person's self or intrinsic intentions and secrets, do not worry about the birthday or the Sun sign. Instead, we are forced to find out where the Moon was located in the chart/horoscope when you were born, and to find that out you have to either contact an astrologer or find an online page where you can calculate this.

Then maybe it's no wonder that most women get happy or confirmed when they contact an astrologer. The "missing" puzzle piece falls into place and the "missing link" is revealed that you did not find in your weekly magazine or even in your little *Sun Sign for Beginners* pamphlet. Perhaps, luckily, women are more curious than men and trust their intuition to wanting to contact an astrologer. Of course, there are also men who are interested, but at the same time they think it may be a little scary to reveal or to analyze feelings if they have a sensitive or delicate Moon in their chart.

Here follows a brief description of the Moon in the respective Signs and also a number of examples of known people or phenomena with both birth signs and Moon signs, so you can see if you recognize or think that this is more appropriate for the person. In some cases, it says that the Moon might be in two different signs, which is therefore marked with "slash" (/). This is due to the fact that there is no actual or accurate time of birth and the Moon maybe was in two different signs during this day. A little unfortunate for some people, mostly older, who do not know exactly when they were born. If you are "lucky" perhaps the Moon was in the same sign throughout the birthday and then it will be easier to describe. Sometimes the differences can be large and easier to figure out, for example, Pisces vs Aries.

I have included both known and unknown people or phenomena (eg., the Tsunami or 9/11) and which Sun signs or Moon signs that apply to that day. I thought it might be exciting to find people who you recognize by name. If not, you might find common denominations between all those who have the same Moon sign as you. Find out the sign where your Moon lies (if you know), and maybe you can find something in common with others who have this. It could be a kind of astrological soul mate.

NOTE: *Physical disposition* must not be interpreted literally. It depends entirely on the Moon's location and aspects to the other symbols.

Rather, call it a kind of *Achilles heel* that may end up in focus during negative periods.

Moon in different Signs

Moon in Aries: Motto - Me first or I am. Symbolically also interpreted as Moon in the first house.

First out is the impulsive and independent attitude that is constantly on the move. They are competition-oriented and like challenges and struggles. Most often they are sincere and forward but not always the best diplomat. Feelings must come out quickly, and they may have difficulty listening to the feelings of others. One of the more physical needs is to be active, and this can give good results if they can apply patience. In the worst case, they are edgy and easy-to-understand, as they can not always control their reactions. Physically, they are disposed towards fever and headaches, or cuts and burns in cases of emergency.

Moon in Aries – examples:

Donna Cunningham, astrologer. Sun Cancer, Moon Aries.

King of Sweden, Carl XVI Gustaf. Sun Taurus, Moon Aries.

Joan Grant, born in 1907. Wrote books about reincarnation. Both Sun and Moon Aries.

Marlon Brando, movie icon. Both Sun and Moon Aries.

Andrew Lincoln, actor *Rick Grimes* in the "Walking Dead" tv-series. Sun Virgo, Moon Aries.

Emile Zola, author. Both Sun and Moon Aries.

Inger Nilsson, swedish actress, "Pippi Longstocking". Sun Taurus, Moon Aries.

Sture Johansson, medium that transchanneled "Ambres". Sun Libra, Moon Aries/Pisces.

"HAL 9000", the computer brain in the movie *2001: A Space Odyssey*. Sun Capricorn, Moon Aries.

James Redfield, author of *The Celestine Prophesy*. Sun Pisces, Moon Aries.

Thomas More, wrote the book *Utopia*. Sun Aquarius, Moon Aries.

Luciano Pavarotti, opera singer. Sun Libra, Moon Aries.

Oskar Schindler, rescued Jews in WW II. Sun Taurus, Moon Aries.

Jim Jones, sect leader who caused around 1000 people to commit suicide in Guyana in 1978. Sun Taurus, Moon conjunct Uranus in Aries.

Kim Ung-yong, Korean infant with an IQ over 200. Sun Pisces, Moon Pisces/Aries.

Rihanna, singer. Sun Pisces, Moon Aries.

Salvador Dali, artist. Sun Taurus, Moon Aries.

Bill Gates, computers. Sun Scorpio, Moon Aries.

John Cleese, Monty Python. Sun Scorpio, Moon Aries.

Moon in Taurus: Motto - I own. Symbolically Moon in the second house.

Moon in Taurus people are into reason and logical rules, and this may be the most practical sign. Achieving things of physical matter and also gaining returns is their strength. Perhaps a bit melancholy and meek, they are also known for having great endurance. Because of a weakness towards the good things in life, they tend to be epicureans who need a lot of activity in order not to gain weight. Sensual and thoughtful, they need physical closeness. Business sense usually is as good as aesthetic interests. They are usually physically disposed towards throat problems and secondary genital conditions.

Moon in Taurus - examples:

Hans Christian Andersen, author. Sun Aries, Moon Taurus.

Gregory Peck, movie legend. Sun Aries, Moon Taurus.

The foundation of Youtube. February 14, 2005. Sun Aquarius, Moon Taurus. 1st video uploaded April 23, 2005, at 20:27, California time. Sun Taurus, Moon Scorpio.

Lindsay Lohan, actress. Sun Cancer, Moon Taurus.

Bob Dylan, musician. Sun Gemini, Moon Taurus.

Mick Jagger, Rolling Stones. Sun Leo, Moon Taurus.

Björn Borg, tennis legend. Sun Gemini, Moon Taurus.

Carlos Castaneda, author, mystic. Sun Capricorn, Moon Taurus.

Greta Garbo, movie legend. Sun Virgo, Moon Taurus.

Bill Clinton, former president. Sun Leo, Moon Taurus.

Edgar Cayce, "the sleeping prophet." Sun Pisces, Moon Taurus.

Julia Parker, astrologer, author of *Astrological Handbook* 1974. Sun Leo, Moon Taurus.

Galileo Galileo, astronomer. Sun Pisces, Moon Taurus.

Charles E.O. Carter, astrologer. Sun Aquarius, Moon Taurus.

Karl Marx, communist, wrote the book *Das Kapital*. Both Sun and Moon Taurus.

Michael Palin, Monty Python. Both Sun and Moon Taurus.

Graham Chapman, Monty Python. Sun Capricorn, Moon Taurus.

Katherine Hepburn, movie legend. Both Sun and Moon Taurus.

Eckhart Tolle, author. Sun Aquarius, Moon Taurus.

Moon in Gemini: Motto - I think and communicate. Symbolically Moon in the third house.

Like a butterfly on a flower bed, these spiritual beings are constantly curious about new discoveries in life and therefore never stay for too long in the same place, work or in a relationship that does not stimulate them. Versatile and with many *balls in the air,* they can be perceived as both superficial and uncomitted, but they think more than they talk. Restlessness occurs if they become obstructed or have to wait, and patience is not their strongest characteristic. Physically disposed towards lung problems and with a delicate nervous system, all stress must be avoided with rigorous routines and planning. Daily walks or exercise are good for both body and psyche.

Moon in Gemini - examples:

Rolf Martinus, Danish mystic born in 1890. Sun Leo, Moon Gemini.

Günther Wallraff, revealing journalist. Sun Libra, Moon Gemini (probably) or Cancer.

Spencer Tracy, movie legend. Sun Aries, Moon Gemini.

Bette Davis, movie legend. Sun Aries, Moon Gemini.

Leo Messi, Argentine football player. Sun Cancer, Moon Gemini.

Alejandro Inarritu, director. Sun Leo, Moon Gemini/Cancer.

Alec Guinness, movie legend. Sun Aries, Moon Gemini.

Victor Borge, pianist/comedian. Sun Capricorn, Moon Gemini.

David Coverdale, rock singer in, among others, rockgroup Whitesnake. Sun Virgo, Moon Gemini.

Sigmund Freud, psychoanalyst. Sun Taurus, Moon Gemini.

Brazilian National Day 7th September 1822. Sun Virgo, Moon Gemini.

Vladimir Putin, Russian president. Sun Libra, Moon Gemini.

State of Iraq, July 14, 1958. Sun Cancer, Moon Gemini.

Johannes Kepler, astronomer. Sun Capricorn, Moon Gemini.

Wayne Gretzky, ice hockey legend. Sun Aquarius, Moon Gemini.

John McEnroe, tennis legend. Sun Aquarius, Moon Gemini.

Ingemar Johansson, Swedish world heavyweight champion in boxing 1959. Sun Virgo, Moon Gemini.

Ingemar Stenmark, skiing legend. Sun Pisces, Moon Gemini.

World Trade Center, 9/11. Sun Virgo, Moon Gemini.

Tsunami, Indian Ocean, December 26, 2004. Sun Capricorn, Moon Gemini.

James Rolfe, *Cinemassacre* Youtube legend. Sun Cancer, Moon probably Gemini.

Franz Kafka, author. Sun Cancer, Moon Gemini.

Groucho Marx, film legend born 2 Oct 1890. Sun Libra, Moon Gemini.

Moon in Cancer: Motto - I feel. Symbolically Moon in the fourth house.

All kinds of feelings control them, and life is a rollercoaster. Sensitive and thoughtful, they suffer from the grief and worries of others and do everything to protect themselves. They can communicate quickly between joy, despair or anger, and they can be amazingly loving but equally exhausted if they are abandoned. They are physically disposed of all problems with the stomach, and obesity may occur with too much self-pity. There is a tendency towards sleeping problems.

Moon in Cancer - examples:

Lois M. Rodden, astrologer and author. Sun Gemini, Moon Cancer.

David Icke, medium and author, featured in the movie *Thrive*. Sun Taurus, Moon conjunct Uranus in Cancer.

Cheryl Strayed, the author who wrote the book *Wild* and wandered along the trail in western United States and wrote a book about her life. She also had a movie made about her. Sun Virgo, Moon Cancer. Emotions and the relationship with the mother were central to her experience.

Frank Lee Morris, one of the runaways from Alcatraz. Sun Virgo, Moon Cancer (Home Prison).

Kurt Cobain, singer with Nirvana. Sun Pisces, Moon Cancer.

Janis Joplin, singer. Sun Capricorn, Moon Cancer.

Facebook, foundation created in 2004. Sun Aquarius, Moon Cancer.

Crown Princess Victoria, future queen of Sweden. Both Sun and Moon Cancer.

Babe Ruth, baseball legend. Sun Aquarius, Moon Cancer.

Isaac Newton, astronomer and astrologer. Sun Capricorn, Moon Cancer.

Harpo Marx, November 23, 1888. Sun Sagittarius, Moon Cancer.

Franklin D. Roosevelt, former president. Sun Aquarius, Moon Cancer.

ISIS, Islamic State In Syria, June 28, 2014. Both Sun and Moon Cancer.

George Orwell, author of *1984*. Both Sun and Moon Cancer.

Jimmy Page, guitarist Led Zeppelin. Sun Capricorn, Moon Cancer.

Shakira, singer. Sun Aquarius. Moon Cancer

Sören Kierkegaard, philosopher. Sun Taurus, Moon Cancer.

Moon in Leo: Motto - I want. Symbolically Moon in the fifth house.

Pride and greatness can provide a good organizational ability and desire to create. They want to shape their visions and are often very productive. Strong, intense feelings can make them protective but also complacent and arrogant in difficult cases. They often have an addictive need for praise. Physically, they are disposed towards heart as well as back problems in excessive loading. There is also the possibility for eye problems.

Moon in Leo - examples:

Islamic Republic of Iran, Khomeini, Feb. 11, 1979. Sun Aquarius, Moon Leo.

State of Israel, May 14, 1948. Sun Taurus, Moon Leo.

Sweden, one of many examples of Sweden's chart, based on the Basics Amendment 1975. Sun Capricorn, Moon Leo.

Paul McCartney, Beatles. Sun Gemini, Moon Leo.

Ringo Starr, Beatles. Sun Cancer, Moon Leo.

Peter Jackson, director "The Lord of the Rings". Sun Scorpio, Moon Leo.

Queen Elizabeth II, born 1926 England. Sun Taurus, Moon Leo.

Felix Kellberg, Youtube phenomenon *PewDiePie*. Sun Scorpio, Moon Leo/Virgo.

Martin Sheen, actor, president in the TV series *West Wing*. Both Sun and Moon Leo.

David Bowie, musician. Sun Capricorn, Moon Leo.

Lana Del Rey, musician. Sun Gemini, Moon Leo.

Marlene Dietrich, movie icon. Sun Capricorn, Moon Leo.

Marilyn Manson, aka musician Brian Hugh Warner. Sun Capricorn, Moon Leo.

Ralph Waldo Emerson, author. Sun Gemini, Moon Leo.

Jack Lemmon, actor. Sun Aquarius, Moon Leo.

Michail Gorbatjov, former Russian president. Sun Pisces, Moon Leo.

Terry Gilliam, Monty Python. Sun Scorpio, Moon Leo.

Terry Jones, Monty Python. Sun Aquarius, Moon Leo.

Evangeline Adams, world famous astrologer born in 1868. Sun Aquarius, Moon Leo or Aries (2 different years).

Mahatma Gandhi, non-violence leader of India. Sun Libra, Moon Leo.

James Joyce, author. Sun Aquarius, Moon Leo.

Emperor Nero, Rome, born in 37. Sun Sagittarius, Moon Leo.

Anne Frank, world-famous diarist. Sun Gemini, Moon Leo.

Tom Hanks, actor. Sun Cancer, Moon Leo.

Moon in Virgo: Motto - I review and analyze. Symbolically Moon in the sixth House.

Here we have the permanent secretary who works better behind the scenes than in the spotlight. The need to serve makes these people trustworthy, conscientious and loyal. Emotionally shy, reserved and excessive caution can lead to inhibition and poor self-esteem. Often they are diligent in school work and love to immerse themselves in and bring order out of chaos. Pedantry can occur, but they are careful with hygiene and cost. They are physically disposed towards bowel diseases and bile disorders.

Moon in Virgo - examples:

Joan K. Rowling, author of the *Harry Potter* books. Sun Leo, Moon Virgo.

Deepak Chopra, author. Sun Libra, Moon Virgo.

Dalai Lama, Tibet's spiritual head. Sun Cancer, Moon conjunct Neptune Virgo.

Serena Williams, tennis player ranked 1st. Born the same day as the author´s *Utopia*, September 26, 1981. Sun Libra, Moon Virgo.

John F. Kennedy, former president. Sun Gemini, Moon Virgo.

Gertrude Stein, lesbian advocate. Sun Aquarius, Moon Virgo.

Richard Burton, actor. Sun Scorpio, Moon Virgo.

Ingmar Bergman, director. Sun Cancer, Moon Virgo.

Shirley MacLaine, author, dancer, actor. Sun Taurus, Moon conjunct Neptune Virgo.

Anders Breivik, mass murderer, Norway 2011. Sun Aquarius, Moon conjunct Saturn in Virgo.

Eva Braun, Hitler's wife. Sun Aquarius, Moon Virgo.

Tycho Brahe, astronomer and astrologer. Sun Capricorn, Moon Virgo.

Toshiro Mifune, Japanese actor in *The Seven Samurai*. Sun Aries, Moon Virgo.

George Martin, Beatles producer. Sun Capricorn, Moon Virgo.

Dr Eugen Jonas, gynecologist and astrologer who by method could determine the sex of the fetus. Sun Scorpio, Moon conjunct Neptune in Virgo.

Moon in Libra: Motto - I weigh or judge. Symbolically Moon in the seventh House.

This is the diplomat in the congregation who detests all forms of imbalance or conflict. These people seek constant confirmation and work best in partnerships, collaborations or groups. They are social and outgoing but perhaps lacking in self-esteem and needing to take care of themselves first. There is much interest in art and music and to beautify their surroundings. They are also known for being strong on patience. Physically, they are disposed towards weight problems as well as kidney and sleep disorders.

Moon in Libra - examples:

Philip Glass, composer of *Koyaanisqaatsi*. Sun Aquarius, Moon Libra.

Kitaro, New Age musician. Sun Aquarius, Moon Libra.

Nat King Cole, musician. Sun Pisces, Moon Libra.

Aileen Vuornos, a prostitute who killed her customers. Sun Pisces, Moon Libra. (The movie *Monster* was about her life.)

Bruce Springsteen, musician. Both Sun and Moon Libra.

Björn Ulvaeus, musician in ABBA. Sun Taurus, Moon Libra.

Ingvar Kamprad, founder of IKEA. Sun Aries, Moon Libra.

George Bush Sr., former president, born June 12, 1924. Sun Gemini, Moon Libra.

George W. Bush, sober alcoholic and former president. Sun Cancer, Moon Libra.

Fidel Castro, communist former leader of Cuba. Sun Leo, Moon Libra.

Robert Powell, actor portrayed Jesus in the TV mini-series in 1977. Sun Gemini, Moon Libra.

William Shakespeare, playwright. Sun Taurus, Moon Libra/Scorpio.

Helena Blavatsky, medium. Sun Leo, Moon Libra.

Rudolf Nurejev, ballet dancer. Sun Pisces, Moon Libra.

Karl Ernst Krafft, Hitler's astrologer. Sun Taurus, Moon Libra.

Sylvia Plath, poet who committed suicide. Sun Scorpio, Moon Libra.

Justin Bieber, singer. Sun Pisces, Moon Libra.

Noam Chomsky, author and humanitarian. Sun Sagittarius, Moon Libra.

Moon in Scorpio: Motto - I wish. Symbolically Moon in the eighth house.

These natural outsiders in society seem to survive all the adversities of life. They are desirous to fight, tough, heartfelt, determined and on the verge of mania. They often succeed in surpassing themselves and others. However, there are deep undercurrents in the psyche that can sometimes make them extremely hot-headed, and emotional outbursts can be catastrophic to both themselves and others. Physically, they are prone towards problems with the genitals, menstrual disturbances and prostate and anus dysfunctions.

Moon in Scorpio – examples:

Jacob Davidsson, the author and astrologer. Sun Leo, Moon Scorpio.

Silvia, Queen of Sweden. Sun Capricorn, Moon Scorpio.

George Harrison of the Beatles. Sun Pisces, Moon Scorpio.

Agnetha Fältskog from ABBA. Sun Aries, Moon Scorpio.

Luis Suarez, football player from Uruguay, not only famous for his skill but also his mental problems (biting his opponents). Sun Aquarius, Moon Scorpio.

Alfred Hitchcock, director. Sun Leo, Moon Scorpio.

Charles Chaplin, movie legend. Sun Aries, Moon Scorpio.

Stanley Kubrik, director. Sun Leo, Moon Scorpio.

Stephen Spielberg, director. Sun Sagittarius, Moon Scorpio.

Francis Ford Coppola, director. Sun Aries, Moon Scorpio.

Ida Lupino, director and actress. Sun Aquarius, Moon Scorpio.

Elizabeth Taylor, actress. Sun Pisces, Moon Scorpio.

Bob Marley, reggae musician. Sun Aquarius, Moon Scorpio.

Robbie Williams, singer. Sun Aquarius, Moon Scorpio.

Italy's national day 10th June 1946. Sun Gemini, Moon Scorpio.

Discovery of the planet Uranus 1781. Sun Pisces, Moon Scorpio.

Robert Hand, astrologer. Sun Sagittarius, Moon Scorpio.

Johnny Cash, musician. Sun Pisces, Moon Scorpio.

Paul Horn, a flutist born in 1930, who recorded inside the Great Pyramid in Giza 1976. Sun Pisces, Moon Scorpio.

Uri Geller, telekinetic medium. Sun Sagittarius, Moon Scorpio.

Michel de Nostradamus, world famous astrologer born December 14, 1503. Sun Sagittarius, Moon Scorpio.

Nils Ferlin, Swedish poet. Sun Sagittarius, Moon Scorpio.

Roger Waters, musician of Pink Floyd. Sun Virgo, Moon Scorpio/Sagittarius.

James Dean, movie legend. Sun Aquarius, Moon Scorpio.

Warren Beatty, actor. Sun Aries, Moon Scorpio.

Jules Verne, author. Sun Aquarius, Moon Scorpio.

Herman Wouk, author. Sun Gemini, Moon Scorpio.

Lady Gaga, musician. Sun Aries, Moon Scorpio.

Björk, musician. Sun, Moon, Ascendant and Neptune in Scorpio.

Bono, musician with U2. Sun Taurus, Moon Scorpio.

Beyoncé, singer. Sun Virgo, Moon Scorpio.

Harry S. Truman, former US President 1945-1953. Sun Taurus, Moon Scorpio.

John Wilkes Booth, who shot Abraham Lincoln. Sun Taurus, Moon Scorpio/Sagittarius.

Rembrandt, world renowned artist. Sun Cancer, Moon Scorpio.

Maria Montessori, child educator. Sun Virgo, Moon Scorpio.

Edward Snowden, whistle blower. Sun Gemini, Moon Scorpio.

Julian Assange of Wikileaks. Sun Cancer, Moon Scorpio.

Roger Federer, tennis legend. Sun Leo, Moon Scorpio.

Moon in Sagittarius: Motto - I see. Symbolically Moon in the ninth house.

These people are the visionaries and the carefree chatterboxes who see everything positive. Optimism and humor are their natural air, and they love to spread good vibrations. Like clowns, they can seem unconcerned and easy going, but under the surface they are often serious and pondering over all injustices. They are freedom-loving and constantly on the way to something or somewhere. An interest in higher education is always possible if the interest is present, as they are always seeking more information which they can then pass on. They are physically disposed towards problems with the back and hips as well as a tendency towards overweight due to too little activity.

Moon in Sagittarius - examples:

William Shaffer, good friend of the author and former astrologer and channeller of the *Akashic Records*. Sun Gemini, Moon Sagittarius.

Liz Greene, author and astrologer. Sun Virgo, Moon Sagittarius.

Michael Newton, author of the book *Journey of Souls*, is born around a New Moon and has both Sun and Moon in Sagittarius.

Paolo Coelho, author. Sun Virgo, Moon Sagittarius.

Are Waerland, health pioneer born 1876. Sun Aries, Moon Sagittarius.

Emanuel Swedenborg, mystic and author. Sun Aquarius, Moon Sagittarius.

Dante Alighieri, author of *Divina Comedia*. Sun Gemini, Moon Sagittarius.

Dan Brown, author of *The da Vinci code*. Sun Cancer, Moon Sagittarius.

Albert Einstein, universal genius. Sun Pisces, Moon Sagittarius.

Mary Shelley, author of *Frankenstein*. Sun Virgo, Moon Sagittarius.

Michel Gauquelin, astrologer. Sun Scorpio, Moon Sagittarius.

Sylvia Browne, medium and author. Sun Libra, Moon Sagittarius.

The cat *Garfield* , born (published) Gemini with Moon in Sagittarius (loves food).

Jennifer Aniston, actress from *Friends*. Sun Aquarius, Moon Sagittarius.

Zlatan Ibrahimovic, famous soccer player. Sun Libra, Moon Sagittarius (many travels and residencies in several countries).

Helge Ingstad, Norwegian explorer and adventurer who lived to 101 years old. Sun Capricorn, Moon Sagittarius.

Olof Palme, assassinated Swedish Prime Minister, 1986. Sun Aquarius, Moon Sagittarius.

Charles Lindbergh, lone flyer over the Atlantic. Sun Aquarius, Moon Sagittarius.

Neil Armstrong, moon traveler. Sun Leo, Moon Sagittarius (long journeys).

Charles Dickens, author. Sun Aquarius, Moon Sagittarius.

Carl Sagan, author Tv-series *Cosmos*. Sun Scorpio, Moon Sagittarius.

Estonia´s independence, February 25, 1908. Sun Pisces, Moon Sagittarius.

Nicolaus Copernicus, astronomer. Sun Pisces, Moon Sagittarius.

Lois de Wohl, the allied forces astrologer in London during WW II. Sun Aquarius, Moon Sagittarius.

Donald Trump, president. Sun Gemini, Moon Sagittarius.

Adele, singer. Sun Taurus, Moon Sagittarius.

Bruno Reuter, musician known as *Karunesh*, born January 10, 1956, *Sounds of the Heart*. Sun Capricorn, Moon Sagittarius.

Jiddu Krishnamurti, philosopher, author of *Freedom from the known*. Sun Taurus, Moon Sagittarius.

Mike Tyson, boxer. Sun Cancer, Moon Sagittarius.

Moon in Capricorn: Motto - I'm using. Symbolically Moon in the tenth house.

This serious person continually takes responsibility for everything and everyone and should more often take a time-out to learn to relax. Ambition or a deep sense of responsibility is usually a bit too high, and they may be as demanding towards others as to themselves. High goals in life and a practical approach can achieve enormous success in the long run. They are emotionally vulnerable at times when it does not seem necessary. However, their sense of duty is colossal. Physically, they are prone towards problems with knees, bones, teeth or skin. Rheumatoid arthritis and indigestion are also problems caused by too much anxiety.

Moon in Capricorn – examples:

Edvard Munch, artist, best known for *The Scream*. Sun Sagittarius, Moon Capricorn.

John Lennon of the Beatles. Sun Libra, Moon Capricorn. Moon Aquarius at alternate time. Birth time in question.

Eric Idle, Monty Python. Sun Aries, Moon Capricorn.

August Strindberg, author. Sun Aquarius, Moon Capricorn.

John Gray, author of *Mars & Venus*. Both Sun and Moon Capricorn.

Lon Chaney, silent movie legend. Sun Aries, Moon Capricorn.

Billie Holiday, jazz legend. Sun Aries, Moon Capricorn.

Rosa Parks, Citizens' Rights Movement fighter (bus protest). Sun Aquarius, Moon Capricorn.

Argentina's National day. Sun Cancer, Moon Capricorn.

Abraham Lincoln, former president. Sun Aquarius, Moon Capricorn.

Al Gore, politician and author of *An Inconvenient Truth*, and *almost* a president in the election 2000. Sun Aries, Moon Capricorn.

Lars von Trier, director. Sun Taurus, Moon Capricorn.

Rainer Werner Fassbinder, director. Sun Gemini, Moon Capricorn.

Peter Gabriel, musician with Genesis. Sun Aquarius, Moon Capricorn.

David Letterman, TV show host. Sun Aries, Moon Capricorn.

Marine Le Pen, French right politician leader of "Front nationel". Sun Leo, Moon Capricorn.

Rod Steiger, actor. Sun Aries, Moon Capricorn.

Lucille Ball, television star of *I love Lucy*. Sun Leo, Moon Capricorn.

Franco Zeffirelli, director of *Jesus of Nazareth* series. Sun Aquarius, Moon Capricorn.

Marc Robertson, astrologer. Sun Aquarius, Moon Capricorn.

Neale Donald Walsch, author of *Conversations with God*. Sun Virgo, Moon Capricorn.

Michael Moore, documentary filmmaker and director. Sun Taurus, Moon Capricorn.

Latvia's independence, November 18, 1917. Sun Scorpio, Moon Capricorn.

William Herschel, discovered the planet Uranus in 1781. Sun Scorpio, Moon Capricorn.

Reinhold Ebertin, famous German astrologer. Sun Aquarius, Moon Capricorn.

Agneta Oreheim, Swedish astrologer. Sun Leo, Moon Capricorn.

Emperor Augustus, Rome, born 63 BC. Sun Virgo, Moon Capricorn.

Adolf Hitler, dictator. Sun Aries, Moon Capricorn.

George Clooney, actor. Sun Taurus, Moon Capricorn.

Mark David Chapman, shot John Lennon. Sun Taurus, Moon Capricorn.

John Fogerty, musician with Creedence Clearwater Revival. Sun Gemini, Moon Capricorn.

Robert F. Kennedy, murdered president´s brother. Sun Scorpio, Moon Capricorn.

Moon in Aquarius: Motto - I know. Symbolically Moon in the eleventh house.

The one who unconsciously and consciously stands out in life. Eccentric and obstinate, they often think outside the box and always choose other ways, though alienation can occur as a result. Socially aware of the world conscience, they often struggle for maladjusted and odd people. Idealism with hopes and desires may be the driving force, but restlessness and inability to cooperate can interfere with the energy. They are the independent freedom lover who thrives best on his own way in life. Physically, they are disposed towards problems with the shins, calves and ankles, but also secondary heart problems in the event of too much anxiety or restlessness. Cramps and hysteria are latent when overloaded.

Moon in Aquarius -examples;

Princess Diana, "Lady Di". Sun Cancer, Moon Aquarius.

Jon Anderson, singer in the rockgroup YES. Sun Scorpio, Moon Aquarius.

Gillian Flynn, author of the book *Gone Girl* which became a movie. Sun Pisces, Moon Aquarius.

Francois Truffaut, director. Both Sun and Moon Aquarius.

Roy Andersson, director, born 1943. Sun Aries, Moon Aquarius.

Vladimir Lenin, former Russian politician. Sun Taurus, Moon Aquarius.

USA, July 4th, 1776. Sun Cancer, Moon Aquarius.

Marilyn Monroe, movie icon. Sun Gemini, Moon Aquarius.

Orson Welles, actor and director. Sun Taurus, Moon Aquarius.

Joseph Pulitzer, author and founder of the Pulitzer Prize. Sun Aries, Moon Aquarius.

Sarah Palin, American politician. Both Sun and Moon Aquarius.

Ernest Shackleton, polar scientist. Both Sun and Moon Aquarius.

Brian Epstein, Beatles manager. Sun Virgo, Moon Aquarius.

Stu Sutcliffe, first drummer in the Beatles, died in 1962 of a cerebral haemorrhage, 21 years old. Sun Cancer, Moon Aquarius.

Woody Allen, director. Sun Sagittarius, Moon Aquarius.

Edward Grieg, composer. Sun Gemini, Moon probably Aquarius.

Johnny Weissmüller, *Tarzan*. Sun Gemini, Moon Aquarius.

Mohammed Ali, former Cassius Clay, boxer. Sun Capricorn, Moon Aquarius.

Charles Manson, sect leader. Sun Scorpio, Moon Aquarius.

Moon in Pisces: Motto - I believe. Symbolically Moon in the twelfth house.

This is the Zodiac's merciful samaritan for both body and soul. They are cautious and a little bit modest, but with a lot of care and dedication to all those who are worse, even the animals. Dreaming and sometimes absent, they are best enjoying their imagination or creative activities. They seek frequent security in religion or mystcism and in the "other side". They are even known to look for loneliness to avoid conflict (the eremite who rather meditate than fight). Physically, they are always sensitive to chemicals that affect the body and the mind as they are vulnerable to all influences. The feet can be fragile, and colds may be hard to get rid of. All kinds of drugs should be avoided as they may have destructive effects. Similarly, medicines should be taken with caution. They sleep for hours when worried.

Moon in Pisces – examples:

Terry Evans, psychic medium and known from television. Sun Scorpio, Moon Pisces / Aries.

Helen Keller, deaf-mute author. Sun Cancer, Moon Pisces.

Leonardo da Vinci, artist and universal genius. Sun Taurus, Moon Pisces.

Michael Jackson, musician. Sun Virgo, Mcon Pisces.

Robert Plant, singer with Led Zeppelin. Sun Leo, Moon Pisces.

Annifrid Lyngstad of ABBA. Sun Scorpio, Moon Pisces.

JRR Tolkien, author of *The Lord of the Rings*. Sun Capricorn, Moon Pisces.

Grace Kelly, actress and princess. Sun Scorpio, Moon Pisces.

Sarah Michelle Gellar, star of *Buffy the vampire slayer*. Sun Aries, Moon Pisces.

Ken Hensley, musician in the rock group Uriah Heep. Sun Virgo, Moon Pisces.

Chris de Burgh, musician. Sun Libra, Moon Pisces.

Diego Armando Maradona, soccer player. Sun Scorpio, Moon Pisces.

Jim Davis, creator of the cartoon *Garfield*. Sun Leo, Moon Pisces.

Edward D. Wood, known as the *worst* director in Hollywood, but also an important person for the LGBT movement because he made films about transgenders and transvestites in the 50's. Sun Libra, Moon Pisces, probably in conjunct with Uranus (change their feelings/gender).

Christopher Lambert, actor of *Highlander*. Sun Aries, Moon Pisces.

Johann Wolfgang von Goethe, poet born 1749. Sun Virgo, Moon Pisces.

Astrid Lindgren, author born 14 Nov 1907. Sun Scorpio, Moon Pisces.

Axl Rose, singer with Guns N 'Roses. Sun Aquarius, Moon Pisces.

Dick Cheney, former vice president of G.W. Bush. Sun Aquarius, Moon Pisces.

Bashar al Assad, dictator of Syria. Born on September 11 in 1965. Sun Virgo, Moon Pisces.

Sweden, appointment of Gustav Vasa in 1523. Sun Gemini, Moon Pisces.

Aleister Crowley, born October 12, 1875, developed the Tarot game Thoth. Sun Libra, Moon Pisces.

Sture Johansson, medium that transchanneled "Ambres". Sun Libra, Moon Aries/Pisces.

Betty Ford, founder of rehabilitation clinic USA. Sun Aries, Moon Pisces.

Chico Marx, born March 22, 1887. Sun Aries, Moon Pisces.

Andrei Tarkovsky, Russian director. Sun Aries, Moon Pisces.

Hermann Hesse, author. Sun Cancer, Moon Pisces.

Vaslav Nijinsky, ballet dancer. Both Sun and Moon Pisces.

Jesus of Nazareth, carpenter. The entire solar system probably in Pisces.

Derek Parker, astrologer, author of *Astrological Handbook,* 1974. Sun Gemini, Moon Pisces.

David Attenborough, television reporter. Sun Taurus, Moon Pisces.

Amy Sherman-Palladino, the creator of tv-series *Gilmore Girls*. Sun Aquarius, Moon Pisces/Aquarius.

Neil Michelsen, computer programmer and creator of the "red" and "blue" Ephemeries. Sun Taurus, Moon Pisces.

Cinderella, naive dreamer. Sun, Moon, Mercury, Venus, Jupiter, Neptune and Ascendant Pisces.

Are you curious about someone you miss in this collection? Go to http://www.astro.com/astro-databank/Main_Page and search!

(Astrologer and client Astromässan Tvärskog 2005. Photo: Alexander)

Aim in Life – MC

" Made it, Ma! – Top of the world!" (quote; James Cagney)

What is the meaning of my life, and where am I going?

I have never dared to claim to know the "meaning" of life, but some theories fascinate me. Purely astrologically, we have to take into account both karmic "homework" and what we strive towards. I do not like the term "homework", though, because to me it connects to guilt or punishment.

In the chart you must first study your MC to see where you are going. But you must also take into account all the messages of each aspect. They tell you more about your predispositions and talents. Often, I tell you about your strongest abilities and capacities, combining this with your MC or your inner dreams and desires. We always strive for something better, bigger or happier in life.

The idea may be that we need to focus on our weaknesses and shortcomings, and work to improve these, while striving to achieve certain milestones or interim goals. I personally believe that life becomes easier the more humble you are. But that's a matter of taste. Trying to strive for less or shorter times can bring faster success and progress, and "success brings success," right?

I think you need both short and long term goals in life. Also, I think it's important to sometimes dare to break your patterns and adopt new challenges. If this is because you feel bored or satisfied does not matter. What *does* matter is trying out your wings in a new profession or trying out something you dreamed about. These thoughts come on and off for most of us, and I often try to find these important break-points to see when it may be appropriate for a new way in life.

Also emphasize the incredible importance of our personal dreams. Dreams may be naive and childish and sometimes even unreasonable, but they come from the intuition and our higher consciousness and should be taken seriously. Not everyone can get all their dreams fulfilled in life, but I personally think it's important to at least dare to listen to your intuition. If you dream about getting to the moon, you may come to the tree tops. In addition, we must all compromise the constraints and demands of everyday life and reality. No one can always work with what they love and dream about.

In conclusion, you may be able to combine your dreams with reality and indulge in a faster success by working both with your shortcomings and to dare to dream about the future as well as by learning to understand yourself and others better. Trust your intuition while accepting the requirements and the compulsion of reality and be patient with your dreams. "It's not the goal but the way that makes the effort worthwhile." (Karin Boye).

If you do not know what you want to do or be, contemplate on your MC, the Sun's capacity and the needs or talents of the Moon. Your Mercury shows how you think and what you want to know. Venus shows your values and what you long for. Mars shows you how to use your will and how to claim yourself. Jupiter can give you a picture of what you can succeed in, and Saturn shows what you need to make more effort with. Uranus points to where and when in life you can find changes, and Neptune shows you where your imagination can be developed. Pluto can also show you what you're heading for or avoiding. This may be healing to learn.

I will not be using the cookbook interpretations here with a number of examples, but rather encourage yourself to use your own imagination and creativity. As a child with watercolors, you can combine your planets, signs, aspects, and houses on your own, and see how the combinations lead to new images and symbols. It's incredibly exciting if you only use the keywords.

Although any universal "Meaning" (Higher Purpose) may apply to all souls, perhaps this should be classified as a purely spiritual experience. Regardless of religious or philosophical attitude, we all have unique, personal and often secret dreams of what we want to be when we grow up, or when we have gained insight into our own lives. Dare to dream and hike on your own country road, but do not forget that you are important to those in your life who love and need you. We all strive for our different goals in life. Everyone has their own road to follow.

I guess I have always been a dreamer. In my childhood, I was playing with my dreams. When I met Love in my teens, the dreams became both rose-colored and idealistic, but they never disappeared. Rather, they just changed color sometimes. Through all the books and all the music, I still dream. Movies are today for me as temporary dreams. As far as personal dreams are concerned, it's probably best to stay here for as long as possible so I can meet some of the ambitions I have left. The ambition of this book was to make a synthesis of my life experience as an astrologer, husband, father, sibling, son, and be able to pass it on to those of you who I have met during my life.

I myself today dream about writing more books, though maybe with a little different alignment. I dream of keeping myself healthy and strong for the children's sake. I dream of returning to my beloved mountains in Norway, to take care of my large garden and to see all the seeds ripen into flowers, fruits, berries and vegetables.

"I'm happy ... I'm strong ... I'm healthy ... I'm calm"

(My own affirmation for the last 15 years during my daily walks. The three dots in between represent just about every step, and I keep count with my fingers and repeat this 20 times every 350m (around my plot) as a pure mantra. I have probably repeated this over 10,000 times and walked thousands of miles. This is my way of positive brainwashing)

Part 2 THE ASTROLOGER

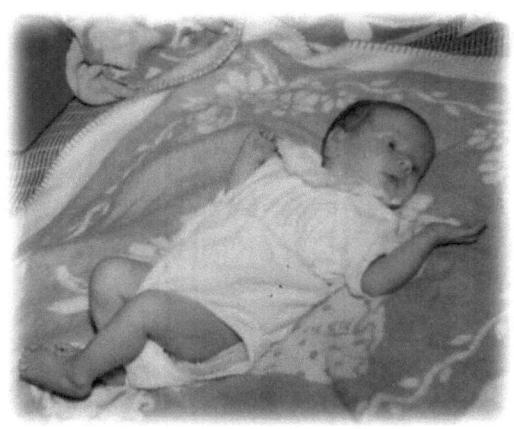

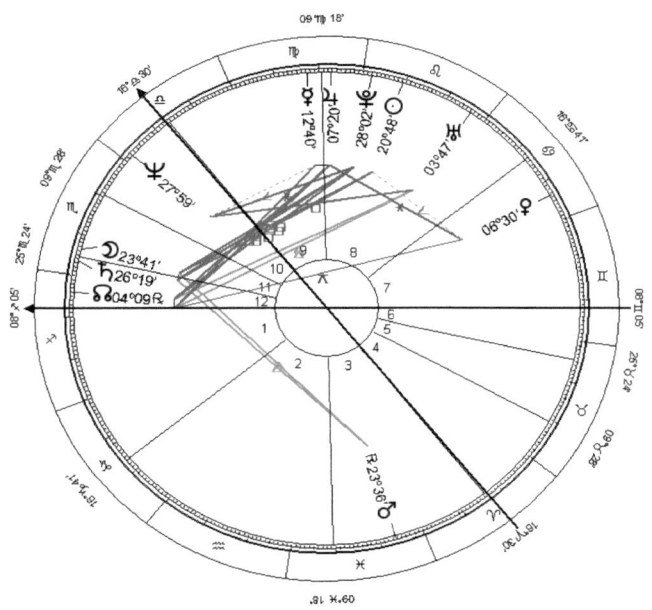

Jacob

I was born on Monday the 13th of August in 1956, at 3.45 PM, at Sahlgrenska hospital KK II, Gothenburg.

Now it may not be up to me to interpret and tell you about my birthchart, but I thought it might be interesting for you to understand my mere astrological qualities. Then you can compare and see if you have something similar in your own chart.

Marsian?

At a glance, you can see that the planet Mars in Pisces is lonely on the lower half of the chart. This is said to dominate the entire chart. It is also placed in Gemini's third house that rules communication and "messages." This incdicates focus and much energy to talk and share my knowledge. Also, there is a minor half-sum that, according to astrologer Ivan Wilhelm, can be like a machine gun if I became upset. I think it is Uranus half-sum Mercury-Mars. Mars in Pisces is physically connected to my feet, and I can not remember every time I injured my feet, whether through cuts, sticks, several times from pieces of glass, stuck on the heel under a lump of concrete and not to talk about twitches and twists. Nevertheless, at least I have never broken any leg.

Mars is also trine with both Moon and Saturn in Scorpio and activates energy. Moon-Mars gives an impatience and impulsiveness to the feelings, and I do not usually have trouble "putting the cards on the table." However, spontaneity may sometimes be embarrassing. My own "truths" and opinions stand out like a fountain, and it's not always fun to be hit. This aspect can cause enormous irritation for most with my inconsiderate comments. I compare myself as an elephant in a porcelain shop. I should have become a satirical comic and work with *standup comedy*. Unfortunately, the Moon in Scorpio may be unpleasant, provocative and sometimes disrespectful if I do not bite my tongue. I have no problem with "talking dirty," but I'm not sure how others will react. To talk about sexuality or secrets is simple, as well as taboo subjects or phobias meant for disclosure and analysis. Out with it, I say! Of course, I use a more diplomatic attitude in my interpretations with clients.

The Mars-Saturn trine is my "survival" instinct. Probably, this is the stubbornness and stamina that helped me survive and endure for long periods of agony, both physically and mentally. I could walk on my knees to Paris if I bet on it, and the only thing that stops me is fatigue or collapse during longer efforts. However, this trine is worth gold if you want to be strong or increase your resistance. Through determined repetition of effort, you become more persistent. During my teens I practiced both soccer and judo. On the intellectual plane, this aspect acts as a fearlessness to focus on Saturn's effects in Scorpio as well as being in the twelfth House. Much energy is thus activated in isolation and on my own. I love to work "alone" with different projects and can usually last for as long as possible.

If you begin with the Sun's position, then you must consider all aspects first and do not begin by just describing Leo. The Sun's square to both Moon and Saturn can give a fragile health, weak self-esteem, poor self-confidence, shyness, insecurity and a cautious attitude in relation to both men and women. My mom ran to the doctor with me when I was constantly tired, and it turned out that I was often suffering from iron deficiency, not to mention all childhood diseases. It started early with colic, followed by chickenpox, measles, tonsillitis, otitis - you name it.

Saturn can constrain both will and attitude; but by taking your own responsibility, this can be fruitful. These people have the potential to succeed by their own efforts, but seldom with the help of others. I can not remember that I ever asked for help with anything, and I still do not know how to do it today. Naturally suspicious and skeptical, these people rarely rely on others, sometimes not even relying on themselves. Sometimes I can be perceived as strict and demanding, but this often includes being the same towards myself. All suspicion of agencies and authorities usually leads to that these people become their own boss and head. Sun-Saturn sometimes indicates that the father-figure is absent, and my father was often at sea for long periods of time. Physically, there is a strong tendency towards both fatigue and pains, and they often need a break to restore power or to recover. Sun-Saturnians always have a tendency to workaholism and do not give up until they die. Therefore, rest and relaxation need to be imposed upon them.

The square (and opposition) between Sun and Moon is sometimes a little mean, referred to as "the divorce-aspect" because the person often perceives different signals from the parents. I obviously could not avoid this in my own three marriages. Even my parents were extremely different and represented quite different things for me as a child. Today, 60 years of age, I must admit that I feel more relaxed around women than men in life. This is despite my delicate Moon-Saturn. It may even be because of my own father's absence.

Since the Moon has a positive aspect to Mars and a strong aspect to the Sun, one can easily see that the feminine energies are easier and the masculine energies are a little more difficult to use. Also, I have never been particularly comfortable with testosterone people or macho types. I simply feel I benefit more from women rather than from men. This is something I can use positively in my work as an astrologer. A comic effect may be that I often feel spontaneously attracted to women. My Venus in Cancer reinforces this.

Mercury in Virgo has a wide conjunction with Jupiter, and this enhances both the desire and the ability to learn more and carry this on through speeches, interpretations, lectures, courses or perhaps a book. Strangely, this did not affect my school ambitions, as I was never interested in shining with my knowledge. I got decent grades, or 4s (out of 5 – a B today), in the subjects I thought were fun. In the other subjects, I almost ignored the grades. Notice Sagittarius's total nonchalance and disinterest. This combination is common for people who work as educators or journalists, and it is good for all studies, even later on in life. I can be both analytical and critical but always conscientious and on the verge of perfectionist at times. Minor difficulties with concentration may occur, and some inability to limit themselves are common. The process of this book was with repeated corrections and edits. Virgo´s influence gives an objective and practical setting, but Jupiter is more about impatience and looks rather towards the whole picture. Therefore, things like cleaning or sorting can take an unnecessarily long time.

Mercury's strongest aspect is the semi-square to Neptune, which is also in the tenth house, concerning career and occupation. This gives a very complicated ability to interpret signals that are not always so concrete. Virgo´s critical information is combined with Neptune's, stimulating suggestions that can easily be both confusing and blurred. Often this aspect has a comic kind of dyslexia where I lose letters or words, I forget about small things and mix up some concepts. As an absent-minded professor, I sometimes seem to be comically confused. Maybe that is why I love humor and the Marx Brothers. However, there is also a very stimulating ability when I interpret freely and words can flow. A square to the Ascencant contributes to some complications. It is not always easy to express myself, and sometimes the message becomes a little too intense. As a strategy, it is better to be quiet sometimes rather than to speak in some contexts. Mercury in the ninth house contributes to my great passion for books, where I can travel everywhere and learn more and more. I have repeatedly gone to adult school. The first time I did this, in 1980, it was of a pure lust for revenge because I wanted to see if I could get good grades in school. I got two A´s in the subjects Social Science and Psychology, considering what was coming.

Venus in Cancer is probably a sore point for me. Feelings are vulnerable and I feel terrible when something bad happens. These people love children and enjoy the family, but they can act like an over-mothering hen on the verge of overprotecting. Deep feelings are important in all kinds of relationships, including school and work, as it is in the seventh house. "The road to a man's heart goes through the stomach," and that's probably correct. There is, of course, a great love to enjoy food, but maybe a bit excessive sometimes. (I've experienced reflux for over 15 years). Sentimentality is strong and is relieved by events, movies and books. These people can be easily squeamish, close to tears and lamenting heavily if something negative occurs in life, such as death or other tragedies (for example, the final scene in the movie *Spartacus*). A strong 150 degrees to the Ascendant can mean a discreet attitude with some shyness in unaccustomed situations. I have always considered myself a "domestic cat" and can feel extremely insecure sleeping away from home.

Venus sextile Jupiter is probably my best natal aspect, giving me a sense of good Karma. Caring for others makes me happy, and I'm happy to help with many practical things, especially with my Jupiter in Virgo. Generosity exists, but sometimes it can be exaggerated. An easy tendency is to enjoy a little too much of life's sweets, like food and drink, and weight problems can occur unless energy is elsewhere. This sextile also shows everything I receive from others in the forms of support, help, advice, love or trust from customers. Jupiter in Scorpio's eighth house sextile Venus in the seventh house stimulate both the sexual needs and increases the amorous empathy.

Jupiter's position in Virgo can mean great willingness, and responsibility is often taken for the sake of others. Located at the end of the eighth house, the intuition and understanding increases the psychological understanding of life. An almost exact square to the Ascendant in Sagittarius becomes a double effect. These persons can be perceived as extremely nonchalant and carefree and seem to just fool around in existence. An unexpectedly successful event may, however, occur in cycles, and the person always comes down with his or her feet on the ground. I have repeatedly "won" in games and speculations for more than thirty years. The only real problem is that radiation hides all difficult experiences, and the person can have difficulties in being taken seriously (the clown's ambiguity). In addition, I am totally uninterested in clothes and how I "look" or how I am being perceived. (Jupiter 90 degrees square Ascendant).

Saturn in Scorpio symbolizes that people may have difficulties in resentment with their destiny as Scorpio symbolizes everything we can not influence or disturb. In the twelfth house, this can be experienced as a psychological banishment or exile from others (symbolically, a fear of ending in prison or monastery – something that may have occured in several previous incarnations). However, there is a toughness to endure; and although fears arise, they can be processed through Saturn's analytical energy. Confronting your demons can be terrible but at the same time very rewarding. In case of more difficult conflicts or problems in life, one has to possibly go into temporary exile or isolation when Saturn is in the twelfth house. (This also results in one going back home time after time). This house also represents what we hide from others. My own view is that I have an easier time focussing on work or more "serious" projects when I'm "outside" the usual social patterns. The twelfth house is often described as pertaining to hospitals, prisons or monasteries. But for my part, it has been very positive with aloneness and seclusion. The Moon's conjuction with Saturn contributes to my serious outlook on life, but also with the tendency to pull me away from the world's crises and concerns. Social arrangements such as parties or weddings are often experienced as cramped effort.

Luck, Bad Luck or Karma?

The Moon's strong square aspect to Pluto early indicated that difficult events would lead me into new ways in life. Contact with women can be abruptly canceled because something is going wrong. Likewise, contact with children can be prevented or altered by sudden circumstances that are not always planned. This combination is a bit for me like *Pandora's box*. Extremely strong emotions can suddenly come to the surface and without warning. This unfortunately reinforced with Moon in Scorpio, and Saturn's presence increases the effect of sheer stress. These traits are common along with pure hypersensitivity in fragile subjects. This triple energy Moon-Saturn-Pluto is also stimulated by Mars, and here things happen below the surface. This sensitive combination, I think, is the reason for my ability to penetrate the depths and just "understand" the phenomenon intuitively.

Looking at the horoscope from just a physical aspect is a bit contradictory. Several clear indications of strong health and resilience, especially from the Moon's energies, give a toughness; but at the same time, there can be a strained inhibition and limitation of physical resources, through Saturn's square to the Sun. I have lived in periods of repeated genital surgery and fragile health, but also long periods without as much as a cold. The major difficulties I have experienced are more often about emotional crises, not purely physical. Should you be a little positive, Saturn in Scorpio can mean a death at an old age. Prostate cancer is unfortunately a potential risk with all these Pluto energies. I have had repeated operations in these regions already.

On the mental level, it can be noted that my IQ has helped me to survive all these extreme phases (and horrors) in life. Through hundreds of books, conversations with good friends and thousands of clients, lots of movies and my own experiences, I have managed to cut out a vision of life today, which I feel relatively pleased with. The books by Michael Newton felt a bit like a magical "explanation" in my search for a purpose of life. This, my very first published book, is perhaps a result, and I hope that I will summarize these collective experiences.

In a karmic sense, I do not think anyone would want to change with me. I've seen and heard people break down and lose the will to live by just the fraction of the energies I have lived around the clock, and sometimes, of course, I've wondered how to cope. Suicidal periods have come and gone. Many "exits" have been passed but always avoided. Was there still any task left? Today I do not want to give up for the sake of my children. However, I believe and hope that my task this time may help make life a little easier to understand and endure, even for you.

As a birthchart, you should try to see this as a discouraging example. I used to compare my chart with the charts of the old Soviet Union or the US. They are quite complicated. Statistically, there are neither perfect nor catastrophic charts. Most of the time we all have a fair mix of "red" and "blue" energies in our charts.

La Familia

(Astrologer's mother and father 1956)

I have for many years had an album, in short called "La Familia." I believe it first related to the strong importance of family ties, not least in the Italian family. In the album that over the years is still growing, I have gathered everyone in the family tree and the most important and best friends of significance to my life. Eventually, the children's and stepchildren's boyfriends and girlfriends came along, and now it's well-stocked.

I don't know if I remember correctly, but I think I heard in one of Woody Allen's movies that "you can't choose your family, but thankfully your friends," but please tell me if it was not Woody who said this. The subject of "Family" is to many people a little taboo, based on our individual, complex Karma. I have over the years met with latent hatred and anger towards one or both of peoples' parents, and even siblings gets a spoonful of bitterness sometimes, usually from the other siblings. One's roots can be sensitive to talk about, and there are many "skeletons in the closet," probably more common than many believe. I have not specialized in relationship interpretations, but every time I tested, I managed to go over my expectations. In addition, I thought that it was both necessary and important to dare to look back on one's upbringing and the relationship with our parents. This was not always successful because many sore toes were trampled on and some did not even want to talk about their past. But I was persuaded and often demonstrated the important thing in understanding why we become who we are. You must not always blame your "stupid" parents. They had their crosses to bear. On the other hand, I think it is important to understand the vibrations or energies that affect our growth, and then it is inevitable to mention what kind of people the parents were likely to be.

I thought it was incredibly exciting just to see what sort of energies, zodiac signs or vibrations my ancestors lived with, not just my parents. The family tree can reveal a lot of our genes and talents, although I'm prepared to establish that they are sometimes skipping a generation. Draw up your own family tree, and you will probably find more signs that will return.

The Family Tree

If I start with the tree on my father's side, then his father Gerhard was a Capricorn with Moon in Gemini while his mother Tekla had both Sun and Moon in Pisces. Gerhard was an entrepreneur and master painter; and with his Moon in Gemini, he was constantly engaged and on the move. Grandmother Tekla was not only the mother of seven boys, she took care of other children in the summertime and also helped old and lonely people with their cooking and washing on her own unpaid time. They were both very religious and actively worked with the district mission parish throughout their lives.

On my mother's side it is completely different. My grandmother Margit was born in 1909 in Stockholm out of wedlock and was placed in an orphanage and never got to know her biological parents. She was taken to Värmland after a few years by Anders and Kajsa Sandström, who could not have any children of their own. Grandmother Margit was a Capricorn with Moon in Gemini (like my grandfather Gerhard and my youngest daughter), and we were very close throughout my childhood. Because my father was mostly at sea and mother got to work extra, grandmother became the obvious baby-sitter. Grandfather Gunbert was born in Glava, Värmland and was an Aquarius with Moon in Scorpio, but they did not spend their last years together because after moving to Gothenburg, he never enjoyed the big city but moved back to Värmland where he ended his life in 1965 due to stomach cancer. However, they remained good friends and never divorced.

My few memories of grandfather smells of a pipe and moped when he took me fishing. He had a recognizably difficult mood, but I neither saw nor heard anything. I was only 9 years old when he passed away, but I can recall when the ambulance picked him up in the middle of the summer. That was probably my first encounter with "death" when they later told us he died just a week later. I didn't attend the funeral.

We children were considered too young. That summer, Neptune was in transit squared my Sun, which was probably both confusing and sad. Neptune symbolizes both sadness and confusion and connects to the "other side."

My father, Åke Ewert, was born as the second child in a brood of seven boys and strangely became the "black sheep" in the family, going off to sea early in his teens while all his brothers formed families and settled here in the area. Dad is a Leo with Moon in Virgo and is famous for his leadership qualities in the kitchen. But at the same time, he was careful not to reveal too much of his heart. This is very typical for anyone with Moon in Virgo. He met my mother Gull-Maj Margaretha, who was a Taurus with Moon in Aquarius, but they had a hard time living together and divorced relatively early as friends when I was in my teens.

Thus, I am a classic "divorce child" (Sun-square-Moon), but this never worried me. I hardly knew my dad because he was seldom home; and when he was home, he did not talk too much (Both dad and I have Sun square Saturn). In addition, as a sailor, he was a bit too fond of strong drinks, and my mother never accepted this. However, I have two siblings born in 1965, and we have always had a strong relationship. Anna & Kajza are biological twins (Aries with Moon in Scorpio like me), and we have always supported and helped each other.

Even if it's not up to me to interpret my own chart, you can surely see that my Moon in Scorpio has many critical points of contact and that I am a Leo may be more of my own Karma. I never experienced either of my parents or siblings as difficult or stressful but rather as a big support.

All three of my wives may be the mothers of my children, but of course everyone came with their own individual karma. My first wife, Madeleine, is a Pisces with Moon in Scorpio like me. She is both strong and kindhearted.

My second wife, Josefine, is a double-Gemini but has both Uranus and Pluto square to her Sun-conjunct-Moon. This became too intense for both of us. However, we still have a very good relationship and are very good friends.

My third wife, Cecilia, is also a Gemini, but with Moon in Virgo. I had perhaps the longest and most intense relationship with her and maybe even the strongest karma. Again, we are still very good friends.

All of my children have unique features. I usually say that they have three basic components: a little bit from mom, a little bit from dad, but mostly their own unique, karmic characteristics. We can only be there for them, hopefully without hurting them too much, because they will go their own ways and have their own unique karma to work with. Today, I'm sad to say that I probably never was a perfect parent, but I have never deliberately hurt or harmed any of them. I was probably never suited to be a parent. When the two oldest children came, I was definitely too young and immature; and when the middle boys came in the 80's, I was not around them long enough. The only one I really lived with is the youngest daughter. This is because I refused to give up again, and I was also a bit older and maybe a little more mature to take my responsibility.

My firstborn, Daniel, born in 1977, is Cancer with Moon in Sagittarius, and today he is a proud father of three children. He made me a grandfather when I was only 41 years old. His wife is Angelica, Leo with Moon in Cancer, and their children are Julia, Pisces with Moon in Gemini, Alexander, Aries with Moon in Taurus and Sebastian, Sagittarius with Moon in Leo.

Sofia, born in 1979, is Virgo with Moon in Libra, and today she has a son, William, who is Scorpio with Moon in Aries, together with her husband Mikael, a Libra with Moon Virgo.

My second son, Andreas, born in 1987, is also Cancer with Moon in Scorpio as his father. Already he has two children, Loke, Virgo with Moon in Scorpio, and Freja, Cancer with Moon in Taurus. He also has a step-son Lucas, Libra with Moon in Gemini, together with his double-Aries wife, Malin.

Alexander, born on my birthday in 1988, is thus a Leo with Moon in Virgo like his grandfather, and like him, he likes to cook. Otherwise, for him it's mostly ice hockey and music on his mind.

"The Little Nine," as she was called, arriving after eight older half-siblings, Amanda, born in 1993, is thus the youngest daughter, a Capricorn with Moon in Gemini, as my grandmother and grandfather, and for practical reasons the one I lived the most with.

Today, as I am writing this in 2017, my only living at home family consists of myself and my five cats. I thrive in what others label as "loneliness". I live in my own house on the same farm as my 92 year old father and help him with everything practical. We are two old Leo's in *Rosenfors* who enjoy the privacy and nature all around us. I live in the house closest to the main road and daddy in the older big house, looking like a "cross" from above in the old photo from the 50's.

(Rosenfors, Anebo in the 50's)

U.T.O.P.I.A.

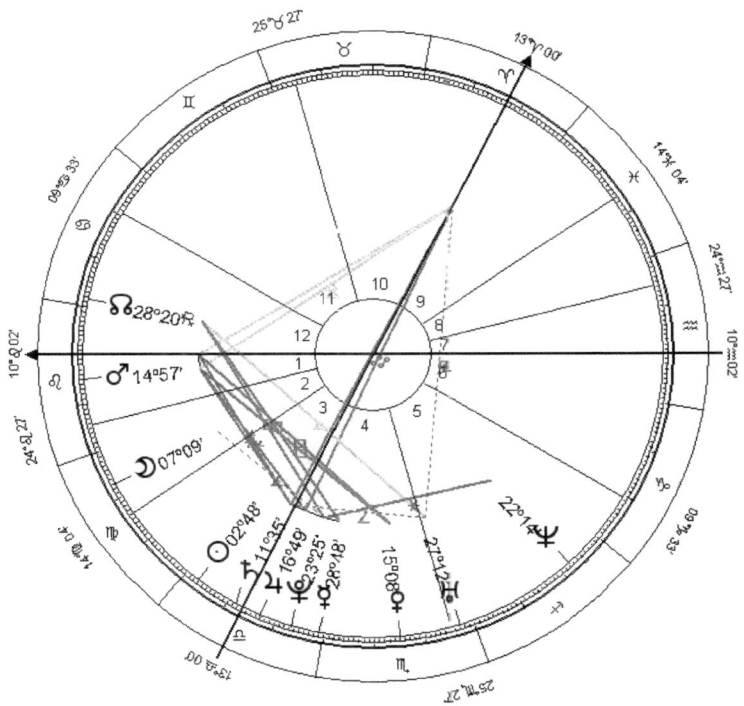

(UTOPIA, 26th of september 1981, at 01.48, Gothenburg)

The name is actually a play with initials I discovered by chance. I just had a clue that it was a concept based on a book by Thomas More, born February 7th, in 1748, Sun Aquarius with Aries Moon and ASC Sagittarius and MC in Libra.

The initials stand for **U**niversal **T**heosophical **O**rientation with a **P**ractical focus on (In/in swedish) **A**strology.

I created this "name" one night living in Angered just north of Gothenburg, Sweden, on September 26th, 1981, at 01.48, local time. A few years ago, I discovered that the tennis phenomenon Serena Williams was born exactly on the same day, just a few hours later, at 8.28 PM in the evening in the United States. She has earned 76 million US dollars and has taken 21 Grand Slam titles alone. Exactly a week later, the Swedish soccer phenomenon Zlatan Ibrahimovic was born in Malmö, Sweden.

This chart was partly manipulated, but only considering that the Moon transited Jupiter in my own chart. I later discovered that the Ascendant ended up in Leo and MC in Aries. I never registered the name UTOPIA until October 24th, 1984 after my move to Småland. By accident, this was registered on the Tax Agency on the day of the New Moon in Scorpio along with a conjunct Pluto. It was a strange day completely without "red" or strong aspects and only conjunctions and sextiles.

Although the name remained for many years, my attitude or presentation of my business has changed from time to time. The company and name disappeared from the registry when I took time off, and in line with the Internet, there were several new names: Astroutopia, the Utopia astrologer, Jacob Astrologer (during my first Hotmail e-mail) and The Anebo Astrologer. Astrologer Jacob finally became in 2016 Astrojacob, which is the name of today's website. http://www.astrojacob.com/(at least when this book was published).

If you compare the chart of Utopia with mine, obviously it is the actual transit in my own chart. Sun sextile my Uranus (astrology), Moon conjunct my Jupiter, Mercury conjunct my Neptune and sextile my Pluto, Mars sextile my MC, Jupiter conjunct my MC in Libra, Saturn slowly increasing a conjunction to my MC, Uranus conjunct my Saturn, Neptune's trine my Sun and Pluto 150 degrees to my Mars. Venus in Scorpio is the only planet without an exact aspect. However, within 8 degrees conjunct my Moon and sextile my Mercury in Virgo. Thus, there are a variety of "triggering" factors.

Interpretation is a little more complicated. With both the Sun and four planets in Libra, it indicates a lot of messages and contacts with others (clients). Sun (the boss), Mercury (communication), Jupiter (social success), Saturn (responsibility, seriousness) and Pluto (psychology) are all in the sign of Libra, which benefits all social interaction and collaboration with clients, customers or patients. Mercury, in addition, conjuncts Pluto, which reinforces both curiosity and many conversations about secrets. Disclosures come up to the surface and are communicated in a diplomatic way, including in my home environment (4th house). The planet that can really be interpreted as strongest is Saturn in opposition to MC in Aries. According to the statistician astrologer Michel Gauquelin, who investigated a lot of planets close to the ASC and Midheaven (MC) axis, this opposition is dominant. It can be interpreted as "lonely work in solitude" as well as a very earnest and serious ambition that is not achieved without great discipline. Saturn emphasizes everything realistically and concretely, while the MC is about career and methods of expression. MC in Aries also emphasizes that I go my own way and work on my own. This is further enhanced by Mars in Leo in the 1st house. There is no question about who rules, and many may see me as being right, outgoing and self-conscious in my attitude. The comic part is that this is mostly a purely external aspect. Perhaps many perceive me as very pushy and straightforward. Mars trine MC emphasizes even more the role of being the entrepreneur. Mars sextile Jupiter contributes with both enthusiasm and a positive attitude to achieving high goals in my career. Mars sextile Saturn contributes with both discipline and perseverance in bridging all obstacles that come in the way.

In addition, both Sun and Saturn end up in the 3rd house, which points to a clear focus on communicating messages, often with a serious emphasis. The Moon in Virgo has a semi-square to Pluto, and this is about emotional depths in a methodical and analytical manner, which also contributes to my income (2nd house).

Saturn sextile the Ascendant expresses "the serious astrologer" in my dealings with new clients. Uranus might have had a more central role because it is about astrological activity, but it has an active energy with responsibility from the semi-square to Saturn and is also in the 5th house. I interpret this as both my greatest pleasure and my creativity. In addition in Scorpio, which reinforces the psychological driving forces of Uranus. A little odd aspect is a great trine between Uranus and the North Node in Cancer in the 12th House, which would mean a lot of sudden and unexpected spiritual contacts, often behind the scenes or in my secluded accomodation. This is undeniable.

Otherwise, maybe the "best" combination would be Jupiter's passage over and conjunct my MC in Libra. When this occurs in life, for everyone around every 12 years, it can mean both the crown of a career and/or the birth of a new successful concept in life. The moment could not have been better. This conjunction was then repeated in September of 1993, December of 2004, March of 2005 (due to being retrograde), August of 2005, and December 1st, in 2016, to reenter in April and July of 2017, due again to retrograde motion. What could that mean? (*blink, blink*) Perhaps a published book?

As it says in Ebertin's little orange book on Transits: "Beginning of a harmonious and spiritual relationship, being in good humor, achievement of a new position, happy change in life, love's joy, success in life." (Big Smile)

For example, throughout the lengthy work on this book, Pluto has equaled my Mercury (write, think) and my MC (purpose, endeavor). Neptune has influenced both my Venus (inspiration, creativity), my Jupiter (optimism, flow) and continued in 2016-2017 to aspect my Mercury (intuition, higher awareness) during the final phase of the book. Uranus started activating my Venus (positive change), then through Aries, aspecting my ASC (change my attitude), my MC by opposition and simultaneously conjunting MC of Utopia (new goals), to end during 2016-17 by aspecting my Sun (great positive changes, creativity with new impulses).

Between 2013 and 2016 Saturn passed through both Scorpio, with my important focus, and Sagittarius, which helped with both discipline and a tendency to be more on my own to be able to concentrate. I actually wrote continuosly during a couple of months while a sextile transited my MC. In the final part of the writing process in June of 2016, with proofreading and a review of my priorities and choices, it was square my Mercury. It returned with the next phase in October of 2016. This triggered a new "critical phase" (I had to adjust to learning new editing methods previously unknown to me and also took full responsability in the finishing of the book all on my own).

During the same years, Jupiter has passed through Gemini, Cancer, Leo and Virgo and transited through my seventh, eighth and ninth houses, which has been positive for the deepened process. In September of 2016, Jupiter entered Libra, Utopia's own month of birth, and later on it transited my MC in December.

Similarly, you can always plan or schedule your projects. Both a shorter or longer trip, an exam, a wedding, or when you move into your new house or start a new job or career. Everything need not be planned in detail, and forget about an exact time of day as long as you have an idea of the bigger, slower energies or aspects at the time. Good luck!

Mediums

The question of "The Meaning of Life" has always attracted people all over the world. To find out about our destiny, we have contacted fortune tellers, psychic persons, witches, astrologers and wizards. We have palmistry, Iris diagnostics, Tarot or common playing cards. Today, the Internet is flooded with *paypal* numbers to Mediums and Tarot Card readers who charge £10 a minute. I usually refer to them in a malicious manner as "VISA - MasterCard witches." Compared to the 70's, there are many more astrologers today, but I have no idea how many.

Britta

My own experiences from mediums are quite limited, but I have probably had a lot of luck. The ones I have met have mostly been both skilled and serious. My first meeting was with "Psychic Britta" in Nybro, Sweden, back in 1990 when I first got to know her daughter Ewa. Of course, Britta was a Scorpio and we got on instantly. On a visit here in my home in Anebo, she saw several fun things, eg., my grandmother who sat and sang down in the old barn. What Britta did not know was that my grandmother Tekla sat every day in the barn singing while weaving. Britta told me several personal things that fit and some personal matters I can not disclose here.

Terry Evans

In the autumn of 1995, on recommendation of my good friends Peter & Pia Palm in Kalmar, I had an exciting meeting with Terry Evans visiting Kalmar. Even Terry was, of course, Scorpio. Immediately when we met, he asked me if I was a teacher or an actor. "No, but I am an astrologer," I said, and then he laughed. "Of course!" He mentioned several personal issues, among many things, my doubt, and my inner wounded child, my perhaps too serious attitude, and suddenly he said that he had a message from a "famous" person who had recently killed himself and he wanted to communicate that it was a mistake. He had never meant to kill himself. Now he wanted me to tell the people involved. I thought spontaneously on the musician Kurt Cobain who died the year before, in 1994, but I never did anything about it. After some serious thoughts, he claimed that my wife could stop fixing flowers at home because we would soon move south. The following year we moved down to Simrishamn in Skåne. "Many new beginnings," he said. I perceived Terry as not only skilled but very diplomatic, sensitive and a good psychologist. Today I know that he has featured in many programs on television.

William Shaffer

The big high, however, came when we lived down in Simrishamn in Skåne. My cousin Kent Markho Davidsson, who was living in the United States, had taken home a guy to Sweden, named William Shaffer, and wondered if I wanted to meet him in his mom Britt-Marie's house outside Värnamo. I drove there on April 15th, 1997, from Simrishamn, and we had some intense hours with both a trans-channeling session and some dinner before my departure.

It would be impossible to account for the whole experience, but some key parts concerned my past lives and experiences. Through the *Akashic Chronicles* and my own *Higher Self*, William addressed my potential, my great Karmic task, and both my positive and negative experiences from many past lives. I had been a teacher, priest, healer, doctor and astrologer many times and apparently helped thousands of souls. Intellectually, I reached my "peak" thousands of years ago and felt "safe" with everything intellectual and cognitively. I can talk my way out of any situation, and I have no respect for power, politicians or the rich. But all was not peace and joy. My *Achilles heel* was fearing and repressing emotional bonds.

I was scared to death of being vulnerable and becoming addicted to someone and used my intellect to talk down to others or hide behind my intellectual mask. I was very familiar with heartache because I had repeatedly abandoned parents, children and lovers in many past lives. However, I also received a lot of shit as a consequence of this repeating pattern. I had many times been blamed for, and got accused of, actions I did not do. This was because I refused to support in astrological assistance in political intrigues, as I was never interested in the games people played for power. I had been accused, punished, murdered (often brutally) for things I was innocent of. Today I can overreact if I'm accused of something I am innocent of.

My "issues" were fears in general and in particular the fear of emotions, as I felt emotions made me vulnerable. Therefore, I have hurt and left so many who loved me. Some of these have followed me in life after life trying to make me feel love while others have wanted their revenge because I left them in past lives. No names here, but some of them I have met during this life as well.

An interesting thing that came up was how to use astrology before, especially during the Atlantis era. Then, a physician would come up to me as an astrologer and wanted an analysis of the patient's previous lives. No physical analysis was made without first looking for the karmic causes of errors or diseases that occurred here and now. If, for example, a woman had breast cancer, you first analyzed her natal chart and searched for her previous patterns in past lives to see how and why this cancer occurred. Thus, no future prognosis was made like you do today. William called this Karmic Astrology. In this version of astrology, the natal chart is like a blueprint of past lives from the *Akashic records*.

Apparently, I've given more to millions of others, but hardly ever for my closest ones who loved me or to myself. This was due to the fear of showing my inner emotions or showing my vulnerability. William referred to Scandinavia as "the land of the emotionally retarded" and said that I felt safe here because everyone conceals what they really feel. Obviously, I should change the environment and start hanging out with living, honest people who dare to show their feelings and take responsibility for their emotions. He mentioned *Gestalt therapy*, *Psychodrama* and *art healing* as possible methods to process my emotional issues. When I asked about regression hypnosis, he said it might be good to figure out the causes of many karmic problems, but I still have to process all the emotions in order to be able to heal and transform them.

During the time William made his channeling, the Moon transited my Uranus in the eighth house. Talk about profound, emotional shock and disclosure! Afterwards, I stayed for a while and was invited for dinner, and then William "revealed" that we were brothers in an earlier life in current Russia. We starved there after trying to survive on beetroot. I hate beetroots today, as does William. Now I understand why. Astrologically William is born in 1952, a Gemini with Moon in Sagittarius.

When I'm being asked about mediums today, I never recommend anyone. I do not know anyone personally today and do not want to take responsibility for sending them clients/patients. William has had the benefit of doing analysis or readings for several in my family. He has now retired from public teaching and lecturing and lives in Wales.

Tarot or Astrology

I do not want to talk back on or underestimate others who predict your future, but just the concept of Tarot has become an epidemic or pestilence in my view. I know several that are both psychic and serious and can mediate the message that the cards may have, but I understand it is also very much up to the ability and insight of the interpreter. On three occasions I have received different interpretations with completely different messages. The first time was at an astrological conference in Söderköping, Sweden, where a manic woman persistently followed me around, asking me to just pick a card from a Tarot pack of cards. I refused several times but on the last day I gave up and picked a card. It was something about having protection from "Superior or Higher Powers," so I said, "There you see, I do not need your cards." The second time was even worse. A woman living in Gothenburg wanted over the phone to exchange services, so I sighed and agreed. After a week, I got a cassette tape with something inaudible and just became frustrated. However, she was pleased with the analysis I gave her. Unfortunately, I let my frustration out on her via a couple of annoyed emails, and before I realized my mistake I had managed to enrage her. I assume and hope this book never reaches her, but for the sake of the universe I apologize for my idiotic behavior. In fact, this was one of very few clients during my more than 35 years as an astrologer that have scolded me. The third and last (I hope) time was one of my best friends, wonderful Maggan in Simrishamn, who laid a Tarot star here in Anebo and it was not only impressive but probably also very suitable for the process I found myself in. I have it copied but remember that the "Death Card" was my main card.

Too many people buy a deck of Tarot cards and put up an ad in the local grocery store. Tarot is also based on the random factor. Astrology is based on exact planetary positions and a concrete schedule of events. There may be a lot of psychics who can interpret the message from a Tarot card, but to talk about serious mental disorders or to help suffering people through a life crisis from these cards seems to me on the verge of distastefulness and a lack of seriousness. I would rather you take your money to a professional therapist.

In terms of energy and time, I will continue to try to help people through the use of my astrology, but I will probably focus more on the past, not the future. Maybe I should work as they did back in Atlantis instead. That is, process why you become the one you are.

Mediums and Books

There are many international mediums and psychic people that have written books. I can highly recommend several books by Betty Shine or Sylvia Browne (see Appendix Book List). Since my teens I have plowed through a lot of spiritual literature and books about parapsychology, so I have perhaps become more critical and questioning. It was a unique experience to read several of Shirley Maclaine's books and then watch the movie *Out on a Limb* about her experiences in Peru, and not least her meeting with Sture Johansson, who channeled "Ambres." But it was not until the 90's that things began to happen. I heard about a new concept, "increase of frequency;" and in just a few years, several exciting books came out.

James Redfield's *The Celestine Prophecy* came out in 1993, Neale Donald Walsh´s *Conversations with God* in 1995 and *Journey of Souls* by psychiatrist Dr Michael Newton in 1994. However, Newton was not translated into Swedish until 2011, and I came into contact with his first book in the fall of 2015. I maintain that I am still very critical and skeptical towards a lot of sensationally spiritual "mumbo jumbo," but this first book by Michael Newton opened up a lot of new insights and really blew my mind. Today, I know that he has published at least four books, of which the third and fourth are compilations by his trained students and their own cases. However, he wrote another book after the first one called *Destiny of Souls,* which came out in 2000. He deserves a separate chapter of his own, but I am pleased to make a minor report here.

Dr Michael Newton

Dr. Michael Newton worked for more than 30 years to help people with different traumas through different hypnosis methods. This also meant returning to earlier past lives, where he often found the causes of the person's problems or emotional wounds in this life. Suddenly, one of his patients in hypnosis began to describe his experience and place in a completely different way. As a result, Dr. Newton repeated the course of action with other patients and provided more and more information about a condition that did not belong to an earlier life, but rather to another dimension more easily described as the state of "in between" the different lives or incarnations. Hence, the name of his groundbreaking research is called *Life Between Lives*, today abbreviated as LBL.

I do not want to describe all the endorphins I experienced and reveal all my secrets and new insights, but I would like to mention a few provocative truths that made me change my mind about life and death.

Death is, of course, an enormous illusion. There is no death such as the one we are taught here on earth. The concept has always been used by those in power to discourage "poor sinners" from comitting mistakes and sins, and not least the church has always used these arguments to keep the masses in check (under their strict control). When we physically "die," the "soul" returns to our "common gathering place," and we meet our own special "soul group." It's like being on a vacation or retreat, and we get to process our last life to learn the lessons from our mistakes. After a certain time, we choose our plans for the next incarnation, while at the same time creating our circumstances together with our important soul group to fit our next task down here on earth.

I can understand if this sounds staggering, but I sense an almost perfect universal logic in the sequences. What fascinates me the most is that all kinds of people with different cultural or religious backgrounds provide the same description of LBL, whether living as a Jew, Muslim, Christian, Buddhist or as a renowned atheist. The descriptions are practically identical. Both people who believe in the afterlife and those who do not describe the same thing.

Likewise, with the phenomenon "Hell," we have yet another giant illusion. If you have "sinned" or done wrong or commited adultery or killed, you are not thrown into hell or purgatory (as Dante so thrillingly described) but "punished" more laboriously and with much more patience and discipline to process and understand what was done "wrong" during our recent incarnation. The "punishment" may be that it takes longer before you meet your soulmates and your soul group, because you must first go through an educational "purification bath" while meeting several so-called "spiritual masters" before meeting your group again.

It's all about understanding what you've done and what this means and realizing where you may still lack experience and wisdom.

After reading Dr. Newton's first book, I quickly got hold of the others and can warmly recommend them to everyone, regardless of your own religious attitude or previous experiences of similar theories. Whether you "believe in God" or not is really unimportant. The insights and experiences one has while reading goes beyond a simplified explanation of God's being or non-being.

The great effect the books had on me was to be less or completely unafraid of death, to worry less about the threat of hell, and not least that we may begin to treat our fellow men/souls with greater respect and love while doing our best with our own life task in this incarnation.

Of course, I got hold of his birthchart, but unfortunately without any correct time of birth. But I enclose the chart below, calculated for 12 Noon.

"It is an immense privilege to gain access to the spirit world and thus giving people knowledge of the souls' stay there."

- Michael Newton

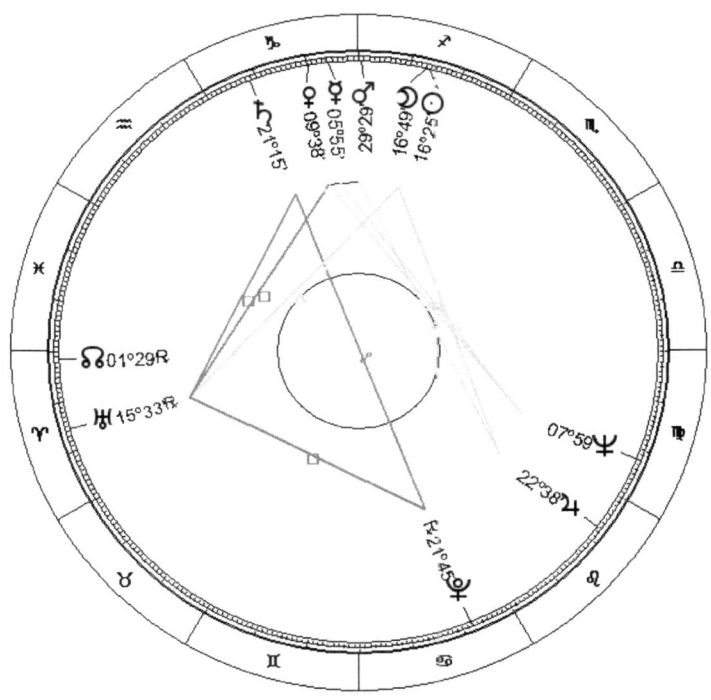

Dr Michael Newton, 9th of December 1931.

Dr. Newton was born around a New Moon on December 9th, 1931, which means he has both Sun and Moon in Sagittarius. The conjunction between Sun and Moon means that his ability to commit is one hundred percent. This conjunction also points to a stable psyche and an ability to balance between insights and feelings. In addition, there is a big trine from the Sun and/or Moon to Sagittarius's own ruling planet Jupiter in Leo. Symbolically, this represents many "long journeys." In the other direction, there is a similar trine of the Sun and/or Moon to Uranus in Aries. This also contributes to his ability to perceive high frequency signals. The Moon's trine enhances his emotional receptivity, and this is common among psychic or sensitive persons. What is even more exciting is his Mercury and Venus in Capricorn, which both form a major trine to Neptune in Virgo. Here, the thoroughly accurate analysis of Capricorn is combined with an intuitive inspiration with critical details from Neptune in Virgo. Venus trine Neptune also enhances both his empathy and ability to a high spiritual morality. With Mars entering Capricorn, one can easily find that much of his energy is expressed in communication and conversation. As an interesting reflection, one can also find that he has an almost exact opposition between Saturn and Pluto, which probably means a very serious and objective attitude towards death and all that is hidden within the psyche (Pluto).

Simply put, this is an incredibly fascinating and "strong" horoscope that has had a tremendous influence with it´s "Sagittarian" message across the world. In addition, it connects to or matches with many of the very best features we associate with the Sagittarius character and the meaning of the"Higher Message."

For those of you in Sweden who are interested, it may be nice to know that I found a regression therapist educated at The Newton Institute, Rita Borenstein, a Scorpio, who receives clients in Stockholm. She is also a licensed Osteopath D.O, a TCM Acupuncturist and a Registered Nurse. I got in contact with her on the Internet and received her consent to participate in this book. Rita is also a "friend" on my facebook.

The Astrologer's Karma

This time I chose a life full of love, children, fear and anger, along with a mother with strong social awareness and a self-centered father with strong integrity. I am also blessed with independent and generous sisters.

With my Moon in Scorpio, I have lived my whole life with so-called mood swings. The roller-coaster of life has been both breathtaking and destructive. Sexuality has been a driving force sometimes expressed with the manipulation of women. This only gave me a guilty conscience. The quest for confirmation was indifferent to me (money as well). Grades in school were never that important. My esteem and my self-confidence were intact until fear came sneaking in. People lied, cheated, were self-absorbed and greedy. They apparently just thought of themselves, and my illusions burst.

I tried drugs, with terrible results. Cannabis just gave me anxiety. I also experimented with solvent-type drugs (i.e., sniffing glue) for a short but intense period. That, however, was a screwed experience. As Roger Waters in Pink Floyd described it, "My hands felt like two balloons." I experienced myself as a drop of water falling in slow motion into a track on a gramophone record. A few years later, I unexpectedly received a flashback when I tested laughing gas after a baby delivery. God, what do they give women during delivery? Pure OBE (Out-of-body experience).

The teens with all the hormones and impressions were probably my most exciting time. I got in touch with spirituality, the occult, astrology and existential issues. What was the meaning of life really? I examined most religions but found no answers, only more questions. Why did everyone believe that their religion was the only right one? As Dire Straits sang: "Two men say they're Jesus, one of them must be wrong" (*Industrial Disease*).

Something happened when I was on a course in yoga. I had started training in soccer and judo and tried to train my body when I saw an ad about yoga courses in Gothenburg. This was the summer of 1972, and it became an important turning point (I was16 years old). The Sun progressively transited over my Jupiter! Talk about a new world view and a glimpse of the *Future*!

I also came in contact with exciting literature during my teens. Jiddu Krishnamurti, who wrote the book *Freedom from the Known*, was one of my first gurus. Later I read an incredible book by Paramahansa Yogananda called *Autobiography of a Yogi*, which opened up new dimensions into my world.

In the 70's, my studies continued in astrology, but there was a lack of good literature on the subject. The only book was *Complete Astrologer* by the spouses Julia and Derek Parker. It was both comprehensive and exciting and addressed most of the important aspects of this giant subject. Later on I went on a course with the astrologer Roger Algehov who taught me more. The best books continued to be in English. I devoured books by Stephen Arroyo, Liz Greene, Donna Cunningham and Robert Hand, whom I later met during an astro conference in Gothenburg that Roland Skogkvist, RIP, and the *Gothenburg Astrologers* arranged.

After my fated car accident in August 1979, life definitely made a turn. A few months after the accident, an acute panic attack occurred and paralyzed my entire existence. Stupid and selfish as I was, I never sought help but thought it would pass, but the problems stayed around the clock and both my marriage and work duties became a problem. Despite a marriage in 1980 and having two young children at home, the relationship did not endure. I hardly had the energy to cope with the psyche through the day. Fear and anger led to a break-up, and no blame is being put on my first wife, Madeleine.

We separated in 1982, and until 1984 I lived in five different appartments in Gothenburg as a bachelor, through several temporary relationships and in very cramped living conditions searching for a fixed point. I learned more about astrology, tried to live as a vegetarian and became a teetotaller for a couple of years before I decided to move from the big city. Symbolically, it was my dad who made the inquiry because his birthplace Rosenfors in Anebo was empty after my grandmother's and grandfather's death in 1975 and 1978. Dad had taken over the farm, was still at sea, and did not finish his job until 1988.

The first years at Anebo was like living in another world. I was commuting for the children's sake to Gothenburg, and my health improved by living in the countryside. After some temporary jobs, I got a job at a gas station named "OK" and started a new chapter in my life. Slowly I developed a reputation as "the astrologer" or "the talkative one from Gothenburg". Soon the local newspapers heard about me, which became the start of a couple of intensive years as a gas station employee and astrologer. Of course, soon I met and fell in love with a "double" Gemini, Josefine, and another two boys were born in '87 and '88.

As I was now both separated from my older children in Gothenburg as well as having two new toddlers, I worked at the gas station and interpreted charts in my spare time. But time caught up with me, and my anxiety attacks came back. I ended up questioning myself as to whether I was on my way *to* or *from* my job. The wake up call led to another unplanned separation. Neither Josefine nor I can place blame for my/our inability to keep all these balloons in the air. Unfortunately, another chapter was soon completed. My birthchart Moon square Pluto foreboded this in both 1982 and 1989.

In the beginning of 1990, I was completely both physically and mentally exhausted and recovered by working and enriching myself in astrology. Unexpectedly I met another woman who meant a lot to my spiritual growth, Ewa, a strong Leo with Moon in Pisces. Her mother was "psychic Britta" in Nybro, and Ewa and I had many interesting conversations during our brief but intense passion. However, our short-lived relationship did not last long, and on her initiative we separated.

In the spring of 1991, one of the major chapters of my life began. Between late 1984 and 1995, transiting Pluto passed through Scorpio, and in 1991 it came in contact with my Sun for the first time. I met my third wife, Cecilia, Gemini with Moon in Virgo, resulting in my fifth child, Amanda, who was born in 1993, Capricorn with Moon in Gemini. This new development intensified both my Karma, my role as an astrologer and a deepening of my real task in this incarnation.

The marriage, with a total of nine children of all ages, both Cecilia´s previous and my previous, suffered. My psyche was back in agony and turbulence, and this led to both recurrent anxiety attacks and physical health deterioration, symbolized by Pluto this time transited both my Moon and Saturn in Scorpio. Today my Saturn is at the same place as my daughter's Pluto, which can be interpreted as a strong karmic link. We call it our common "sting point" (inside joke).

During the vast majority of the 1990s, my physical health, probably due to stress and work overload, also worsened with constant emotional mood swings and reoccuring conflicts in the family situation. I was both a father of five and stepfather to four others and tried to support us as an astrologer, taking the dog out, and supporting my wife Cecilia who tried to maintain a balance within the family. There were two children mainly living in Gothenburg. I tried to go there when I was "free" from work, and two others in Målerås who stayed at our place when there was opportunity. My body spoke up in a strange way. The anxiety attacks succeeded and increased via a urinary problem that required an urgent operation. The first time was in 1992. This procedure was repeated several times until 1998, which was the last time. Having trouble peeing and constantly needing to go to the bahroom for several years was a mere hell without exaggeration. Tragicomic or simple clearliness, I have my Moon and Saturn in Scorpio, which are both linked to the genitals, bladder and the anus.

With this in mind, it was strange that my role as an astrologer increased. I was covered by the local press, the local radio station in Kalmar and even had time for a fun visit to Växjö on local TV4 in May of 1994, where two young men worked who later appeared in other national tv-channels, namely the sympathetic Rikard Sjöberg and Peter Jihde. They fought during air-time breaks to keep little newborn Amanda, five months old, in their arms. It remains a funny memory, and I am still good friends with Rikard. An edited videoclip from this session is available on Youtube and my website.

By the mid 90's we tried to solve the situation by moving to Simrishamn in Skåne, and it was shortly after a meeting in the fall '95 with the medium Terry Evans visiting Kalmar, who claimed that we should move south. The amazing Österlen in Skåne gave us an extra honeymoon, and Amanda was allowed to grow up in this amazing landscape with the sea, beaches and new friends for life.

Sad to say, it's a little hard to live solely on love alone, and both our work, our economy and our relationship faltered and finally came to an end after only a few years. Disease, stress, minimal economy and shortage of jobs eventually ended up too much for me, but I stayed until the summer of 2002 before I finally gave up Skåne for Anebo again. However, Cecilia and Amanda stayed until 2006 before moving back to Kalmar, and Cecilia and I are still very good friends. We had to go through many important events together and know each other inside out today, but I can easily say that this karmic love relationship was absolutely my most important.

The contact with mediums and psychics increased in the 90s and in 1997 I met William Shaffer visiting Sweden. The meeting with William was bewildering. He peeled off my personality and confronted me with both my demons and my earlier lives, and this was the first time I received a real confirmation of all my strange fears. A funny point, however, was when I found out that he was an astrologer before he started transchanneling. When I asked if he had any good books to recommend, he laughed right in my face and said I only tried to fool myself. I did not have to read any "damn" books anymore. I channeled myself all the time and needed no more unnecessary knowledge.

(The talkative Astrologer at Tobisvik Camping in 2001)

Yes, the meeting with William solved many issues and might also help me through future crises. Astrology was a little low for a while, as it was difficult with a new clientele. I worked two seasons at Tobisvik's camping (photo above) until the ominous day 9/11 in 2001. Transiting Pluto reached a square to my Mercury. Also, in the fall of 2001, I accidentally damaged one of my knees (Saturn), which ended in an operation in January of 2002. Even Uranus was opposite my Sun in the fall. While waiting for surgery, I took some strong pills, unaware that they were prescribed as narcotics. When I stopped taking them after the surgery, I ended up in an acute abstirence condition with infernal hallucinations and clammy nightmares. Uranus squared my Moon during the winter, and I decided to move home to Anebo again.

Back home, I had to lick my wounds and go through all the emotional "garbage" I had collected since my move from Gothenburg in 1984. Autumn of 2002 became a catharsis practically, physically, emotionally and economically. I even found the strenght to reinstall myself in my little summer cottage without any heating except for a small fireplace. Dad decided that we would install water pipes and a toilet, and this was finished just before christmas of 2002. I had new freedom, but with a heavy conscience.

The accumulated result since the near-fatal car accident in 1979 now added up to three divorces, five children, countless removals and a fragile health. I continued to commute to Simrishamn until 2006 for Amanda's sake, but bodily agony and non-existent economics made me live as a zombie with the anxiety constantly latent. I met some lost psychiatrists, but the best help I received was from my best friends: Sannmarie in Kalmar, Maggan in Simrishamn, Kent in Gothenburg, and above all, my best friend since 1990, Kerstin Lilja.

My own rehabilitation went slowly but in the right direction, even though I literally encountered the infamous "wall" in 2006. Even today, I am surprised that I never got myocardial infarction or cerebral haemorrhage. In 2006, after helping out with a move, my psyche collapsed (again) and this time I had to seek some sort of help. Because I refused all sorts of heavy sedatives, I only took Sobril and the milder Atarax, but for four years until 2010 I barely took Sobril more than once (only in case of acute panic disorder). If you wake up in the middle of the night convinced that you've got an infarct, Sobril can be the only way out to overcome the fear. As of today I have lived without pills or drugs for more than seven years, feeling at ease and more pleased with life than since the 70's. However, I do not recommend this kind of self-torture where I balanced 'on the edge" for many years. It was simply my own pigheaded way cf compelling myself through self-discipline when dealing with all the difficult situations. (Moon in Scorpio).

But what about the astrologer? Yes, the strange thing was that when I was working with clients, all the anxiety sort of "disappeared" and my focus went to interpretation alone. I simply felt good and could once again bear in mind that astrology was a way out of "hell." I believe that my collaboration with clients simply refueled my aura and filled my vitality - my Chi.

Well, if all this was "scripted," you might wonder if I was totally intoxicated when I made my choice in the archives in the *Akashic Chronicles*. I had apparently chosen almost lifelong anxiety, more than thirty different dwellings, three failed marriages, multiple love affairs, even more brief sexual relationships without any depth of meaning or consequence, several operations, pills, drugs, car crashes, employment services, health insurance, physicians, psychologists, psychiatrists, lawyers, police and men and women of the Church. Anyone want to swap karma with me?

Secret Dreams of the Astrologer

or the influence of Neptune

(Dawn in the east in Anebo)
" Without hope you cannot start the day"
(from YES album *Union* 1991)

The quote above is from a record with one of my absolute favorite groups from the 70's, the rock group YES. They are classified as "difficult" and end up in the genre Symphonic Rock. For my part, they represent a more spiritual part of my music experience and with a high emphasis on the actual lyrics and message. I read many years later that singer Jon Anderson read the book *An Autobiography of a Yogi* by Paramahansa Yogananda and afterwards with the others in the group, made the album *Tales from Topographic Oceans* in 1973. The strange thing was that when I read the same book, I had no idea about this.

Why I begin with this is important to my story. This record and a few years later reading the yogi's autobiograhical book is probably one of the first and most important components of what would be my view of life. The lyrics are both poetic and advanced, filled with a cosmology and universal love that was like pure endorphins for my spiritual development.

I have often tried in my astrological work to highlight the importance of dreams and the importance of having hopes as well as a longing for something. This is not to be mistaken with the 10th House or MC, which is more about the way and the practical goal. The MC describes our efforts in the physical world and how we accomplish something with our ambition. This endeavor connects more to employment and occupation, but we do not always work with something we love.

Our innermost dreams and secret longings, on the other hand, are not just about the perfect sex experience, millions on Lotto or winning the World Cup or the Olympic Games in some extreme sport, but more about the soul's longing for achieving some kind of peace and balance, maybe, even, pure love. Love also has many faces: Eros, Filos and Agape. I believe that dreams are important for our aspiration to grow and gain insights into all things we do not know or understand. The dream can break and disappear if life or love do not turn out as we intended. Then it is important to dare to dream new dreams.

Anyone with the least insight into astrology understands that this is mainly about the sign Pisces and the planet Neptune. They both represent "the other side" and all things abstract that one can not really touch and see in the physical reality. From these come not only our dreams but all kinds of inspiration and creativity important for musicians, artists and writers.

Dreams are important for your survival. They are the driving force and motivation that gives you energy to keep on growing with everyday wear and tear. Hard work combined with a belief in what it takes can lead to worldly and spiritual success. Even though the optimist and pessimist are likewise wrong, the optimist has more fun in the meantime and does not care as much if things fail. Here are some of Neptune's typical effects. If the world seems to be hard and inhuman, one can shut off and dream away. However, dangers occur when using any means to escape the hard reality. It's too easy today to have a glass of wine, a beer at the pub or smoke a joint to relax, which of course calm down for the moment but easily lead to a cowardly way out of everything realistic. (Read more in the chapter Drugs.)

Neptune's contrast to Saturn is obvious: water against soil and dreams against reality. If Neptune represents our idealism and innermost longing, Saturn describes how we perceive and handle the reality we are forced to be in. I sometimes address this conflict by highlighting the necessity of balancing these extremes. Some people call this getting down to earth. I prefer to commute between "physical effort" (Saturn) and inspired experiences when I'm relaxed (Neptune). For me, this is letting me be absorbed by music, a good book or movie. Yoga is, on my part, a fun combination of these energies, the body's focus in a conscious relaxation.

What aspects in the chart?

I must emphasize that this is merely symbolic key interpretations where you can not take into account all other aspects that may exist to respective signs or planets. The following examples apply to all sorts of aspects between the respective planets.

Sun - Neptune

Different combinations or aspects between the Sun and Neptune are common in creative people. Nevertheless, at worst it can lead to a complicated role in existence if you "escape reality" too often. These people often have a deep and empathetic understanding of all living beings and may have it easier than others to indulge in spiritual or religious experiences. You can call them dreamers, but they are often harmless. They wish everyone well and can be almost excessively sacrificial and self-destructive. Here, you can sometimes find what I call "the Christ complex". They both consciously and unconsciously try to live like Jesus with an all-embracing brotherly love for all.

Dreams can be more real to these people than reality itself. They may even see the reality through rose-rimmed glasses and may perceive beauty in the small details easier than others. No wonder they want to create and reproduce their imagination with different tools, whether it comes through words, sounds or pictures.

Moon - Neptune

The Moon's contact with Neptune is the very symbol of the Virgin Mary. These people can be the role model of the perfect mother and suffer in silence if others suffer. They are always risking self-extinction if not more practical energies can ease up this strong emotion. Here we definitely find both the day dreamer as well as the blue-eyed idealist who believes nothing but the best of everyone. If disappointment occurs or if the reality becomes too harsh, the result can often become difficult. When they start comfort-eating, drink or take drugs, it may be difficult to break the habit. To their "better" or easier qualities, however, their empathy and compassion must be counted. They love animals and all living creatures and can create a castle out of a hut. Contentment is not uncommon because their ideal is not of "this world." They are altruistic rather than egotistic.

Mercury - Neptune

Here we emphasize both communication and "the message." A funny description is the English expression "Divine Inspiration." Depending on the kind of aspect, these people are often inspiring and committed, almost unrealistically. They can also be skilled at manipulating or duping others (lies). They can talk in riddles and seem confused, but always with a creative mindset. They both misunderstand and get misunderstood and must remember not to cross over too much between lies and truth. They can easily day dream and create something out of this; but at the same time, they need a practical ability to express clearly between their images and their imagination. It is not uncommon to have both a strong intuition and a slumbering medial talent with this combination, especially with any conjunction in a water sign (Cancer-Scorpio-Pisces). I associate this with the image of the absent-minded professor in the animated series *Tintin,* where the professor is constantly being misunderstood.

I have been gifted with a semi-square between these energies or planets, and this might be one of my most "important" aspects as it gives me both the ability to be inspired as well as to be able to associate freely. This may even contribute to my ability to channel thoughts I'm not always aware of. My own Neptune is relatively neutral, with a weak (7 degrees orbis), positive sextile to the Sun and a weak (8 d 30 m) but "sweet" trine to Venus. Otherwise, it's the semi-square that represents where I control my thoughts and values. Both my family and many clients often perceive me as slightly distracted or confused, and I often stumble across words and violate many grammatical rules, both speaking and writing.

Venus - Neptune

Here we have both the highest form of Love (Agape) and the deepest of sorrows. This combination can sometimes almost dominate the life of a human being and must be analyzed and understood correctly in order to be processed in times of adversity and sorrow.

As I said, the positive effects are an immense gift to humanity. These people are not only deeply compassionate and empathetic, but often they have a high moral and positive view of life. There is not only a hazy dream world but also a bitter reality. These people stand up for refugees and the homeless without any need for their own pay and struggle spontaneously for the weak in society. The love of Man is both a goal and a tool at the same time. When it comes to personal relationships, they are usually prepared for great sacrifices for the one they love and always put themselves last.

The risk is, of course, that it will not always be as you dreamed. If it turns out that reality does not match your ideals, the consequences can be disastrous. Here we have the very basis of the experience in the song *Love Hurts* (Nazareth). The sadness and sorrow you are experiencing is absolute hopelessness and despair. Life loses both its meaning and purpose, and here many suffer from either being forced to medicate or initiate a self-destructive form of drug addiction. In the worst case, the effect of this aspect can lead to a completely distorted view of life, and the stability of the psyche itself is put to the test.

I must admit that many of my most tragic clients and patients have had some of these phenomena. Perhaps this is not so strange since it is most often during crises and difficulties you contact the astrologer.

I also need to admit that my own ideals are both complicated and somewhat confused. At best, I can feel the euphoric ecstasy when I fall in love, but I also experience the optimal disappointment when the fog lifts and only tears remain. However, I can remember a very creative period in my life where I read a lot and used the music as a soothing "drug." I even had a brief infatuation during one of these periods. A transit period with these energies can be experienced as listening to the Vivaldi *Flute Concerto in C Largo* or conversely like listening to REM and their *Everybody Hurts.*

Mars - Neptune

This combination can give a fascinating effect, namely the ability to anchor your fantasies and goals, thus having the opportunity to realize your dreams. People with this strong combination often succeed in realizing their goals in life, just through some form of physical exertion.

Mars symbolizes the body's energy; and when it stimulates Neptune, it can easily lead to visible results. This is common in effective and productive individuals as well as people who use the body during their creative activity, such as dancers or working with animals. Athletes uses this effect optimally when they succeed.

An inharmonius or tense contact between these planets can lead to both frustration and misdirected anger because the ideal is not achieved despite all the effort. In relationships, this is one of the more difficult, but it works best on the sexual plane. These individuals are usually labeled with having the "macho effect" as the masculine energy is released in an aggressive and ruthless way. During dreams, these can indicate both "wet dreams" (about sex) as well as nightmares. This all the more not unusual when under any kind of toxic influence. Mars' contact with drugs and a Neptune aspect can thus trigger a strong self-destructive side unless energy is channeled through more inspiring projects.

I, myself, have no contact between these two influences, but Mars in Pisces in my 3rd house symbolically means spending a lot of time and energy on creative and inspirational projects, like talking, other forms of communication and interpreting charts.

Jupiter – Neptune

Now we approach "Nirvana" in symbolic form. Jupiter traditionally ruled over Pisces before Neptune was discovered, and it thrives in Pisces and is said to be strong and at home here. Since Jupiter is also about visions and hopes, it has the same energy as Neptune. Neptune's idealism and abstractions are enhanced, and here we can talk about "heavenly inspiration." I found this in Goethe's chart, and he is famous for his dynamic poetry. He wrote, for instance, the amazing *Faust*. Born a Virgo, he had Jupiter in Pisces trine Neptune in Cancer and in addition connected to a major trine with Pluto in Scorpio. In addition, is his Moon in Pisces, all of which led to his imagination having an enormous impact both socially and historically.

Jupiter has a tendency to enlarge and strengthen the planet it comes into contact with, and Neptune can float freely with inspiration and empathy. Of course, there is a backside of the phenomenon if wrongly used. This also occurs in extremely successful people's charts and can lead to excesses such as extreme fame, obesity or carefree indifference. Also common here is all forms of gambling and scams. A counter-balance with a lot of earth signs or a strong Saturn is often required to keep the feet on the ground and remain realistic.

Personally, I perceive these people as very good-hearted, almost on the verge of martyrdom and self-destruction, but they are always honest and sacrificing in their idealistic ambitions. Can be successful both on the humanistic and creative levels. Commonly occurring among musicians, poets and artists. Actually, all creativity that requires imagination and empathy. Since both Jupiter and Neptune are longing away, they can also repeatedly engage in many trips.

Saturn – Neptune

This complicated combination can be experienced as a bit difficult. This aspect can show how to balance your dreams with sheer reality. The result can be either catastrophic or successful. As Saturn demands realism, this can hold back inspiration, while at the same time providing a realistic ability to shape your own inspiration. It is rather like learning an instrument or dancing ballet. It requires a lot of patience and discipline in order to improvise and release creativity. If you mix the elements earth (Saturn) and water (Neptune), you can create clay and build many practical things with your imagination. Unfortunately, many who have this combination seem to hold back their creativity because it requires too much (Saturn) or they are too fluttery and impractical to actually create results. These aspects are common among ambitious idealists in the New Age genre today. They want so much and have such high ambitions and dreams but often lack the realistic attitude to being able to manage or handle their own business.

When it comes to dream sequences or a temporary experience of this phenomenon, people can react in different ways, everything from insomnia and sleep disorders to a workaholism where you simply ignore sleeping or resting. This is common with Saturn in Pisces. The key interpretation should nevertheless be that these people often feel a kind of conflict between their dreams and ideals and the sheer reality of their lives. This must be balanced or accepted in order to achieve any results.

Uranus – Neptune

This exciting combination is usually experienced in the subconscious, not in absolute consciousness. As Uranus is associated with the higher thinking and intuition, these effects can be very creative. Uranus speeds up thoughts and inspiration but can also lead to mental stress. At the same time, Neptune's thoughts can be stunned, and the ingenious creativity can get out if the person has any artistic or creative talents. As I was writing about this, I recalled a special woman with this aspect in square, the singer Kate Bush, who has the Sun in contact with this Uranus square Neptune. She is very original and innovative as an artist with her enormous creativity, but I know that she also suffered from a lighter social phobia and fears, which is typical of this aspect.

My colleague Ivan Wilhelm described this aspect as Neptune's putting us to sleep and stunning us, and Uranus is the alarm clock that awkwardly awakes us. That's a very good description. Properly used, this aspect can give a lot of innovation in artistic areas and also lead to major changes in different art forms. The opposite effect can be confusing news, and sometimes changes in life that can lead to disappointments and sorrow at worst. But most of the experiences usually take place on the subconscious level, most probably during an active dreaming period.

Pluto – Neptune

This combination rarely occurs, due to their relatively slow orbits, but it is taken into account if they form contact during a certain phase of life. The conjunction in Gemini in the late 1800s created many geniuses and inventors, but it also created an increased spiritual awareness as well as an increase in mediums and different mystical orientations. Neptune was discovered as late as 1846 and Pluto not until 1930. Their influences are most noticeable in the collective subconscious. Neptune is for example associated with the start of using anesthesia during surgery as well as widespread free religious activity.

Pluto's *transiting* contact with Neptune often attracts bits of the subconscious and can sometimes indicate a kind of religious crisis, as Pluto would like to transform everything that it comes into contact with. As for me, like many born in the 1900s, I have these in a weak sextile, and personally these contacts have always been exciting. I read a lot of spiritual and occult literature and "woke up" after years of slumbering mental hibernation.

Everybody Needs to Have a Friend

Wishbone Ash (album *Wishbone Four* 1973)

Trust in me I´ll try to do
Everything to help you that I can
Broken wings can heal and mend again
Don´t be afraid to cry your tears out loud
Everybody needs to have a friend

It´s only love that I can give
And I give to you the only love I have
When I see you´re in misery
It makes me want to try and understand
Everybody needs a helping hand
When I see you´re so unhappy
It makes me want to try and understand

If everything should turn around
And it´s me who feels so down and out
You could be the kind of company
To share a load and know how bad it feels
Everybody needs to have a friend

Part 3 The WORLD

Social media

It is certainly not easy to keep up with all the various social networks today. You must log in to *facebook*, check your *twitter* account, all your different email accounts and search *Spotify* or *Youtube* to find your favorite music or other information. Then you may also check *Snapchat* or *Instagram*, not to mention all upgrades, updates and endless texts and conversations with your cellphone - your only true "friend" today. The *Internet* is a fantastic and gigantic library that is open 24 hours a day. I have saved many hours by searching on *Google* or *Wikipedia* to find information for my book.

Even if I do not enjoy the constant need to be mean and sarcastic, this virtual world adds to both laughter and irritation. I had a mixed hatred from the beginning to *facebook*. As a display window, you decide to show what would be displayed. Here are many comic variants: the "Jojo" who logs in starving for blue thumbs 5 to 10 times a day, the difficult "Flashers" are hard to distinguish from the "narcissist" who drowns in his own display image permanently adding new selfie profile images on themselves, their platter, their wine glasses, their destinations or pets. Astonishingly, I was surprised by how many people absolutely "must" have their provocative big "boobs" displayed in their pictures. Have I entered a dating community? "Peeping Toms" rarely update, but as a NSA employee they scan everyone else´s lives totally anonymously. How many friends does my new boyfriend have, and "why" is he still a friend with HER? Why hasn't he changed his status? The "Reformer" preaches wholesome food, political change, "saving the whales," and spamming with endless variations on "Share this if you have the world's best daughter or the world's best budgie,"etc. It's like one massive pyramid game. I am no saint myself, and I have probably tested most of these caricatures.

Maybe it's just all about a need to want to share our experiences with others. Or perhaps it is a desperate way to seek attention or to be loved, appreciated or to just be seen. Then it perhaps means that people with good self-esteem rarely use facebook. In the future, there will probably be some new diagnoses related to the phenomenon: "lack of blue-thumbs," "inlogging Tourettes mania," "overdose posting," "shortage of surrogate friends disorder," etc. You are sent to facebook rehab centers where you will learn slowly and pedagogically to avoid constant logins and try to live without the need of blue thumbs up. Perhaps you begin with a facebook-free day per week. What a horrible thought. "Do you not have facebook? Who do you think you are? Burn the witch!" With my natural talent to constantly be obstinate and a "pain in God's ass," it's surprising that I still have facebook.

In the name of honesty, I have enjoyed myself through most of these caricatures. If you're like me at the age around 60, it's not that smart to show new, current pictures on a hoary has-been with a bulging belly. I'd rather post a picture of one of the cats. Had I not had facebook, I also would have missed out on my adult children's and all the grandchildren's entire world. Before, I used to get everything through simple phone calls. Facebook is also efficiently "easy" on birthdays and tributes. You can avoid buying a carefully selected, beautiful greetings card, buy a stamp, and put down the effort to get it off on time. Instead, you just click a little blue thumb, or better, a cute emoji in the shape of a heart. It just needs to take a few seconds. It's so fast, cheap and painless, something stingy Taureans and stressed Geminis love.

Strangely, however, in my role as an astrologer, I have not even received five new orders via facebook since I joined in 2009. On the contrary, I tried to be restrictive in adding new "friends," as I quickly discovered that the "starting page" was hundreds of miles long. Should you monitor all your friends' latest updates, the hours flew away, and, horrible thought, what if you missed out on something important? I still think facebook is a fantastic phenomenon today. You can post questions or quick messages whenever you want and can get the answers the next time you log in. Of course, you can also try to spread some "important" info to your relatives or clients. Then again, "important" is something relative. Facebook is nevertheless an effective opinion maker today where you can reveal corrupt politicians, greedy or immoral companies and disclose hidden secrets. *March against Monsanto* should all be aware of, otherwise they will soon take over the world in a global world government. That is a fact, and unfortunately no exaggeration.

However, life is too short. When this book is published, I will probably terminate my facebook account and join *the world* out there instead. The garden outside my window has lapsed and needs my attention. It looks almost uninhabited. I prefer to ride my car and visit my children, spend more time with the grandchildren and get more time for relaxation and meditation.

Astrological info and history of the most common and most visited phenomena on the Internet today:

Google (No. 1 on Alexa's list of most popular pages)

Google was founded on September 4, 1998. Virgo with Moon and Uranus in Aquarius. Founded by Chad Hurley, Sun Aquarius, Moon probably Aries, Steve Chun, Sun Leo, Moon probably Aquarius and Jawed Karim, Scorpio, Moon Capricorn/Aquarius, who uploaded the very first Youtube video in 2005. He also has Venus-Uranus conjunct in Scorpio, a typical "fame"-syndrome.

Youtube (No. 2 on Alexa)

The phenomenon of Youtube was born on February 14, 2005, with Sun in Aquarius and Moon in Taurus, and the first clip ever was uploaded on April 23, 2005, at 20.27, local time California. Then the Sun was in Taurus and Moon in Scorpio. As you can understand, you can easily make horoscopes even for companies, associations and various situations, if only you know the day and/or the time. As you can see, much on Youtube is about aspects of Aquarius (everyone has access), Taurus (profitability, advertising) and Scorpio (business and secret information). Youtube is owned by Google.

facebook (No 3 on Alexa)

facebook's founder, Mark Zuckerberg, is no sucker. He was born on May 14, 1984, Taurus with Moon Scorpio. Unfortunately, there is no correct time, but the Moon was in Scorpio all day. If he was born early in the day, the Moon will be conjunct Saturn, or late conjunct Mars, both in Scorpio. What is interesting, however, is his Mercury at the end of Aries in a strong opposition to Pluto and trine Neptune at the beginning of Capricorn. Here we can talk about being a messenger for the new age communication.

The facebook phenomenon started as a "Business: facebook web site" already on March 28, 1997 at 2:00 pm in San Francisco local time, and was intended for the students at Harvard from the beginning. The facebook we use today first started on February 4, 2004. In the chart of 1997, the Moon is conjunct Pluto in almost the same spot in Sagittarius and Sun-Venus-Saturn within a few degrees in Aries. This signifies "crazy," manic, light-footed women and impulsive but slightly shy men (Venus-Saturn).

In the map of 2004, the Moon in Cancer is trine Venus in Pisces and a quincunx to Pluto. It was all about getting "inspired by girls" (Moon-Venus). The Moon in Cancer is focused on emotions, women and the family. Sun-Neptune in Aquarius within two degrees is relatively passive and neutral. Neptune's influence, however, is on the spot. This shows men with illusions, imaginations and fantasies. With these energies, facebook started a site that has as of today in 2017 around 2 billion users.

Another interesting date is when facebook was introduced on Wall Street on May 18, 2012. The Sun was in Taurus, just four days after Zuckerberg's own birthday, and the Moon, MC, Mercury and Jupiter were also in Taurus as it was just before the New Moon, within 13 hours. With the Ascendant in Leo, the first shares beat all records, and the exchange curve grew steadily, even today.

YAHOO! (No. 5 on Alexa)

Yahoo! is a multimedia portal that started already in January 1994 and changed it´s name to Yahoo on March 2, 1995. Both Sun and Moon were in Pisces while Venus conjuncted Uranus in Capricorn. It was founded by Jerry Yang, born November 5, 1968, Scorpio with Moon in Taurus, and also by David Filo, born April 20, 1966, with both Sun and Moon Aries.

INSTAGRAM (No. 23 on Alexa)

Instagram is owned by facebook, released on October 6, 2010. It is Libra with the Moon in Virgo, and it was purchased by facebook in April 2012 for 1 billion US dollars. The original creators were Kevin Systrom, a Capricorn with Moon in Scorpio, and Mike Krieger, Pisces with Moon probably in Sagittarius (possibly Capricorn).

TWITTER (No. 10 on Alexa)

Twitter Inc. was founded on March 21, 2006, and was launched on July 15, also in 2006. "The SMS of the Internet" had over 300 million active users by January 2016. The chart for March 21 has Sun Aries and Moon Sagittarius, while the chart for the launch has Sun Cancer and Moon in Pisces. Both the founding and launching have Jupiter in Scorpio indicating a huge collective impact and profitability. The CEO and one of the founders, Jack Dorsy, is Scorpio with Moon in either Libra or Scorpio. There is an interesting Mars on the Sun and both are opposite Jupiter in Taurus. In addition, the Venus in Capricorn is almost in an exact sextile to Uranus in Scorpio.

Only in 2016, 90 billion tweets had been sent up by May. This compares to 32,600,000,000 billion e-mails.

Vine

Vine was launched on January 24, 2013 as a video application to Twitter and is a microblogging service where you put up 6-second clips that run in a loop (i.e., repeated all the time). In May 2016, "King Bach" had 15 million followers. Vine's chart has the Sun in Aquarius with Moon probably in Cancer.

PODCAST

Podcast is a combination of iPod and Broadcast and, at the very least, is messy. Originally an *Apple* service, that meant that you could listen to audio files. Today, however, there are also video podcasts and *vodcasts* with image clips.

APPLE (No 53 on Alexa)

Apple was first founded on April 1, 1976. Sun and Mercury were in Aries and trine Neptune in Sagittarius. The Moon was in Aries or possibly in Taurus. One of the founders was the legendary Steve Jobs, who died in 2011, a Pisces with Moon Aries. Out of Apple, Macintosh were developed to all computers that today are products called Mac. The first Mac computer was launched on January 24, 1984, with the Sun in Aquarius and the Moon in Libra. It has Jupiter and Neptune in Capricorn in sextile with Mars and Pluto in Scorpio, signifying a huge collective impact. Mac Book was launched May 16, 2006 and is very popular today. The latest model Mac Book Retina was launched on April 19, 2016.

TUMBLR (No. 45 on Alexa)

No, it's not misspelled. It is actually spelled this way. This is a relatively new so-called microblog platform that has become very popular, where you can add pictures, text and multimedia and also be private. This was created February 19, 2007 by David Karp, who was born in 1986 with both Sun and Moon in Cancer. The chart for Tumblr has the Sun, Moon, Mercury, Venus and Uranus in Pisces, indicating much creative work with great imagination. In May 2016, there were over 292 million blogs. Users can also link to their twitter and facebook accounts.

BLOG

This has become a very common phenomenon today where pretty much anyone can get a blog and spread their opinions, thoughts and any messages. The word "blog" in English comes from a play with the word "web log," meaning a log online, where someone divided the word's letters and instead wrote "we blog." Hence the word "blog." Today, there are a lot of blogs in all genres, from personal to strictly political, but most are in the form of newspapers and are funded through advertisements. Blogging can also be done via your cellphone and called "mob logging." Blogging is now considered widely as a media. Over 5 million blog posts per day are an enormous spread of information.

Even in the celebrity world, it seems to be a must to have a daily blog with followers who slavishly follow every breath, hangover, clothing choices and spontaneous opinions. I found Beyonce Knowles, born September 4, 1981, Virgo with Moon Conjunct Uranus in Scorpio;

Supermodel Coco Rocha, born September 10, 1988, a double Virgo; and Posh from Spice Girls (Victoria Beckham, who is married to soccer player David). Victoria was born April 17, 1974, an Aries with Moon in Aquarius. Even Jay Z, Lady Gaga, Katy Perry, Paris Hilton, Miley Cyrus and the Kardashians have their own blogs for those of you who are curious.

VIMEO

Vimeo was one of the first pages to share movie clips and is still active. The term "Vimeo" is an anagram of the word "movie." Unfortunately, I have no specific starting date for Vimeo. I only know that they started in October and launched the site in November 2004. It was founded by Jake Lodwick, born July 25, 1981, a Leo with his Moon in Taurus; and co-founder Zach Klein, born September 26, 1982, a Libra with Moon in Capricorn. Sorry, no user numbers have been found, but they offer both free accounts up to 500 MB and more professional variants.

NETFLIX (No. 36 on Alexa)

Netflix already started on April 14, 1998 as an advertiser of DVD by mail and launched streaming movies in January 2007. Unfortunately, I have no starting date. In 2016, it had close to 75 million users worldwide. From 2013, several series were produced directly for viewing on Netflix, and *House of Cards* with Kevin Spacey was the first.

WIKIPEDIA (No. 7 on Alexa)

Needless to say, I had to add this giant database, where I surprisingly found that the Swedish language variant was second to the number of articles, among 292 languages. The entire Wikipedia contains about 40 million articles and was launched on January 15, 2001 making it a Capricorn with Moon in Libra. It's Mercury conjunct Neptune in Aquarius trine Jupiter in Gemini is well suited for spreading information to the masses.

TOP 10 Top web sites

This is the compilation of **Alexa Internet** in March 2016.

1. Google Services & Products - USA.

2. YouTube Video Sharing - USA.

3. Facebook - Social Networking - USA.

4. Baidu - Search Engine - China.

5. Yahoo! Portal and Media - USA.

6. Amazon - Trade and Cloud - USA.

7. Wikipedia - Encyclopedia - USA.

8. Tencent QQ Portal - China.

9. Google India - Search Engine - India.

10. Twitter - Social Networking - USA.

Outside TOP 10 we find Microsoft Windows Live (11), MSN (13), LinkedIn (17), Bing (19), eBay USA (24), Netflix (36), Microsoft (40), Imdb (56), CNN (84), and Adobe (95).

Music

Music has always been important to me, and in some periods, it became almost as a drug or addiction. During my childhood, my eclectic taste in music varied from Tages to Lollipops and Hepstars with the Beatles, but it was not until I listened to Pink Floyd in my mid-teens that strange feelings awoke in me. I discovered early that I was attracted to both more aggressive rock music as well as a more poetic and romantic inspirational genre like classical music and ballads.

Growing up in Gothenburg, I was lucky enough to see many bands Live on Scandinavium or Ullevi, bands like Deep Purple, Led Zeppelin, Uriah Heep, Emerson, Lake & Palmer, Rolling Stones, David Bowie and Genesis.

Later my musical taste altered a little harder rock with The Moody Blues, Genesis or Yes, which I fortunately watched Live in 2005 on *Sweden Rock*. When my nine year younger sisters danced ballet, I became familiar with classical music; not just *Swan Lake*, but all the great masters. As for myself, I never had the patience to learn any instruments but struggled on an acoustic guitar with some simple riffs, but it never became more than "The World's Most Known Riff*," Smoke on the Water* or the four chords of *The Hunt for the Dalai Lama by* Swedish band Hoola Bandoola Band. Today, I am still inspired by all this different forms of music and can even improvise on my daughter's digital piano with great pleasure. Actually I can play perfectly the intro to the Beatles song *Hey Bulldog.*

Music can trigger some strange feeling surrounding love or infatuation. Teenagers are linked to the hormones as well as to the planet Venus, and the music you listen to during your teen years often carves deep grooves into your psyche. I remember songs like *Vincent* by Don McLean, *Everything I Own* or *Guitar Man* by Bread, Morning Has Broken by Cat Stevens, Your Song by Elton John or *Killing Me Softly* by Roberta Flack. In addition, at my funeral, *Could It Be Magic* by Barry Manilow will be played.

Later I discovered some odd artists like Peter Gabriel from Genesis, King Crimson, Manfred Mann's Earthband, Jethro Tull, Stevie Nicks from Fleetwood Mac, Kate Bush, that David Gilmour from Pink Floyd discovered. There were also our Swedish poets Ola Magnell, John Holm, little fairy Barbro Hörberg with *Eyes Sensitive to Green*, Jan Johansson's soft piano play, fairysmurf Ralph Lundsten in his pink castle, desperate but beautiful Supertramp, wonderful City Boy, Steve Harley & Cockney Rebel with the song *Sebastian* and the poets in Wishbone Ash.

In the late 70's, music became a kind of drug that opened me up to unusual chakras and probably made me more open to my intuition. I discovered the so-called New Age music that became a great inspiration when I interpreted and analyzed birthcharts. The Japanese Kitaro (Aquarius) was one of the first and was followed by several, such as Enya, Björn Melander (who in 1994 did the beautiful *Dolphin´s Song* with real dolphins), Donna Bradley with so-called *Metamusic*, Karunesh (born January 10, 1956) with his amazing *Sounds of the Heart* in 1984, Deuter, Paul Horn (who played the flute inside Egypt's pyramids), Tim Story´s *Untitlea*, Mike *Tubular Bells* and his brother Terry Oldfield, Clannad, Howard Blake (a Scorpio who also wrote the beautiful song *Walking in the Air* from the animated movie *The Snowman* (1982), Jean-Michel Jarre's huge concerts with image and sound, Philip Glass (Aquarius with Moon Libra) who made avant-garde film music and perhaps primarily Medwyn Goodall, born in 1961 and who since the 90's has been one of my favorites. In the 2000s I also discovered Jon Mark.

Many of you who received my interpretations on cassette tapes during the 80's and 90's can probably hear Kitaro's notes in the background. Since returning to Anebo in 2002, Jon Mark has mostly been heard in the background of the tapes, but after 2005 I dropped the background music because of difficulties mixing to audio programs in the computer.

John Lennon had his "artistic depression" and wrote his best songs when he was depressed with his Moon in Capricorn or Aquarius. Ulf Lundell (20 Nov 1949), whom I did not discover until the 80s, has provoked and inspired many with his lyrics and songs, and has always frankly expressed what he thinks and knows. On my website you can read more (in Swedish) about this strange person who has his Moon on exactly the same degree as me. Uffe is a "double Scorpio" (born around a new Moon). Perhaps we are kindred spirits. Today I am enjoying both his music, lyrics and his books.

Lyrics - what is the message? Mercury the Messenger

Even the intellectual "message" attracted me early. It was important to me what the music writers wanted to say or speak out with their voices. I was very moved by political protest singers from the 1960s, such as Joan Baez or Barry McGuire when he sang *Eve of Destruction*.

Unlike mainstream pop, these writers really wanted to say something, or for example, protest against the Vietnam War. Woodstock became a symbolic end to the intense 60's where both drugs and flowers were mixed with new spirituality and an increased interest in meditation, TM (Transcendental Meditation). Bob Dylan, (actually Robert Zimmerman, May 24, 1941) had his own way of describing existence, but he was not a pure protest singer, with some exceptions, such as *Masters of War*. Rather, he was more of a poet with his sometimes religious ruminations. However, I am still listening with great pleasure to everything he did, both the older *Lay, Lady Lay* or the recent *Workingman's Blues #2*. During the editing of this book, I learned that Dylan was awarded the Nobel Prize in Literature in 2016. But hell no, he chose not to show up in Stockholm to receive his prize. He has too much inner turmoil and phobias to pretend to be social among the intellectual elite in a smoking or dress jacket.

Today I listen, depending on the mood, to both Ulf Lundell's many songs and much of my new music, such as Evanescense, Lana del Rey, Tom Odell, RED, Thriving Ivory or Three Days Grace. I also enjoy the old heroes Pink Floyd and perhaps mostly Roger Waters with his protests against the Iraq war, President George W. Bush, Jr. and all global social injustices. I could write a separate chapter about Roger Waters. Thankfully I had the chance to see his epic concert *tour "The Wall"* at Ullevi in 2013 with my youngest daughter Amanda.

I still choose my music based on my moods. If the energy is high or strong (Moon Scorpio), I increase the adrenaline with intense hard rock, such as Rammstein, Metallica, Black Sabbath, **Grand Funk Railroad** (1971 *Loneliness*), Jimi Hendrix, Led Zeppelin, Rush, 30 seconds to Mars, Whitesnake, Marilyn Manson, Nine Inch Nails,

Audioslave, Korn or Nightwish. Other days, I only play Venus-Neptune music that stimulates my intuition. I can experience pure astral trips to Vivaldi, Edvard Grieg, Chopin, Debussy or Leo Delibes little beautiful *Flower Duet* from *Lakmé* (Thanks Ewa). Composer Gustav Holst even wrote a whole suite based on his associations with the various planets, called *The Planets*, which clearly shows that he really knew something about the astrological significance of each of the planets.

Film music

Another genre is music as film soundtracks. What would the movie *The Wall* in 1982 be without the music of Pink Floyd or the songs from all the musicals we have enjoyed: *The Sound of music*, *Mary Poppins*, *The Wizard of Oz*, *Grease*, *Cabaret*, *Fiddler on the roof*, *Les Miserables*, or any of Disney's movies, such as *The Lion King*, *The Jungle Book*, *Beauty and the Beast* or *Aladdin*.

As for myself, I have a fondness for older black-and-white movies where it might be even more important with an engaging soundtrack to highlight the image and experience. Here are a lot of wonderful composers, such as Alfred Newman, Bernard Herrman, Max Steiner, Franz Waxman, Ennio Morricone or Nino Rota. What is *Jaws* or *Star Wars* without John Williams? What is Hitchcock's movie *Psycho* without Bernard Herrman's screaming strings? Or *The Godfather* without the music of Nino Rota? Charles Chaplin (Aries with Moon Scorpio) himself wrote a lot of music to his own movies, for example the immortal *Smile* from the movie *Modern Times*.

Today I can listen to entire original soundtracks from movies, abbreviated OST. This is something my youngest daughter actually started with when she got the original soundtracks from her favorite movies. For example, everything with Thomas Newman, born Oct. 20, 1955, and a Libra with Moon Sagittarius: *The Shawshank Redemption*, *American Beauty*, *Road to Perdition*, *Finding Nemo* and *Skyfall*. We also enjoy Howard Shore, born Oct. 18, 1946, another Libra but with Moon Leo, who wrote all the music to *The Lord of the Rings*. Today there are many wonderful composers for film alone: James Horner, born Aug. 14, in 1953, RIP (Leo with Moon in Libra, who died in an air crash in 2015), Alexandre Desplat, Clint Mansell (*Requiem for a Dream*), Jerry Goldsmith (*Alien*), James Newton Howard, and perhaps one of the prime composers in my opinion, Hans Zimmer, born Sept. 12 1957, (Virgo with Moon Aries), who created music for the epic *Inception*, *Hannibal*, *The Dark Knight*, *Gladiator* and *Interstellar*.

If I want to be sentimental or sad, I prefer Billie Holiday (April 7, 1915), Aries with Moon Capricorn (Queen of Blues) or Edith Piaf (December 19, 1915), Sagittarius with Moon Gemini, or the wonderful Nat King Cole (March 17, 1919), Pisces with Moon Libra. His version of Chaplin's *Smile* is timeless.

By accident, Alexander (one of my sons) and I in 2005 were lucky enough to see Denmark's own "Billie Holiday", Kira Skov, born June 6, 1976, together with her former group The Kindred Spirits (2001-2007), live in Middelfart, Denmark.

Also fantastic was the adored Egyptian icon Oum Khaltoum (birthday varies with different dates, but she was born either December 31, 1898 or May 4, 1904).

For many, classical music is just music of composers who have been dead hundreds of years, such as Beethoven, Grieg, Chopin, Mozart, Strauss or Bach. But much of that music is both timeless and unbeatable. Has anyone missed the world famous intro to Beethoven's *Fifth Symphony* or the fourth movement to his *Ninth Symphony*, *Ode to Joy*, which Kubrik used in his movie *A Clockwork Orange*? Many children have heard Tjajkovsky's *Swan Lake* or Prokofiev's *Peter and the Wolf*. Many also have probably heard *Also Sprach Zarathustra* by Richard Strauss, a Gemini, that director Stanley Kubrik used in the space film *2001: A Space Odyssey*.

Music is important. It channels our feelings, gives us energy and inspiration, empathizes with and within us, helps us comit and/or connect to anger or help us escape reality when needed. Luckily, I have some musical children who can play the guitar, piano and/or sing.

The combination of music and message can be exciting. For example, consider John Lennon's *Power to the People* or *Working Class Hero* or Bob Dylan's many protest songs. In Michael Jackson's amazing music video for *Earth Song*, he highlights how Man is destroying and devastating almost all the wildlife of the Earth. Check it out on YouTube! There have been 156 million views in 2017 !!!

Music itself is linked to several planetary energies. Although Pisces may dominate with the Sun or Moon, other occurring signs are Taurus, Libra, Cancer or Sagittarius. Combinations between Neptune, Uranus and Venus are common, but also the Moon must be included in the picture as it reinforces the need to express feelings. Moon-Saturn or Moon in Capricorn can indicate melancholy or a more serious view of life, while a strong Mercury tends more to put the weight on lyrics. Bob Dylan's Moon-Uranus reflects his concerns and protests.

I also have a few spot-on combinations that often occur. Combinations mainly between Venus and Uranus are often found in so-called "famous" peoples' charts; so if you hope to become famous, look for this combination. A strong Mars in the chart also reinforces the more aggressive need and is common among hard rockers and those drawn to a bit more intense music. I'm probably a big mix, as I change in mood, depending on inspiration. Driving the car I switch between some intellectual IQ on P1 and "rock-classics." My Neptune has no strong contacts beyond a semi-square to Mercury, so I might listen more to the lyrics than the music.

One last fascinating reflection: I heard many years ago about something called "*The Backster Effect*"(Google Cleve Backster). It was a person who measured electromagnetic charges in flowers and compared their "reaction" when subjected to different types of music. He started out as an investigator in the CIA with a detector and polygraph. He not only discovered that the plants responded to music, but they even used telepathy. They reacted intensely if only the test person "thought" of hurting the flower, and they would react if a plant in another room was subjected to torture. Mindblowing ... As for the music test, the flowers "enjoyed" classical music, got "scared" from rock music and reacted "not at all" to country music.

"The Balance"

(From The Moody Blues album *A Question of Balance* 1970)

After he had journeyed,
And his feet were sore,
And he was tired,
He came upon an orange grove
And he rested
And he lay in the cool,
And while he rested, he took to himself an orange and tasted it,
And it was good.
And he felt the earth to his spine,
And he asked, and he saw the tree above him, and the stars,
And the veins in the leaf,
And the light, and the balance.
And he saw magnificent perfection,
Whereon he thought of himself in balance,
And he knew he was.
Just open your eyes,
And realize, the way it's always been.
Just open your mind
And you will find
The way it's always been.
Just open your heart
And that's a start.
And he thought of those he angered,
For he was not a violent man,
And he thought of those he hurt
For he was not a cruel man
And he thought of those he frightened
For he was not an evil man,
And he understood.
He understood himself.

Upon this he saw that when he was of anger or knew hurt or felt fear,
It was because he was not understanding,
And he learned, compassion.
And with his eye of compassion.
He saw his enemies like unto himself,
And he learned love.
Then, he was answered.
Just open your eyes,
And realize, the way it's always been.
Just open your mind
And you will find
The way it's always been.

Film – Neptune´s Reality

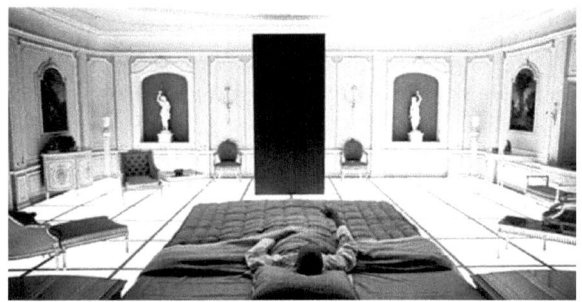

(From *2001: A Space Odyssey* 1968)

"It looked like our dreams ..."

(Quote from the TV series about the film's history, *The Story Of Film: an Odyssey* from 2011).

First, I want to explain why I devote a whole chapter to this cultural form. At the back of the book, in the Appendix Movies, I deliberately omitted most of my major favorites and even more popular films. Otherwise, the list would flood the entire book.

I have already planned to do a more detailed treatise on Film and Film History in my next book. Then we will get more into the epic directors: Akira Kurosawa, Charles Chaplin, Buster Keaton, Ingmar Bergman, Victor Sjöström, Dreyer, Stanley Kubrik, Alfred Hitchcock, Erich von Stroheim, Frank Capra, Frank Borzage, Orson Welles, Vittorio de Sica, Billy Wilder, Fritz Lang, F.W. Murnau, Josef Sternberg, Tod Browning, Jean Vigo, Jean Renoir, Marcel Carne, Fellini, David Lean, Francis Ford Coppola, Christopher Nolan, Peter Jackson, Milos Forman, Clint

Eastwood, Werner Herzog, Kieslowski, Sergei Eisenstein, Andrej Tarkovsky, Mike Leigh, Ken Loach and many others.

In the Appendix, I do not have so many older black and white and silent movies, even if I love the old masters. However, you will find a couple of interesting animated movies.

Film and theater have always played a big part in my own development, both personally and as an astrologer. A film can, for a while, bring me to another world away from the here-and-now with its anxiety, sadness or void. Almost like being under the influence of drugs, I experience everything from grief to exalted happiness. Due to my mood, I can choose to get entertained, scared or get new experiences from other people's lives in films. The reasons may vary, and the supply is infinite.

The priorities are, of course, individual as well as the likes and genres. Some people enjoy fun gags, slapstick or stereotypical dramas where women are naively foolish in their gender and men are successful muscle-cluster with a huge sex drive. I am aware that the flavor is divided, but I think the movie's own message can give you immense experiences. I myself may prefer the genre drama or documentaries, but I also love old black-and-white melodramas told with humor or excitement. Even the classic silent movies have brilliant messages if you can take them to your heart.

The difference between older black-and-white and color films is big. During the film's own development, both lighting, camera angles and cutting techniques changed. In addition, the requirements were both higher and different to the actors themselves. If they did not have *charisma* like Marlene Dietrich or Greta Garbo and could personify their role, it did not matter how the shape looked. The same problem is also found in contemporary movies. Lots of action and explosions and colorful CGI (Computer Generated Images) can never compensate for bad actors or a lousy script (the story).

Certainly there is a difference between movies and their messages. I watch with tremendous curiosity on the genre documentaries, where so to speak "God Himself" is the director (according to Hitchcock). They are often revealing, provocative, questioning and informative. You find out about the causes of war, political consequences, inhuman animal breeding, dolphin slaughter, or simply finding out more about unusual lives.

Another of my favorites is the simple drama: a story about ordinary people, their lives, conflicts, crucial events or experiences as well as love, hate, pain, broken illusions, sorrow, death, longing, dreams, etc. If a movie attracts you, then you can maybe identify with one of the roles. The crucial liberation in the experience is that within an hour or so you actually get to see "how it resolves." To summarize, you can call it a "review of a person's life or its situation and how they succeed or fail to learn something about the event." I liken it to reading a key or as a fast journey through time and space.

What I find most fascinating is to find out "how things turns out." Whether you can use this experience or knowledge in your own world is another matter. I personally believe that we can actually learn a lot, just by seeing how others solve the same situation. One can get inspiration, energy, motivation or just an increased joy of life from different movies.

Considered as a "drug," film is, perhaps, relatively harmless. There is no hangover, if you can avoid sitting up all night and having to get up early the following morning. Economically, everything is about your own choices and priorities. Today you can lend old VHS/VCRs or DVDs from friends and acquaintances. Well, sometimes I still watch an old VHS. I have an almost new VHS video recorder, where we sometimes watch older movies that you simply can not find on DVD. Today you can also rent movies, even if it was more common before. Many libraries have a smaller selection of the slightly not-so-commercial films. These films were not always popular or successful, but they were ambitious, artistic or old classics. Today there is also a wide range of so-called streamed movies, like Netflix, where through a subscription you can get unlimited access to lots of movies.

I myself had a period over several years where I collected both VHS and DVD movies. I was a customer at a now abandoned site, lovefilm.se (forerunner to Netflix), where you rented unlimited a month for only 79 SEK. (My films were received by post). For five years, I rented altogether a huge collection of mostly older and rare films that were not available for purchase anymore. I gathered over 800 movies in these years, and of course I "ripped off" most of them to my computer before sending them back. In principle, this was illegal, but it was never done for commercial use. From the start the ambition was to help my own teens. If I wanted them to see the best, then I might have to go through a number of them to find the really good quality movies. In addition, my two youngest children (now 29 and 24 years old in 2017) continued their studies in the world of films. Additionally, too, for the sake of honesty, I must admit that most of my movies in my "movie treasure chest" have simply been downloaded, most of them for free. These films were not always with Swedish subtitles, but non-English films are usually with English subtitles. Today's range of movies is unlimited online.

What energies are involved?

For those of you who already guessed on the planet Neptune, this is obviously right. Neptune is linked to both our subconscious and our dreams, as well as to our imagination and inspiration. Art, literature and music belong here, and Neptune's passage in space is also said to influence the fashion trends of the day. Through Neptune's position in the chart, you can see your ability to create or imagine. Neptune is often very strong in the charts of filmmakers, artists, writers and musicians, as well as, unfortunately, also in addicts and people who may be dependent on medicines of different kinds.

Through Neptune's progressive (forward in time) movement in the chart, you can see periods of active creation as well as periods of fatigue, illness or depression. Everything depends on how you use and channel the energy you come into contact with. Some have it easier to "dream away," while others may think it's unpleasant or scary. Those who live with an ever active Neptune can have a little difficulty with reality and unfortunately suffer from some form of addiction. I have repeatedly met clients where I found some kind of Neptunian influence, and it can be an unsettling mix of disease, fatigue and disappointment.

I myself have a relatively neutral Neptune in Libra in my 10th house, which suggests that I can use its positive energy in my work. It only has a wide sextile to the Sun at 7 degrees, so it's really too big to actually consider. There are interesting correlations here when I look at my social career as a chauffeur, having many contacts with customers in the oil industry in Gothenburg (Neptune) and having worked in Nybro for six years at a gas station (Neptune again). I also did a year's service as a church verger. Neptune is related to all things concerning religion. Additionally, my very first summer job in 1973 was in a larger hospital (Neptune), even though it was in the kitchen. Hospitals are also ruled by Neptune.

What, then, does this have to do with movies? Well, because Neptune is in my 10th house, it has meant a lot for both my personal development and my social career. Neptune has a higher vibration associated with dreams and healing, and this energy I can use with my intellect because I have a semi-square (45 degrees) to my Mercury in Virgo in the 9th House. You can also see it in a little funny way and point to "my naive dreams about the balance in life between individuals, with a great urge to express this in speech and writing." This aspect is probably also mirroring my ability to channel and interpret charts and to use both suggestions as well as a healing power in the mental process.

Neptune's influence in the world of films is obvious: to create and build illusions and dreams and to convey both message and learning with inspiration and empathy. The connection to pure entertainment is obvious. Making money from giving people a moment's illusion or escape from reality has always been ruled by Neptune. Jupiter-Neptune aspects are very common throughout the film industry.

Movies at home or in the cinema?

(Or: why did I not buy shares in Netflix?)

Movies should of course be experienced in the cinema. But this is not always true. If the experience is based on colors, sounds, music or great image perspectives like in *The Lord of the Rings* or in the *Harry Potter* movies, it may be a pleasure to sit inside a big cinema. But if it is about deeper feelings or a more low-key poetic experience, then perhaps it feels better to be at home on the couch. How often have you not been forced to listen to "idiotic comments" from acquaintances when leaving a cinema? In addition, you can cry unrestrainedly in your own sofa at home in the dark.

Another advantage of today's technology and the internet is the incredible range of viewing possibilities. Today you can both download and/or buy any tv-series you want, both new and older. If you glance through the offer today, the number of series on TV has completely exploded, and producing for TV has become as common and profitable as producing expensive movies. Actors today can shift between the stage, television productions and film parts. Since the supply of DVD has increased, boxes (collections of complete series) have also come out of the old series from the 50's and 60's. You can overindulge in the old black and white *Twilight Zone* or Alfred Hitchcock's productions. But you can also buy everything from the 70's and 80's to see all seasons of *Dallas*, *Dynasty* or *Falcon Crest* if you want.

The range today is almost immeasurable. There are banal soaps such as *Glamor* or rural idylls such as *Emmerdale Farm* that have run decades, but in the 21st century all Grammy and Emmy records were beat by more so-called quality series. *The West Wing* and *24* were given more space in the media than new movies, and a whole new money carousel had a renaissance with the world of the TV-series.

Today, in 2017, you have to search for or google special lists to get an idea of the ratings or the polls of any new series. Today the lists are topped by several different genres: *Game of Thrones*, *Fargo*, *The Walking Dead*, *Breaking Bad*, *True Detective*, *The Wire*, *House of Cards* or *Downton Abbey*. Every season brings new series, so this minimal list will be old when this book is on sale. Even cartoons are profitable to produce, and my favorite, *The Simpsons*, holds the record for the number of seasons. I believe they are in their 28th year. For my part, I have only had the time to focus on a few single favourites. Among them, which I can see at any time, are the old *Fawlty Towers* and the epic saga *I, Claudius*. But I also enjoy the later *West Wing*, the feel-good favorite *Gilmore Girls*, the sci-fi thriller *Battlestar Galactica* and the skillfully unpleasant *American Horror Story*. I still have to add that I have great difficulty understanding how to get time for this leisure activity.

GAMES - VR - Virtual reality

Another aspect of the concept of movie experience is today's TV or computer games. There are games for both the television and the computer. Online games are very popular among younger people. The phenomenon of *World of Warcraft* (*WoW*) led to a whole generation's deteriorated school grades (the Pisa investigation), when they preferred to spend the day (and for several years!) played online in this virtual reality. I saw and heard for myself my two youngest sons in this "addiction."

New games are constantly coming out for your PC or for Nintendo Gamecube, XBOX ONE 360 or Sony's Playstation, PS4.

Since my own experiences of this particular world are limited, I can not comment on all the various games that occur. It would probably be a whole book, but of course I've tested both Nintendo's older console and the Gamecube. I had a period when I sat and played *Super Mario* with the old console with my youngest daughter. Later, the new Gamecube came and I learned to play with a newer console and improved graphics. The favorite game was the horrible *Gauntlet: Dark Legacy* that my youngest daughter was not even allowed to watch her older brothers play, but she heard the cool music and the horrible sounds when they played. "Blue Wizard is about to die!". Having tested both XBOX, Gamecube and Playstation, I know how fast you become addicted.

My favorite games in recent years from all categories are *Resident Evil* or *Biohazard*, which became a mega success all over the world. I have played the first, a remake of the first, number two, three, four, five and six, but mostly the legendary fourth. Leon, Ada, Krauser, Wesker, Merchand, Saddler, Ashley and the others almost belong to the family today. In the same year (2017) as this book is published comes the long awaited *Resident Evil VII*.

Even the horror genre is big in the gaming world. My daughter forced me to play *Outlast* on PS4, and it was extremely realistic and almost scarier than a normal horror movie as you have neither weapons nor the ability to defend yourself. You could only sneak and hide when "bad guys" or psychopaths came. In addition, this is performed in an abandoned mental hospital where the doctors are almost crazier than their patients. This game is not recommended for the timid or nervous. I see it as pure self-harm. I have also tested *Alien*, *Dead Space*, *Deadrising, The Walking Dead, Until Dawn* and the epic *Silent Hill*.

I must admit that I have nevertheless had a wonderful time together with my now 23-year-old daughter when we sat and "fought" together through dangers, solved riddles and problems on different paths. The favorite is still *Resident Evil 4* on Gamecube, PS4 or XBOX 360, which I can play for hours as a pure pleasure and relaxation. I read, by the way, last winter, that soccer player Zlatan Ibrahimovic is a "gamer addict" for many years. He recently played *Far Cry*, mainly on XBOX.

Movies are a pure escape from reality, but they can also teach you more and increase your understanding and awareness of yourself and of Life on multiple levels. You can choose the way you want to fully utilize these energies. Some listen to music or play themselves, others create something, some takes drugs while others watch movies as pure relaxation or as a pure pleasure.

(scene from PS4-game Outlast)

229

Easter Egg 1
GILMORE GIRLS

Here is a little exception from my principle not to write so much about films. This may be placed under the heading "Positive Energy," which we all need. In fact, this is a little secret bonus "Easter Egg" to my own family.

I discovered this series a few years after my youngest daughter Amanda had been persuaded to watch this show by one of her sisters,

Tildy. At first I was a little doubtful, but then I said "ok" and gave it an honest chance. The concept of *"feel good"* is quite simple: do well, giggle a little bit, recognize yourself, sometimes get a tear in your eyes and most of all laugh at purely human weaknesses and comical situations. These are situations we all can recognize inhabited by a personal gallery of the most typical characters of today.

However, this is not the only benefit. The casting of the roles is superb. A single mom, Lorelai, 30-something, lives with her 16-year-old daughter, Rory, who is just about to start at a new (more expensive) private school. The problem is that they do not have enough money, so Lorelai must humiliate herself by asking for help from her well-off parents, something she refused to do earlier because she wanted to be independent.

In the ensemble there are coworkers, schoolmates, the small town's many kooky and self-centered individuals, including the sullen cafe owner Luke, a dance teacher, Rory's Korean best friend Lane with her super-strict mom and Lorelai's parents who live in their own little world without economic worries. Somewhere along the way comes a cute teenage boy who contacts Rory and the play can begin.

There were seven seasons for this award-winning and celebrated series that ran between 2000 and 2007. In 2016, 9 years later, they released a spinoff with most of the series characters back, called *Four Seasons*. It may not be quite the same, but it still was a dear reunion with people who have been like the closest family relationship.

There are several special gimmicks in the series, i.e., quirky traits that gave much character to the show, and one of these traits is the fast paced momentum in the dialogue. This reminded me of the contemporary series *West Wing,* where fast talk or long dialogues was in focus. I read somewhere that they have records in the number of words or sentences in script by episode, something that not least the main character Lorelai loves. Secondly, there are frequent references to well-known writers, musicians, movies and celebrities. You're almost waiting for their funny posts. Already in the first episode, they mention the films *Rosemary's Baby* and *Mommie Dearest* and use a quote that refers to the movie *West Side Story* when Lorelai mentions Officer Krupke.

Unfortunately, for those who have never seen the series, I can not reveal which people appear later on in the ensuing seasons, but all twists, both awaited and unexpected, are incredibly exciting, hysterically fun and above all emotionally charged. Love is not always as you think, and we are revealed troublesome, constantly verbalizing unfortunate slips and constant conflicts on a regular basis, like we all experience sometimes. I can only say that the one who can get through all seven seasons can't be disappointed. As the saying goes, the one who waits for something good...

Astrologically, the "birth" of the series was on October 5, 2000 with the Sun in Libra and the Moon in Capricorn. The show reflects these astrological signs through relationships (Libra) and serious or responsible women (Capricorn). The Sun trine Jupiter in Gemini means both humor and much "talk" and a positive flow. On the other hand, the Sun forms a trine to Uranus in Aquarius, which indicates many positive changes for the better, because Jupiter forms an interconnected major trine between these three air signs that stimulates thoughts and communication.

The exact location of the Moon is around 18-20 degrees in Capricorn and may have a positive aspect to Mars in Virgo (Rory) and a weak sextile to Venus in Scorpio (much talk about sex). The Moon in Capricorn actually reflects both "girls." The daughter Rory is very responsible, loyal and puts much responsibility on all her obligations in life. Mom Lorelai is her own boss and also with her own responsibility for her little family, which is a perfect interpretation of Moon in Capricorn. Even grandmother Gilmore represents an "elderly woman" of both seriousness and a certain authoritarian and conservative attitude.

Mercury in Scorpio is often sick humor with biting irony, easily vulgar and reveals many truths. There is a light sextile to Mars, which reinforces a straightforward openness and "cards-on-the-table" attitude. In addition, a weak aspect to Neptune in Aquarius can be interpreted as misunderstandings and confusion, but also extremely ingenious imagination. Venus in Scorpio in a sextile to Mars in Virgo provides energy, creativity and good interplay between the sexes. Mars in Virgo may be critical but mostly correct and responsible, which may be reflected in the grandmother's attitude. Jupiter in Gemini is in almost exact opposition to Pluto in Sagittarius, which can lead to tremendous success on the social plane, reflecting the popularity of the series. In addition, "rich and wealthy" often figure in the series from time to time. Funny enough, Saturn at the beginning of Gemini is completely neutral and almost without aspects, which I interpret as almost carefree, or at least without "more difficult" problems, even though everyone happens to encounter a lot of misery along the way. Simply put, one can say that the show lacked Saturn.

A quick analysis of the main characters' charts:

Mom **Lorelai**: Lauren Graham was born on March 16, 1968 with her Sun in Pisces and her Moon in Gemini. She has a so-called Large Trine between the Sun in Pisces, Jupiter in Cancer and Neptune in Scorpio. This indicates lots of travel, humor, generosity and emotions. Mercury in Pisces trine Mars in Scorpio points to a great spontaneous imagination and boldness to express her thoughts. Venus in Aries square Jupiter is overflowing in love but unwise in handling money. Everything points to a big heart, intensity in everything she does and being somewhat unrealistic from time to time. Plus, she loves all kinds of food.

Daughter **Rory**: Alexis Bledel was born on September 16, 1981. (just 10 days older than my *Utopia*) with her Sun in Virgo and her Moon most likely in Aries. Her Sun square Neptune is common among dreamers and idealists, and it also indicates that she is probably a bit too gentle and kind. Often she can be reserved and shy. The Sun sextile Uranus still provides an independent setting that helps her act on her own, while her Moon in Aries can ignite quickly but probably transient. There are no other visible aspects to her Moon. She may often want a lot and be a little impulsive and have a hard time waiting. Mercury and Jupiter conjunct in Libra give her strong intelligence and exquisite diplomacy. She has a good reading head and usually has a positive attitude. There is much charm, and she is easily popular. Venus in Scorpio square Mars in Leo is common in quick, passionate love, but passion can pass very quickly. There is a strong sexuality but also a strong will that comes first in relationships. She has Venus in Scorpio like the series, and love is often a complete roller coaster. Mars in Leo sextile Saturn in Libra strengthens her ability to self-discipline and gives her an incredible strength and stamina for long-term projects. Pluto's only aspect is a weak conjunction with Mercury, which can amplify her slightly mysterious image. For her, "talking is silver, but silence is golden."

Rest of the ensemble (participated in at least 37 episodes):

Lane: Rory's best girlfriend, Keiko Agena, was born on October 3, 1973. Her Sun is in Libra and her Moon is either Sagittarius or Capricorn, due to her uncertain time of birth.

Sookie (le chef): Melissa McCarthy was born on August 26, 1970. Her Sun is in Virgo and her Moon is in either Gemini or Cancer, again due to the uncertainty of the time of her birh. Later Melissa was nominated for an Oscar in the movie *Bridesmaids* (2011).

Luke (Cafe owner): Scott Patterson was born on September 11, 1958 with his Sun in Virgo and his Moon in Leo.

Michel (receptionist at the Inn): Yanic Truesdale, was born on March 17, 1970 with his Sun in Pisces and his Moon in Cancer.

Emily Gilmore (Rory's grandmother): Kelly Bishop was born on February 28, 1944 with her Sun in Pisces and her Moon in Taurus.

Richard Gilmore (Rory's grandpa): Edward Herrmann was born on July 21, 1943 with his Sun in Cancer and his Moon in Pisces. RIP December 31, 2014.

Dean (Rory's boyfriend): Jared Padalecki was born on July 19, 1982 with both his Sun and Moon in Cancer. Later he became well-known for the series *Supernatural* (2005 and still running in 2017).

Miss Patty (dance teacher): Liz Torres was born on September 27, 1947 with her Sun in Libra and her Moon in Aquarius or Pisces, depending upon the accurate time of her birth.

Kirk: Sean Gunn, was born on May 22, 1974 with both his Sun and Moon in Gemini.

Paris Geller (Rory's classmate): Liza Weil was born on June 5, 1977 with her Sun in Gemini and her Moon in Aquarius.

Logan: Matt Czuchry was born on May 20, 1977 with his Sun in Taurus and his Moon in Gemini.

Mrs. Kim (Lane's mother): Emily Keiko Kuroda was born on October 30, 1952 with her Sun in Scorpio and her Moon in Pisces or more likely Aries.

Babette (neighbor and catlady): Sally Struthers was born on July 28, 1947 with her Sun in Leo and her Moon in Sagittarius.

Jess: Milo Ventimiglia was born on July 8, 1977 with his Sun in Cancer and his Moon in Aries. He was later in the series *Heroes* (2006-2010).

Zack: Todd Lowe was born on May 10, 1977 with his Sun in Taurus and his Moon in Aquarius.

Christopher (Rory's father): David Sutcliffe was born on June 8, 1969 with his Sun in Gemini and his Moon in either Pisces or Aries.

"*Smells like snow*?"

Money

MONEY ... This is the magical word that everyone loves and loves to hate.

Perhaps I was never meant to have material abundance in this life. Both my parents, my siblings and all five of my children have a better economy and a more stable existence, while I live in my own little world with a fraction of their income.

In one period, I was contacted by several clients who speculated in shares, and it was an exciting world. It was quite easy to test among the big companies, if you only had real "birth data" on the company or the day of the listing. But when I had neither the resources nor the time to get into the rules, it did not matter. However, I know that there were many full-time astrologers on Wall Street in America working for companies in the past. As for today, I do not know. There is also astrological literature on the subject describing the economic cycles. The Sun's activity with solar storms has an 11-year cycle that usually follows the world-wide economic cycles. Even in the world of football, astrologers calculate. In Nils Liedholm's book *Soccer, Stars & Wine*, he described how they often contacted astrologers before they would make an expensive player purchase. They would not pay millions for someone who astrologically may be shown to injure themselves easier than others.

What then controls economics and material success in the horoscope? First of all, there are a number of factors that need to coincide, but there must also be a few basic prerequisites if you are now keen to speculate. You who contacted me may remember that I usually compare love and economy, and I usually mention that you should not chance or speculate in lotteries or anything else unless you fall in love.

To explain this phenomenon more closely, I have to use the terms "luck and bad luck," although it may be about karmic consequences. Why do some people win money while others are being robbed of their possessions?

First and foremost, you look at the Moon's location and aspects. As the Moon symbolizes our basic needs and habits, it often symbolizes our ritual economy. That's where income comes from. The second house, the house of Taurus, often symbolizes our own money and sources of income, while the eighth, Scorpio's house, represents others' money, such as banks, shares and inheritance. Winning something is usually linked to the money of "others," not our own; therefore, this is traced firstly to the eighth house. However, there are also elements of both the ninth and twelfth houses when experiencing unexpected income as profits or dividends. This is because Sagittarius represents the ninth house and Pisces the twelfth house.

Even if the Moon triggers economic effects, Venus and Jupiter should probably be included in the picture. Venus is about money and love, or what makes us happy, while Jupiter often leads to unexpected profits and successes, especially in terms of business or quick profits. In order to win, one has to chance, which mainly refers to Sagittarius, who loves to put all the eggs into one basket. Pisces, on the other hand, profits in a slightly more strange way. Here it may sometimes experience a massive surprise. Hence, the phrase that "one should take care of small wounds and poor friends." Here, of course, the poor friends are a symbol of our humble Pisces. You who have, for example, Moon, Venus or Jupiter in Pisces are more likely to gain from unexpected incomes more than once in life.

Equally likely, Taurus, Virgo and Capricorn never win unexpectedly. They are "too wise" and sensible and think it's just a waste of the scarce resources they have. Aries and Leo may, however, be able to buy on impulse a lottery ticket if they consider themselves able to afford the chance. The Aquarian believes that the whole system is clearly unfair. Why should someone win millions when one has to take responsibility and work for the money? Libra can never decide if they should play roulette, and Gemini can buy a ticket on the go if they see one at the store. These are of course simplified generalizations.

Throughout the years I studied these conditions, I often found that people who seem to have a little more luck than others are often not always interested in speculation. While at the same time, those who may miss the extra ride can ruin themselves on the lotteries. Karmic humor? If you care to study what losers look like, go to the horse races and observe the shine in the eyes of the players who hope to find a winner. Way over ninety per cent of the visitors are losers.

The aspects of the planets in the horoscope

Some simple rules regarding prerequisites:

The Moon's contact with Mercury can provide a wise and sensible attitude towards economics, or they love talking and gossiping about other peoples' money.

The Moon's contact with Venus or Jupiter gives greater chance of luck. A cosmic justice may be that generous and happy people have a little more luck than others.

The Moon's contact with Mars is usually unstable. Here the impulse buyer or gambler often only acts on a feeling, usually completely without logic. They want quick profits and are not interested in long-term investments. Perhaps it is no wonder that this is common among criminals.

The Moon's contact with Saturn can mean both shortcomings or a limited economy and is not recommended to join major gaming companies. Their motto is that money is acquired only through hard work and effort.

The Moon's contact with Uranus can cause rapid fluctuations, as both financial gain or as bankruptcy, so they should not speculate too much or too often. Emotional excitement could mean a negative talent towards game abuse if they win too easily at the beginning. However, income may come from unusual terms.

The Moon and Neptune can collaborate, although empathy may lead to greater generosity and the person would rather share an unexpected gain. This combination, however, indicates a bigger misery economically. They lose their wallet, miss the date of payment, get robbed and, in the worst case, they end up in the social office because of the inability to handle the practicality of the economy. They should never really gamble because then the risk of blotting can be great.

The Moon and Pluto in contact are really like playing Russian roulette. It may be a financial shock for both good or evil, but it is likely they will be exposed to theft, scam, pyramid games or extortion. However, inheritance is in the picture when Pluto is linked to the eighth house. Here we find the ice-cold businessmen who manipulates and gets you to buy a broken car.

Of the other planets, there are some combinations that may be of extra interest. Most contacts between Venus and Jupiter can bring increased prosperity, but unfortunately they have a little trouble keeping the slings. Especially the square between Venus and Jupiter often occurs in very wealthy people's charts. However, I have also found this in the poor, so it is a bit ambiguous. Their good hearts are sadly bigger than their wallet.

The best link between the others is between Jupiter and Neptune. This occurs very often in people with not only big but sometimes unreasonable income, such as professional athletes, musicians or movie stars. The link between luck and success generates both material as well as spiritual prosperity and is also common among religious people.

The last and perhaps even "best" should be the link between Venus and Uranus. It represents our hormones, ovulation, puberty and love, and is activated when we become "infatuated or in love" in life. Everyone does not have this in their basic chart, but everyone can have it active either in a progressive transit sometime in life or during a transit several times a year. At these times it may be worthwhile to at least try. Mathematically, all people have Venus in good transit to their Uranus between four to eight times a year. It is often these periods that we remember the best of the past year.

The planets in different signs

As for the placement of the planets, they work a bit differently. Everyone who ends up in Scorpio, Sagittarius or Pisces sometimes seems to have some extra luck. Both Venus and Jupiter in Scorpio, Sagittarius, or Pisces occur in people who are sometimes almost undeserving to have financial gain. Specifically, Jupiter suggests in Scorpio the possibility of inheritance and luck with major economic transactions. Saturn usually points to the opposite but can also indicate a solid income in the longer term. I often point to the differences between Jupiter and Saturn, where Jupiter stands for huge income without any effort, as through a lottery win, while Saturn represents rewards and gains after a long-term effort, such as a doctor's degree or an investment that gives a dividend after several years. In this context, my very first win in the 70's (1500 SEK) was unexpected when transiting Saturn passed over my Jupiter.

Wealthy people

I have of course also studied so-called filthy rich people who have too much, and both Scorpio and Pisces aspects occur with them. For example, Bill Gates is a Scorpio, and he has both Venus and Saturn in Scorpio. The Gates phenomenon, incidentally, has another combination that interests me, namely the conjunction between Jupiter and Pluto. I used to call this the "Beatles effect," because Jupiter symbolizes an incredibly worldly success while Pluto symbolizes the collective mass. This conjunction took place in 1955-56 in Leo and also ended up in Gates' second house, which controls his own income. This conjunction is also linked to the phenomenon "Swedish athletes born in 1956." However, I "escaped" this aspect because the conjunction is close to 9 degrees in my chart. However, it is in my eighth house and may point to my income from gambling and astrology.

A funny observation is that my own "Utopia" as well as our soccer phenomenon Zlatan Ibrahimovic have this Jupiter/Pluto conjunction in Libra within a 5 degrees orb (my Utopia has it with 7 degrees), indicating his enormous popularity as well as his huge income. Indeed, these Jupiter and Pluto effects are currently (May 2016) in a large trine between Virgo and Capricorn, both material earth signs. So all people born now will have this trine somewhere in their charts. The same aspect, inverted between Capricorn and Virgo, I also found in the musician Bono's chart (U2). He has Jupiter in Capricorn in an almost exact trine to Pluto in Virgo, and with his group U2 he has had immense successes.

Another example is the founder of facebook, Mark Zuckerberg. This Taurus has his Moon, Mars, Saturn and Pluto in Scorpio. But I don't have his time of birth and therefore I don't know in which houses. He doesn't have the trine, but Jupiter in Capricorn is in a positive aspect to his Moon, Mars and Saturn in Scorpio.

A little more comic interpretation to these particular aspects is also the connection to all crime, which is more or less focused on Scorpio, the eighth house and its effects. As always, you are dealing with "other people's money."

In addition to Saturn's transit over my Jupiter, I've been fascinated about different world events over the years. The simplest but most comprehensive are bigger extravaganzas such as the World Soccer Cup or the Olympics, but it's extremely time-consuming to analyze hundreds of charts before finding the golden grains. As a matter of fact I predicted Italy as winners in the 2006 World Soccer Cup. It's a little easier when there are far fewer participants, like a song contest or with an individual athlete, as it is easier to see the daily fitness and eventual tendency of both "luck" and "bad luck" on the same day. It may seem immoral to already "know" who wins, but I am always only interested in seeing if I was right. Had I wanted to make money, I also needed a nice starting capital.

Has money replaced God today?

Sure, it's nice with some extra money sometimes. But the one who sees money as the only driving force for happiness, I think, suffers more than others. On the contrary, I sometimes think that money is the root of all evil. How many times have you read about people who have become extremely wealthy overnight, only to get rid of their wealth in a short space of time? It seems almost like a symbolic curse throughout this phenomenon. However, we must realize that we live in an uneven and unfair world today, where most people fight for their existence. Therefore, I have a difficult time looking at descriptions and reality shows in which wealthy, unconcerned people are at the center. I read at some point that Aries Ingvar Kamprad, the founder of IKEA, still makes his own sandwiches when traveling somewhere, even though he is good for billions.

In conclusion, I have to admit that I am still quite satisfied with my lot in life. In total, I have had over 25 different jobs since my teens. It is extremely difficult to support yourself as an astrologer. However, if I had not been gifted with generous parents, siblings and children, I would never have survived.

I have a good life today with nature around me, my cats and my own time to enjoy life. I have no major debts, the house and car are paid for and I only have current expenses. When I get a little extra Japaneese YEN or many clients, it can be fun with a little extra and to enjoy things I otherwise cannot afford.

"Everyone is blessed with their own income". However, one can't live on only money, as many Taureans seem to believe. We need love, friends and a purpose with our lives. What ultimately is most important is to mean something to others and to make an effort for those who are in need. Just like air and water, love and care do not need to cost.

PS. I'd rather cry in an old used car that is paid for than in a luxurious Rolls Royce that is expensive with tax and insurance. DS.

Easter Egg 2

"Zlatan Ibrahimovic"

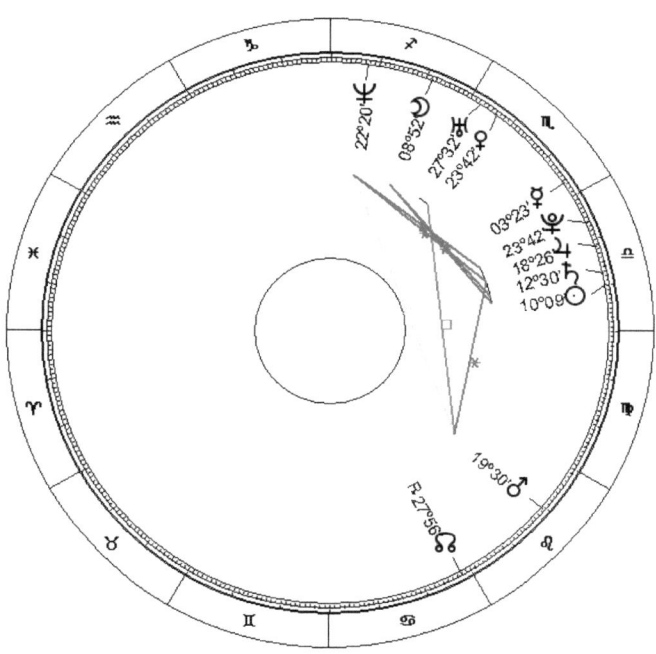

Since I mentioned Zlatan on my website several times, I thought it was advisable to see astrologically why he is the way he is. Since I was active during my teens for a few years with soccer at IFK Göteborg, I have experienced soccer from the inside, with winter sneakers in snow, heavy wet autumn passes and the sweet liniment smell in the dressing room. Unfortunately, I did not have a real "killer instinct" so I quit too early.

A soccer game is a constant artwork where anything can happen. I have many sweet memories from the sports radio in the 60's and my first visit to the stadium Ullevi. I was only 12 years old in 1968 when my "home team" *Blue-white* went on a 3-9 loss against AIK in Stockholm, but that match became a turning point. I recall that *Blue-white*'s Håkan Eklund became overjoyed after his third goal because he did a so-called "hat trick". The year after that, they won Gold and Reine Almkvist became top scorer in the Allsvenskan. Then many years followed with idols who came and went: Libra Ralf Edström, Cancer Torbjörn Nilsson, Scorpio Glenn Hysén, Capricorn Glenn Strömberg and the coach and Aquarius Sven-Göran "Svennis" Eriksson and the magical years of the 80's.

"Certainly, you will win Blue-whites!"

An astrologer colleague of mine, Roger Algehov, who barely knew what soccer was, was asked to give an astrological prediction before the *Blue-white*'s return game in Hamburg in 1982 in the UEFA final (then the Champions League). *Blue-white* had managed to win 1-0 in the first game in the drizzle of Nya Ullevi (Tord Holmgren scored), but they would not stand a chance in the return game in Hamburg. The Germans had already printed posters and sweaters with the text "Winner UEFA 1982" on them, so to the Germans it was just a formality. My colleague Roger was given the task of checking out the teams, the day of the game and the players. He actually had the stomach to say that *"Certainly Blue-white will win!"* with big bragging headlines. Probably there were many who mocked the astrologer. *Blue-white*, with Torbjörn Nilsson in the best playing form of his life, won 3-0 and shocked the whole soccer world.

Since then, I remember many soccer World Cups every four years, even if Sweden did not join and idols came and went, especially Scorpio Maradona with his "hand of God" in 1986 and the humiliation of Sweden in Italy in 1990. Who does not remember their bronze medal in the USA in the hot summer of 1994, with Scorpio coach Tommy Svensson quoting Scorpio poet Karin Boye: "The satisfied day is never the greatest ..." (from the poem collection *In Motion*).

Soccer is the world's largest and most popular sport, and Zlatan Ibrahimovic has now both amused and teased millions for over 16 years since his debut in Malmö. Through success in Holland, Italy, Spain and France, he has managed to win wherever he made his way. Today, in May 2017, he has achieved an unbelievable 30 titles and left Paris SG after 4 years where he almost beat all the records that can be beaten. The future "is written in the stars," and everyone is wondering where he will continue his career. But first, he will play EM in his current country in France, and you who read this already know how it went. (They lost out in the early group stage.)

During my investigations, I have unfortunately not found any correct time of birth for Zlatan. If there is anyone who knows or can ask his family, please contact me. The chart above dates from 12 Noon.

Zlatan Ibrahimovic was born in Malmö on October 3, 1981, and on the same day, the goalkeeper Andreas Isaksson was born in Trelleborg. They are what you call "Star Twins."

Whatever the time of his birth, his Moon is in Sagittarius and probably in a harmonious sextile to his Sun in Libra. His parents comes from former Yugoslavia (Sagittarius). In addition, he has both lived and worked in a number of countries since his career accelerated: Holland, Italy, Spain, France and from 2016 in England. Throughout all these years, he has traveled (Sagittarius) criss-cross. All this perfectly fits with a Moon in Sagittarius. In addition, it is well known that he is privately very playful and humorous and also loves kids.

His Sun in Libra really only has one strong aspect in addition to the sextile with the Moon, and that is the conjunction with Saturn, which makes him a Capricorn-Libra. Here we have his seriousness with the wrinkle of the forehead, his focus, and above all, his extreme self-discipline. He can sometimes be a "pain in the ass" and fault-finder, critical and gnashing against everything and everyone when it does not go as he wants. When he fails, or conflicts arise quickly, he feels attacked or assaulted. He hates other authorities (i.e., referees) and must have both trust and respect to those who "rule" over him, otherwise it will not work. He is his own boss and needs to check on things with accuracy on all details. Often he talks about himself in the third person with both humor and irony ("No one tells Zlatan when it's time. Zlatan decides when it's time. ") By the way, another legendary, soccer legend, Nils Liedholm, was also a Libra with Saturn on the Sun. They both have Venus in Scorpio and Jupiter in Libra. Nils Liedholm wrote a book where he takes up the astrologers' great influence over soccer in Italy, *Soccer, Stars and Wine*.

Even though the Moon in Sagittarius is noticeable when he becomes happy, perhaps his Mars in Leo may be the most typical of him. Only to have Mars in Leo is enough to be both strong and energetic, but he also has Jupiter in Libra in an almost exact sextile to Mars, and it generates constant success. This sextile in a chart generates both popularity (Jupiter in Libra) and his physical ability (Mars), so it's no wonder that he is a physical phenomenon. Also, if Mars is located near the Ascendant, this represents how he also uses his body as a tool. He loves martial arts and trained in Taekwondo in his youth. Mars near the Ascendant I usually call the "Cagney effect" (often appearing in the charts of gangsters), and apparently he has a reputation for being both tough and forceful with his body.

His Mercury is quite neutral in Scorpio, and he is not known to speak unnecessarily. He can sometimes sound clever and sometimes say very provocative things. Sometimes he can be downright disrespectful and sarcastic when he gets upset. He speaks like a Scorpio without much of Libra´s diplomacy.

Venus in Scorpio gives him both glow and passion, and he also managed to get a conjunction with Uranus which I always call the "celebrity aspect," as it often occurs in celebrity charts of both musicians and film stars. It is also a "luck aspect," which gives him a little extra luck in many situations. Also located in Scorpio, you can figure out what it means purely economically. Income from many, unusual and unexpected ways.

Mars in Leo is probably his greatest asset, and it also has a weak sextile to Pluto and a major trine to Neptune, which further enhances the ability to strive and achieve results.

The socially most powerful aspect might be the conjunction between Jupiter and Pluto in Libra. It is approximately 5 degrees, but Mars gives them both energy, and social or even worldly success can be generated anyway. I call this conjunction the "Beatles effect," and it is very common among extremely successful people. For Zlatan's part, it is the result of all his discipline, his physical efforts and his constant concentration.

Here are a couple of interesting details about other important people in his world, but not from his family (for reasons of professional integrity):

His constant "gunman" and good friend since the beginning of his career in Ajax, Holland, is Maxwell, born just a short month before Zlatan on August 27, 1981. He is a Virgo with his Moon in Leo and with probable tangents to Zlatan's Sun and Moon. Maxwell has both Venus and Jupiter in Libra exactly on Zlatan's Sun. This indicates a lovely "karma" at the very least.

I will not go through all of his career, but I do want to mention his latest coach, Laurent Blanc in PSG. He is a Scorpio and has the Moon at 14 degrees in Libra between Zlatan's Sun and Jupiter, so you can say they were good for each other. Paris SG's owner Nasser Al-Khelaifi is also a Scorpio with Moon in Gemini and has the mighty Jupiter-Pluto trine between Aquarius and Libra. Not forgetting Zlatan's own football agent for many years at all Zlatan's transfers, Mino Raiola. What sign do you think he is? Scorpio, of course, with his Mercury in almost the same place as Zlatan's and with the same Moon in Sagittarius.

Now let's hope he can finish his unlikely career with a year or more in England and the prestigious club Manchester United.

Good luck Zlatan! (At this book's print in the spring of 2017, he has already exceeded all expectations and has already scored 28 goals in 46 games played, of which 17 in the league).

Astrology and humor

Humor has always been an effective anxiety release valve. At one of my lectures in astrology in Simrishamn in 1998, I ended up emphasizing this and displayed a book on the subject. (The book was Görel Kristina Näslund's *Laugh and Feel Good*). No sound or laughter was heard. That was fun...

Have you heard of the man who got his death sentence by the doctor and asked how long he had to live? "A maximum of six months," said the doctor. So the man retreated and isolated himself and spent all his time reading funny books and watching comedy movies until he almost laughed himself to death! Back at the doctor's office after the six months had passed, he found out that all the symptoms were gone and he was healthy. (I heard this many years ago and do not know if it's true or an urban legend, but I love the message). It's surely healing to laugh... Endorphins help and strengthen the immune system.

I claim today more than ever that humor is vital. In a world full of dishonor and violence, it's not just the bottle that comforts. Laughing is both beneficial to the body and the soul. The role of the clown has always been important. Look at the jesters of the Middle Ages or the King's fool. Today it is standup and mainstream comedy series selling for our pleasure. Situation comedy have always calmed some of us, as our insensitivity tolerance threshold has become lower and lower. So-called wicked humor has distorted sometimes into cruel abuse. Chaplin dared to do this politically when he made the movie *The Dictator* in the 40's where he mocked Hitler.

A more notorious comedian from the 1960's was Lenny Bruce, Sun in Libra with the Moon in Virgo. Bruce mocked almost everything and challenged all possible taboos and prejudices. He provoked, and the intention was to reveal everyone's own prejudices. Because of drug abuse and constant conflicts with the authorities, he died prematurely by overdose in 1966, aged only 40 years.

How many of you do not remember the old silent movies from childhood, with Chaplin or Laurel & Hardy? I myself most enjoyed the series of comic books, "Donald Duck & Co." Donald is, by the way, a Gemini with the Moon in Aries (hot tempered) and has his Saturn in the 2nd house (a rich elder relative). Animated movies became popular in line with the film's development; and when TV came, it was fun with music or a quiz, and always the great humor. Nowadays, one can not show a song contest without the need for awkward humor that is expected to be fun. There may be limits to what's considered fun, and it's definitely very individualistic from person to person.

In many movies I've seen, both cynical and irrational comments are often uttered by the protagonist who is in a hopeless dilemma. Thinking of James Bond, who before he is executed or dying does not cry out to God, but instead casts a fierce comment about the weather or perhaps his wicked career choice.

The Monthy Python gang produced a blasphemous and detested (by Christians) film about Jesus called "Life of Brian," in which it all transpires that Brian was mistakenly designated as the savior. It was hysterically funny and quite daring to joke about Jesus, God and Creation itself. Pisces George Harrison from the Beatles was, by the way, co-producer for the film.

Another of my animated gurus was Grelber, who lived in a hollow log in the "Broom-Hilda" series if I remember correctly. He had a sign outside saying "Free Insults." I don't know his birthday, but he probably has most of the planets and definitely the Ascendant in Scorpio.

Another charming "bastard" is the extremely mean cat "Garfield." He was "born" (published) for the first time on June 19, 1978 and is a Gemini with his Moon in Sagittarius (loves the lasagna). His creator Jim Davis was born on July 28, 1945, and is a Leo with his Moon in Pisces.

Of all the humor giants on the silver screen, I can only list them without deeper analyzing. The four (actually five) Marx brothers may be in the top and really deserve a separate chapter. I read with laughibg hysteria Harpo´s memoir, Harpo speaks and one of Groucho´s, where he at one point mentions when he was on a date. He invited the girl to the movies on the other side of town, and they had to take the tram, but the money was not enough so she had to walk all the way home. Or the classic: "Once I shot an elephant in my pyjamas, but I don´t know how it got there" and "But why-a-duck?" See their respective Sun and Moon in the chapter Wrong Astrology.

Anyone remember the Danish piano comedian Victor Borge? He was born the day before my wonderful grandmother, on Jan.3, 1909, a Capricorn with his Moon in Gemini.

Two favorites of mine, both now deceased, are my hero Lasse Brandeby (Kurt Olsson/Gotten Flowers), Sun in Taurus and Moon in Scorpio and Rolv Vesenlund (Marve Fleksnes), Sun in Virgo and Moon in Libra. He was one of my spiritual gurus, and my favorite of his is "Volvo Sonett Has Four Carburetors and Is Italian" ("At the Dentist").

The Monty Python with John Cleese (Scorpio with Moon in Aries) consists of several maniacs. Among my older favorites, there are not only the Marx Brothers and Charles Chaplin (an Aries with the Moon in Scorpio) but also Buster Keaton (a Libra with his Moon in Aries) and Harold Lloyd (an Aries with his Moon in Gemini). All of these men belong to the greatest comedians ever. But let's not forget our own Swedish humor genius Nils Poppe (Sten Stensson Steen and Fabian Bom), with both the Sun and Moon in Gemini.

Our worst traits

If there is something we humans are good at, it's often that we more easily recognize characteristics that are labeled as "bad" (i.e., undesirable), and I think we Swedes are particularly good at this, probably because of Martin Luther and/or the *Jante law*. But if you are asked to describe your positive and negative qualities at the same time, most of us more easily recognize our negative ones. Why is it like that? Perhaps we do not dare to talk about or boast of our positive qualities for fear of being perceived as egotistical or self-righteous?

Here is a "funny" list of the most typical "bad qualities" of the signs. I must emphasize that this list is oversized and with excessive irony so you won't recognize yourself too easily!

Worst qualities of the signs

Aries: Together with Leo, Aries is the symbol of selfishness and self-esteem. You shall have no other Gods except yourself. I can recall when they asked Aries Agnetha Fältskog (ABBA) on TV whom she admired, she quickly replied, "Myself!" Aries enjoys all the attention and will kill themselves rather than come in second in the Eurovision Song Contest. The funniest thing is to point out their shortcomings and lack of empathy and then watch their shocked reactions. As partners, they make weird self-promoters who only look for their own needs first and foremost. Facebook can both give them endorphins and depression, depending on how many blue thumbs up they can count. The surface appearance is the most important thing, so they change their display image as often as they eat.

Taurus: Taureans are something of the stingiest and greediest since Scrooge McDuck. They can earn five bucks extra if they sell their used dish racks on eBay. Being a sensual epicurean can unconsciously lead to both extreme obesity and food abuse; and if they can stop worrying about everything they can't win or earn, then all enjoyment could become a pure art of living. A gourmet becomes gormand, and the taster becomes eventually alcohol-damaged. They hate all effort if they do not get paid and fully live by the motto: "Love over Gold to Gold Over Love." They hate the phrase "You can't bring anything with you when you die." Do you dare mention their tendency to fart from time to time?

Gemini: Here we find the sexual one-night stands. The Gemini prototype of the term "temporary liaisions" can lead to pure prostitution. They do not worry about tomorrow if they can party seven days a week. They preferably have seven extra jobs rather than one permanent job, and they will never stay long at any job if they get bored, which is all the time. Likewise, Geminis are the same with their accomodations. As a traveling funfair, they move criss-cross. They love their own voice and get upset if you interrupt their lectures. They are a disaster to marry because they are already "outside the church" thinking about the next exciting life companion. From one companion to another, whether a man or a woman does not matter, as long as you are having fun. They can find most of their sexual variations here. Unreliable and with an easy tendency to dupe, they talk down both customers and their best friends but flutter smoothly as butterflies on a summer bed, completely light-hearted. Here the expression "borderline" is created. This sign is the reason why psychiatry has become so popular.

Cancer: If they do not end up in the social services office, you can see them recycling empty cans and bottles at the supermarket. They are not necessarily stingy but scared to lose their assets, and emotionally they are the most unstable and vulnerable among all signs. Gastric catarrh is not a disease but more a natural condition among Cancerians, and they also tend to compensate for all deficiencies with food and drink. USA is born Cancer and has statistically millions of obese people. Feelings are important, and they often care to the smallest extent that they love their partner to death. Here we find the phenomenon "mother hen." Depressions are common, and they are of course regular customers with their therapists.

Leo: Convinced they have all been born as kings and queens, they see themselves as both chosen and best in everything they do. This ego bloating easily becomes comical, similar to *The Emperor's New Clothes*. If they can't rule, they close up completely and go away with self-pity, their tails between their legs. Like Aries, they love the attention and must constantly be at the center of all parties and meetings. Give them power and they take over the world. Arrogance is an understatement, and they love both luxury and exaggeration and can sometimes be more material than Taurus. A Leo with bad self-esteem is probably one of the most difficult patients at the psychiatrist´s because the lack of self-love is like breathing without air.

Virgo: Hypochondria was invented by Virgo. If there is nothing at all to worry about, they seek for anything that is wrong. Like Sisyfos, with his stone, they love to put energy on everything that never becomes done or ready, like cleaning, laundry or dishes. As a lover, you have to "take them" while they clean, as they are probably completely worn out when they think they are ready at last. Life is never and will never be perfect, and this is the cause of Virgo´s suffering. They are looking for perfection and are not shy to constantly point out your shortcomings as well as everything you DO NOT OR SHOULD DO, so get some earplugs if you live with a Virgo. Scared of everything from diseases to the apocalypse, they end up either in a mental institution or on the street.

Libra: Librans don't know how "loonliness" (conscious spelling mistake) is spelled, so they will marry a lamp post rather than live alone. They will ruin themselves because of a desire to constantly beautify their appearance or wardrobe. They are trapped in a ritual need to go through the wardrobe a couple of times a year to make space for all new clothes. They have facebook as a starting page on their computer because they are constantly looking for everybody else's confirmation. If you want to bother a Libra, then ask them to make up their mind. It's the best torture ever. Their decision anxiety can lead to apathy, and often you have to push them forward as they need constant encouragement. They are the best life partner if you have good finances and if you also hate loneliness. Unfortunately, the lack of balance can inevitably lead to both gluttony and wastefulness, so the weight and bank account are constantly their source of concern.

Scorpio: Sex is not just a matter of life and death. It is also more important than air, food or sleep. Prohibition or taboos are meant for breaking, and the term *crime* is just an expression by those who govern. If you can beat records or push yourself tirelessly, you do not get much time for your partner. Here we find not only the sex addict and the fox, but all economic "parachutes," money under the table and dirty money. They can trick the shirt of you with one big smile and make you believe they made you a favor. They are excellent as mean policemen and manipulative psychologists because their curiosity does not know any limits. Living with a Scorpio is like living with a ticking time bomb: you just never know when it's going to blow up.

Sagittarius: They believe in optimism in all glory, but this infamous blind optimism often leads them to repeated bankruptcies and scandals. They are imaginative but sloppily dressed. They look like a traveling circus act. This Saggitarian clown in the gang can not take anything seriously. They live as if every day were the last one and would like to hit the heels on the roof even as the world goes by. Party!! is the key word. Everything is exaggerated and obesity is a normal condition because there are no limits for either appetite or pleasure. Often winning at the lottery of life, they waste everything as fast as they can get it. Game addicts and generally indifferent, they walk unnoticed and constantly hope that the grass is greener further afield. Sagittarius founded the travel industry and best enjoys the holiday, so they must constantly be encouraged to keep their jobs. They never live as they learn but still laugh at the face of death.

Capricorn: Their addiction to commitment is a little pathetic. As an obedient dog, they are tricked into working 80 hours overtime a week if the boss so demands. They rarely smile and see life as a single huge exam. Their black eyes and skepticism make them perfect as inspectors and judges, and their lack of imagination makes them easily fooled. Because they have difficulty relaxing, they easily get sleep disturbances, and all the requirements of life must first be completed before they spend time off on holidays or vacations. Perhaps loyal as a sex partner, if you have to really want to make love punctually at 11 pm every Sunday, but only "if it is absolutely necessary." Because of their heavy minds, of course, life is never a rose garden, and they love the funerals and visits to the lawyer. They will finally end up in a wheelchair or in the long-term care because they refuse to realize their own limitations and often survive everyone in their own family.

Aquarius: Welcome to the most sexist character of all. The name itself excludes the woman. Genius can be found here, but only as the crazy one no one wants to be with. They must always go their own way in life, even when there isn't any road to walk upon. They will change their roommates as often as they change their status on facebook, but they never worry about it. News is like a sparkle, and they love to gossip and come up with extreme stories. You will find them obstinate mostly just for the desire to upset. They tease the gall on most everyone. Aquarians founded the word "Why?" They are political chameleons with constant turnarounds, both in career and privacy, and they are constantly moving and are never really happy with anything at all. If you can change anything, you do it. However, they stand out as both perverse and innovative in all relationships, somewhat like having sex in a lift between two floors. Total freedom is the greatest illusion among these self-absorbed idealists. They love to save the world – as long as the neighbor can take care of himself and not interfere or question everything the Aquarian does.

Pisces: Finally, we arrive at the madhouse. Season two *"Asylum"* of the series *American Horror Story*. It is here, in the madhouse, where Pisceans end up sooner or later because ife is so cruel and ruthless against these fragile souls. They can't handle either their hygiene or their finances, and they need practical help with almost everything. They usually live in their own bubble with the help of all their thought-tools, i.e., drugs. They hate routines and are fired as often as a result of negligence as pure indifference. However, they love to sacrifice themselves for others and easily spoil their self-absorbed boyfriend/girlfriend, which naturally leads to undue depression due to disappointment. They can only stay in relationships as long as their life-mate stands out with their self-deception and emo-mentality. As for sex, I heard a good comment from a female astrologer, Donna Cunningham. Pisces often ask after the sexual act, "Was it good for me too?" The lack of ability to claim for themselves is obvious, and they end up early in care, from child psychiatry and adult psychiatry to countless counseling therapists. Life is a constant suffering, so it's just as good to put the head in the sand and snort away from reality. Many Pisceans are perceived, unfortunately and incorrectly, as a bit autistic.

What points to humor in the horoscope?

Purely astrological, there are many ingredients to mix. Sagittarius and Gemini, however, appear to hold a lot of the humor rather frequently, probably because they like to communicate and also because they like to spread insights around them. In planetary terms, there should be links between Mercury and Jupiter, but preferably with influences of both Neptune (imagination and intuition) and Uranus (genius ideas). A humourless person never buys lottery tickets. I wonder why?

Geminis are not just the first astrological "human sign." They also symbolize the nervous system and the ability to communicate. They speak, write and read and would like to convey everything to others, hence the need to provide knowledge. Sagittarians are more visionaries and maybe more of clowns and often mix humor with seriousness in a reliable way. The arrow of Sagittarius symbolizes all the knowledge he/she wants to send away, and a strong Jupiter is common with both authors and journalists as well as with ordinary teachers.

However, there must be a combination of intelligence and deep gravity for the comedian to find the punchline, and therefore a little Uranus is needed. Especially the combination between Mercury and

Uranus is common when it speeds up. This is also excellent at improvisation.

Then you can of course generalize all the signs. Capricorns may be wrongly accused of dry humor. They might have a strong Moon, and all Scorpios need not be sarcastic and mean.

Any political advice you might recognize?

This is an extended version of the poster with cows that was popular a long time ago.

Socialism - You have two cows. You give one to your neighbor.

Communism - You have two cows. The state takes both of them and gives you some milk.

Fascism - You have two cows. The state takes both of them and sells you some milk.

Nazism - You have two cows. The state takes both of them and shoots you.

Swedish Democrats - You have two cows. You refuse to accept one more because it is Arabic.

Surrealism - You have two giraffes. The state is teaching you how to teach them to play the harmonica.

Bureaucracy - You have two cows. The state takes both of them, shoots one, milks the other one and spills the milk.

Traditional capitalism - You have two cows. You sell one and buy a bull. Your herd grows and your economy grows. You sell your cattle and live well the rest of your days.

Modern capitalism - You have two cows. You sell one and press the other to produce the same amount of milk as four cows. Then you rent an expensive consultant to analyze why it has fallen down dead.

IT Factory capitalism - You have two cows. You sell three of them to your listed company, because a bank guarantee convinces investors that you actually have four cows. That's why you pull off the feed for five cows on your declaration. The right to milk six cows is now transferred via a bank in Polynesia, owned by a shell company, which sells the right to milk seven cows to the first company. The auditor-approved annual report states that the company owns eight cows with an option for several more. You claim that you have a bull that has won first prize in an animal show, after which you sell the bull and disappear.

French activity - You have two cows. You are striking and blocking the roads because you want three cows.

Italian business - You have two cows, but you do not know where they are. You decide to have lunch.

Chinese business - You have two cows. You have 300 employees to milk them. You claim that you have the right staffing and high productivity. You put down the newspaper that writes the truth.

Indian business - You have two cows. You worship them.

Australian business - You have two cows. Everything seems to work fine. You close the office and celebrate your success with a few beers.

Japanese business - You have two cows. You redesign them so that they have one tenth of a normal cow and can produce 20 times as much milk. You then create a manga figure and increase your income by launching it as a children's toy under the name Cowkemon.

Iraqi business - Everyone thinks you have lots of cows. You are telling them you have none. Nobody believes you, so they bomb you apart and invade your country. You still have no cows.

Part 4 Rated "R" (Adult)

(Anebo midnight *"Light in the dark"*, photo by Amanda)

These first sections in Part 4 are not necessary to
read if you are too young or lack experience in
Life's difficulties, for example, with drugs or
severe anxiety.

Drugs – Illusions of Neptune

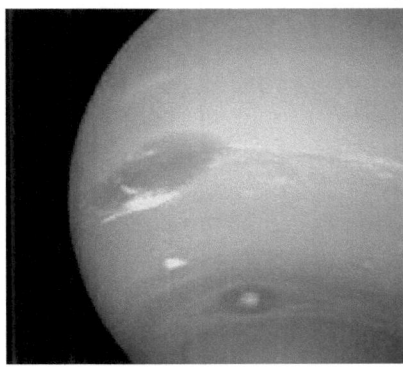

This is a difficult and extremely complicated area where much consideration has to be given to individual situations. You who have had or have problems with variations of addiction need to keep in mind not to interpret everything literally and that all my examples are extreme key interpretations; therefore, not necessarily absolute truths. Nor do I take responsibility for claiming the solution to your complex problem. Everyone is different, reacts differently and needs different strategies. I also wrote this with particular affected relatives in mind. Abuse of all kinds is a most often invisible suffering.

Why I chose to include this difficult area is probably due to the fact that I have experienced many downsides with these energies myself, but also that it still reminds me how many forms of abuse are glorified and taken as something playful or harmless in film and media. Both children and adolescents receive norms that are harmful and destructive in the long run.

In terms of abuse, it´s not only enough to mention alcohol or drugs. Addiction to pills today is an epidemic as well as gambling. All, of course, can be graded to a degree of habituation and proportion. However, the consequences are similar, whatever the abuse. Almost all addictions end up as potentially life-long suffering and requiring rehabilitation or detoxification.

I name the astrological codes at the end of this report but start with pure facts for an overview.

Even though drugs and chemical substances are common today, it is nevertheless alcohol that accounts for the most common form of addiction, probably because it is more culturally accepted and it is thought to "not be as dangerous as narcotics." The list of movie stars who suffered from alcoholism is endless. We Swedes also have a split attitude towards alcohol. People from other cultures dare to claim that the Swedes can not handle alcohol. That I can agree to. If you go abroad, you rarely experience the offensive behaviour that you find with inebriated Swedish Midsummer celebrations.

Tradition

There may have been in our genes since the Viking period where people guzzled the alcohol from a skull and then broke it into pieces, carrying on in this matter often days in a row. No wonder the church constantly accused alcohol of being the temptation of the devil. Double morality is another area in which Swedes are skilled.

When we grow up, it is obviously considered to have alcohol around all important weekends, such as Christmas, New Year, Easter, birthdays, weddings, baptisms, Valborg, St. Lucia Day or Midsummer.

Children get used to the fact that adults are drinking, and children do as we do, not as we say, right? They also learn that adults are happy when they drink, which aggravates the illusion that alcohol is the best way to be happy. That some respond like *Dr. Jekyll & Mr. Hyde* and lose his/her head is another matter. Others simply do not seem to tolerate alcohol at all.

Today, not only in foreign films and shows, however, it is shown that drinking is accepted worldwide and almost a must if it is going to be nice. Alcohol advertising is everywhere, although Swedish rules are a little stricter than abroad. In Swedish TV, they sometimes have a wine taster who judges and tastes new varieties. This, to me, is incomprehensible. "It is informative and pure product information," the defenders say. How many times have I not seen beer glasses and wine bottles on facebook, titled "We Are Really Happy". These are signals you send your children.

It is not just about alcohol. Narcotics may not be as common but exist even in little Sweden. However, these drugs are more dangerous, and the effects are significantly more physically visible and also reduce the life of the body drastically. Pills, on the other hand, are a more invisible form of addiction. In the case of different types of "luck pills" (Swedish expression) or stronger sleeping pills for pain relief or for soothing the nerves, this addiction does not always show when the person is affected -- an obviously hidden form of addiction. Many do their jobs without suspicions from others, like the German pilot who flew into a mountain wall in France or Princess Diana's driver who crashed in Paris. He apparently had anti-depressant drugs in his blood.

Psychologically, this is difficult to handle, most probably because it is so nice and comfortable to "take something" to better relax or relieve other symptoms, such as anxiety, stress, pure apathy, sleep disorders or physical pain. Often, you may not have any other options. In case of grave panic attacks, exhaustive sleep disturbances or painful body pain, there are sometimes no options.

The tragic thing, however, is that readily accessible pills, the acceptance of others to take the pills and your own lack of self-discipline will make you "take one more" as soon as you return to the box again. The emotions and fears re-surface, and the emergency solution quickly becomes a bad habit as well as an emotional dead-end where you neither dare nor have the ability to break your ever-spiralling habit.

In the end, we discover that we can not work "without" the emergency solution and set our lives thereafter. For pill addicts, it may be easier to conceal their addiction, but anyone who finds it is good with a beer or a glass of wine in the middle of the week does not always understand why. "But that is how they do in Greece, France, Denmark, Italy or Spain!!!" The worst thing is perhaps the unconscious behavior, where you go year after year to repeated Friday or Saturday parties, and during the week you behave normally and sober with the usual fears and perhaps a latent anxiety under the surface. "Soon it's Friday, then we'll be happy again." Those of you who have never been **too** drunk and regretted the following day do not have a clue to what I mean. *(Life Is a Party* - Nationalteatern/Swedish rockgroup in the 70s).

Cold Turkey

Even if you have begun to accept your own addiction, it is not easy to stop. When do you dare to tell your best friend or fellow mate that they drink too much or too often? Probably you'll only get a lot of scolding back. "Shut up - it's my life!" Or you'll be punished instead.

Many factors must be correct in order to break your addictive patterns. You might need to dare to do a doctor's check-up to see how the body feels, or debate your feelings with a professional therapist in order to proceed. Working conditions may need to change. You can not just quit if you have an employment. It may perhaps become necessary to take an extended leave of absence from work or a vacation or timeout.

Your personal relationships are extremely important. If you do not have support and understanding from your immediate environment, it will be considerably more difficult. In extreme situations, a combined physical and psychological rehabilitation may be required with a forced weaning at a rehab clinic. In the past, alcoholics were often rehabilitated just through hard physical work (Saturn), and the idea had its good points.

Delirium Tremens may occur during a prolonged alcohol rush as well as during the detoxification phase. They often occur 24 to 72 hours after a prolonged intake of alcohol. I have read that you can even die of heart failure during a *Delirium* attack. The ironic thing is that the anxiety you wanted to subdue returns, but this time with multiple strength. Nevertheless, the addict will sometimes try to ignore everything else they've been able to destroy around them, including their health, their work, their marriage, their finances, their sex drive, their friends' trust and really everything else.

There are two old black-and-white films that deal with these phenomena in a skilled manner. The first film is *Lost Weekend* from 1945, which won 4 Oscars, including Best Picture and Best Actor, starred Ray Milland and was directed by Billy Wilder. The second film is *Days of Wine and Roses* from 1962 with Jack Lemmon. Both films are very well-sighted, often uncomfortable and unpleasant but superbly objective.

The one who thinks he/she is able to get rid of an addiction without anyone's help just fools him/herself. The organization AA (Alcoholics Anonymous) has passionate employees who themselves have been in the shit and know exactly how it feels. There are similar organizations for drug and pill addicts. Indeed, there are many who are prepared to assist if needed; but because alcohol is God, everything else is actually less worthwhile. An alcoholic is forced to be an extremely selfish and self-absorbed person who does not care about anything except the next drink and will easily manipulate anything and everyone to continue the addiction. Additionally, it's much easier to be unfaithful when you drink and maybe risk a marriage just for a temporary sex drive. Was it worth it?

Shadows in the past

After reading this far, you probably think that this does not apply to me, right? That's just what happens in movies and, I'm so young and just party sometimes. Yes, the body is a phenomenon that needs long-term accumulation, but it´s mostly the attitude I turn against. Why do you need to get extra help to have fun and socialize easily? Is life so boring and frustrating that you have to drug yourself in order to look bright on things? Maybe it's not only due to a lack of chemicals in the blood. The problem may be elsewhere. A bit critical, one might say that it may be due to lack of self-confidence or self-awareness. I still have to point out that most drunkards are a little pathetic. Have you heard a bunch of philosophers in the middle of the night after a few drinks or some wine bottles? More intelligent debates are heard in the sandbox at the kindergarten. I firmly claim that if not all, then at least most alcohol consumption depends on fear or shyness and not just because you want to be happy.

I may seem biased and condemning, but I have my reasons. My own dad was rarely present during my childhood, and the few times he came home from the sea he was usually drunk. Alcoholism was called "dipsomania" at that time. Today, my father has not been drinking for nearly 40 years. Several of my school and childhood companions succumbed to the "ghetto" at Hisingen in Gothenburg, a notoriously infamous area where paint thinner sniffing, beer and drugs flowed. The crime rate was high, and many of my peers disappeared in the "swamp" from various types of addictive self-abuse. I witnessed when they injected their needles and knew the sniffing guys with their smelly thinner rags, so I was never afraid of them. Beer cans were in power over the weekends. It's a little like "today" after Valborg (ritual drinking event). I must have had several guardian angels who watched over me, because I never fell for any of those temptations.

My own Neptune energies emerged as experiments with cannabis and stronger drinks, but by then I had reached my upper teens and thought I saw myself as exceedingly self-confident and "invulnerable." One "partied" only on the weekends in those days. Sound familiar today? Nothing really dramatic happened until I reached 20 and started working in a real workplace. It soon became apparent that my boss Lasse was an alcoholic (after a fatal car accident); and although he was kind, you learned to live with constant lies to customers and daily purchases at the drugstore (Systembolaget). During a few years I was a "regular customer" on the Systembolaget. But it was part of my "duties."

The ultimate turn came in 1979 when I was drunk together with my cousin Simon and totally crashed our car. We managed to get away with just the fear and a bit of cuts and bruises. I was convinced I was protected by another guardian angel (they had their hands full). However, the hangover became worse than the car accident. I was creating a humiliated and sabotaged family. A new sober life awaited, but instead I filled it with guilt and anxiety. After that I did not actually hit a drop for many years. I have later tried to live "like everyone else" and have been slightly drunk even later in life, but always with a sneaky, treacherous anxiety in the background. Also, I sleep worse with alcohol in the blood. So, all of you who think I seem dull and skeptical when you unpack your bags at our celebrations may have a little oversight like this retroactively.

Today, I'm not a renowned fanatic or absolutist and can very well take a mulled and spiced wine on Christmas Eve or a glass of champagne on New Year's Night; but for the rest of the year, I simply do not want to confuse my poor brain. It's confused enough. Through my Neptune, I prefer to channel sober sex, yoga, movies, music, books and outdoor work among plants. I also avoid celebrations with drunk humans acting like zombies.

King Neptune or Poseidon

All kinds of stimulants end up ike drugs and herbal remedies in the drugs category. A drug is a means that is delivered to the body and causes it to react in different ways, either as a soporific or for healing. All this is connected to the planet Neptune and most often also to the sign Pisces. The discovery of the planet Neptune also coincided with the use of anesthesia in operations.

Why do we use drugs? The natural reason is to try to heal whatever does not work. Whether it is the soul or the body that is not in balance, we may need to take something to complete, mitigate the pain or heal. In terms of physical causes, both natural remedies and ordinary medicines are available today, but often with pure mental imbalance, I personally think you have greater freedom of choice. In severe conditions, it may be vital to medicate, such as psychoses, more severe neuroses, panic attacks or other diagnosed mental illnesses. Unfortunately, there is a plethora of mental disorders. Many people can also live with brain damages or other mental illnesses that require daily medication. Is it no wonder that "fully healthy" people voluntarily take drugs?

Although mental health and psychiatry are currently available, I believe that many easier or transient crises in life can be tackled with another strategy. Today there are a lot of therapists who are skilled in Reiki, touch healing or distance healing. There is everything from color therapy and flower essences to physical exercises like yoga or Tai Chi. There are many methods to achieve mental peace without taking medication. Natural remedies can be a good compliment for a while, but be careful not to let the body and psyche become too much attached to these temporary supplements. For example, I tested Valeriana for a while for sleep disturbances. I hardly dare to write that the drug cannabis has been found effective against some cancers, because cannabis's misuse can easily lead to severe reperucssions. In addition, the person gets daft and slow in his mind in the longer term. So, in the long run, cannabis are nothing to recommend.

I know many who basically never even take ordinary Panodil or Alvedon (paracetamol), and there is something in this too. Crises in our lives in different ways make us aware of something wrong or incomplete, and we will not learn anything if we put "blinders" on or try to deny or reject the discomfort. As a Capricorn said about the women's menopause: "Evil shall be lived out and through and not become deaf through hormone preparation". (Ex Flushes).

Not all crises in life require any treatment. How did people survive during the Stone Age when they faced crises? There was no Sobril then. I think it's not always positive with today's ease of getting any preparations or medicines. Perhaps our pain threshold has plummeted.

How does my own Neptune work?

Now, you may not know what signs or aspects your own Neptune has, but you may recognize any of the following descriptions. If you have your chart, you can easily recognize the trident icon.

Neptune can be experienced a bit differently depending on the type of aspect. If it is a conjunction with the Sun or Moon, it gives greater receptivity to both physical and mental influences. This aspect can indicate that it is easier to suffer from viruses, bacilli and infections, but at the same time be easier to receive support from the help of psychics to increase their own healing energy. Physically, this is one of the instances that lowers the body's own resilience. Great caution must be observed in every form of medication. The danger of different drugs, of course, can be extraordinary, not only for one's physical health but also because of the emotional instability that even other, easier forms of abuse may cause.

All of these Neptune people must not become addicts or hypersensitive to medicines. They can also find great pleasure in indulging in their own little inspirations, whatever they may be. The ability to be absorbed by and absorb what they love makes them passionately absent from this world. But it is not necessarily a destructive reality escape. This is just one way for them to live their creativity, their endorphins or imagination in their own intense way. To achieve this little ecstasy, you do not have to use drugs when you have music, dance, books or anything else that naturally stimulates. The problem is just that it *seems* to be faster and easier to experience the stimulation if you get some "chemical help."

I read once a parable about meditation exercises. Learning to meditate and find an inner peace can take a long time, but by taking drugs, in this case, LSD, was like "coming to the experience" in no time. This simply can't be good for the soul, not in the long run. It's like getting a driving license and then immediately attempting to drive a car.

The connection between drugs and God is not that strange. Drugs take us "somewhere else," and religious experiences are often about "another world." Neptune may stand for the higher Love, but it also associates with much suffering, social misery and illness. Too much of

Neptune can at worst lead to a weak physique and therefore an overly delicate physical body. But even these people can strive towards physical achievements that are not "of this world" through discipline and endurance. Thinking spontaneously on the Pisces Ingemar Stenmark, he swam gracefully down the snow (water) in the slalom slope.

There is also a tendency for severely alcoholic or other addicts to completely turn over and become devoted believers. You might understand why: It is the same source of energy they focus on.

I was afraid that this whole chapter might be perceived by the reader as some form of moral preaching, but the offsprings of addictions speak their own clear language. The list of names of people who have been victims of various types of addictions is endless.

R. I. P. (Rest In Peace)

Musician Jimi Hendrix, singer Janis Joplin, Sid Vicious of *Sex Pistols*, singer Whitney Houston and her daughter Bobbi Kristina, writer Ernest Hemingway, actor Spencer Tracy, actor Richard Burton, author Truman Capote, actor Errol Flynn, jazz singer Billie Holiday, author Jack Kerouac, actress Veronica Lake, singer Jim Morrison, singer Amy Winehouse, actor William Holden, soccer player George Best and poet Dylan Thomas. These are just a mere few to mention.

Even the list of sober alcoholics can be equally long; former President George W. Bush, Anthony Hopkins, Stephen King, Eric Clapton, Alice Cooper, Robert Downey Jr., James Hetfield of *Metallica*, Samuel L. Jackson, Al Pacino, Trent Reznor, Ingvar Kamprad (IKEA founder), and on and on and on.

Anxiety in the Chart

Ångest, anguish or anxiety, angoshe, angst: These loaded words are spelled almost the same in different languages: Swedish, English, Italian and German. One picture you can't forget is Edward Munch's "Scream," and it symbolizes this difficult subject.

Why even address this difficult and complicated taboo subject? Yes, I firmly argue that anxiety is one of the most difficult and most important processes we humans have to go through sooner or later. There is no definite linear time in the birthchart, but it is purely individualistic, depending upon several factors in your own chart. Where and when in life this happens is probably determined by individual karma and circumstances. Also, I consider experiencing anxiety from different degrees of personal experience, and everyone can't be so bad that they end up in severe abusive behavior if they have no disposition for this since birth in their chart.

"It's too bad about the people," said Strindberg. He was Aquarius and had his heavy Moon in Capricorn. If I should count on all occasions I experienced anxiety, many would think I was crazy. Most of us survive these periods of life and can also learn how to handle different forms of anxiety without totally collapsing. So, you don't need to constantly worry about it in advance. Anxiety also has very important lessons to teach, so listen rather than automatically shutting down.

If you read a clinical explanation of anxiety, you will get a variety of descriptions. Anxiety is both a state of being as well as a reaction, depending on the situation. I read that doctors can get anxiety from a fear of anxiety, probably due to the great responsibilities they carry for their patiens, for performing an operation or the like. Then there are different degrees of anxiety. Everything from latent and weak anxiety that can be interpreted as pure fear, to pure acute panic disorder, agony or so-called existential anxiety. Unfortunately, I have to admit that I have experienced the whole scale. However, this is not obvious for everyone. I myself have a proper grave form of latent disposition and usually use my own chart as a deterrent (my Sun conjunct Pluto, Sun square Saturn, Sun square Moon, Moon square Pluto, Moon conjunct Saturn). Having only one of these aspects in your chart can suffice to make life complicated. Many of my clients have had at least one of these aspects enabled in their prognosis when they came in contact with me. Maybe that is why I could better understand them.

What to do?

The problem is not the anxiety itself, but more what we do with it and how we handle it. You can escape by taking pills to numb yourself, stumble into different drugs, manically comfort-eat yourself full, time and time again (Moon aspect Uranus), or try to work the brain with a range of distracting activities. I could fill a whole page with distracting activities. All of these are examples of escaping reality and trying to avoid or totally deny a slumbering, underground latent anxiety. TV viewing may sound harmless, but when you go through box after box of any TV series, both new and old, you are attempting to make time go quicklly so the anxiety will hopefully disappear. Another escape route is to log into facebook ten times a day and see if someone "likes" you and everything you do (posts). Even forced exercise can be an expression of this "escape." We may pay expensive prices to go to the gym just to squeeze off the kilos before sunbathing or just try to become more beautiful. I realize that my daily hikes for many years were clearly an anxiety valve as well as for the pure pleasure. But primarily, it was to sleep better and at least believe that I could keep my potbelly in check. In addition, I felt better mentally after a long walk, whether in rain or in a snow storm. No obstacles ever interfered with my fresh-air mania.

All of this we do in an attempt to eliminate something that is actually quite vital to our physical health and spiritual growth. I myself have handled it in all possible and impossible ways. When I was young and "unwise," of course I sometimes took the "easiest" way out: through alcohol, drugs, sex or some form of fun (something termed as "special interests"). It becomes a bit more complicated the more responsibility you have, responsibilities for your children, coworkers or classmates make the anxiety more difficult to handle. One can't just suddenly escape. Maybe you write a sicknote and blame it on a sore throat or headache. Or maybe you are so intense in your belief that you actually are sick that develop real symptoms in your poor body. You get a stomach ache, a headache or an allergic reaction of some kind. Fever is common not only with hypochondriacs.

Then, of course, there is a difference between occasional and chronic anxiety. You can get an anxiety attack at the dentist's office or finding yourself at the height of 10,000 meters in a crowded plane. What do you think they experienced in the "showers" in Auschwitz? Or if you're knife-threatened, or in the middle of an ongoing rape? Anxiety is a vital symptom that forces us to try and change the situation. If you are threatened by an attacking predator, you must run. The brain then secretes substances that can give the body abnormal strength or the ability to flee.

I myself have like Nils Ferlin's (famous Swedish poet) *Anxiety Is My Inheritance*, who lived with anxiety since his teens. (Ferlin had his Moon in Scorpio). As a child, strangely enough, I never perceived anxiety. Or perhaps I had but never was aware of it? In my chart I have several indications that are linked to my childhood. One of the more important indications is the conjunction of Moon and Saturn. Purely astrologically, it is more common with combinations between the Moon and Uranus that can lead to anxiety. For more than forty years now, I have experienced and learned from other peoples' experiences during these processes, and Uranus is usually the classical energy that can easily trigger slight or grave anxiety. I saw a German program on astrology many years ago where the astrologer in the studio was allowed to analyze an unknown person, a so-called blind test. Impressive and unpleasant, she told the unknown person that he probably lived or had lived with various forms of anxiety ever since childhood, and the man responded spontaneously, "Yes, that's right." Then the TV viewers were shown the chart, and indeed the Moon and Uranus were in conjunction, and in Cancer as well (emphasis on the feelings).

Now, you may be terribly curious about your own location or contact between these positions, but do not worry. Everyone experiences different degrees of this during different periods of life and under different circumstances. It all depends on a planet's relative aspects or location in the chart. However, astrologers can often pinpoint these periods in advance or give a clear message if you suddenly would go through a period of different forms of anxiety. This is the strength of astrology, to show a timetable for the different periods. Then it's up to you to try to make the most of these terms. You can avoid global trips or different physical challenges, such as the *Santiago de Compostela* walk or bicycling through Europe.

I hope you don't think it's hopeless or pitch black, but there's a "divine justice" in the phenomenon. Nobody gets off, you can say. Sometimes you can see others who look happy and pleased in life (facebook is a good example of what we want to display). Even though you do not have any direct aspect between these or similar positions in your chart, there will still mathematically be a time or opportunity in life when you will need to deal with these important emotions. Whether this occurs in childhood, adolescence, adulthood or old age is completely individual.

The task of the astrologer will then be to analyze the time period and to pilot the client through this process in the easiest way. Then you may have to take into account all the factors around. Maybe it's time to take a *time out* or just a longer period of vacation. For example, are you responsible for family or employees, or are other people dependent on your presence? How many times have you read about people who "skipped," took a *time out* or "smashed into the wall?" I may have my own prejudices, but I am convinced that the computer's rapid development in the 90's helped create the number of "burned out" or long-term sick people today. All that concerns computers and the Internet is also linked to Uranus, which speeds up time. With the help of the computer, everything just goes faster.

Why are these periods happening then? I usually emphasize the "message" or "meaning" of these processes. Uranus's symbolic task is clearly to force us to change of all kinds. Nobody will get away from the winds of change. We age, gain weight, get depressed, lose interest in our spouse, get tired of the job, lose our loved one, get fired, divorce, end up at the lawyers, are deceived, raped, bullied in school, get a stomach ulcer or just feel older and tired. Yes, as you see, "we have all our problems," as the Norwegian comedian Marve Fleksnes said. Uranus represents the change and development taking place so that we do not stagnate or get stuck in our lives.

Now, this may sound negative, but I am addressing these phenomena that most of us sometimes encounter as examples of how Uranus often "force" us to work on our Karma (as everyone has, no matter how full of self-esteem they are). Of course, there is both meaning and a higher purpose with Uranus. I usually ask my clients if I see a similar period at a time, to be alert, listen and look out for everything that breaks the pattern. You often get signals "from the future." Maybe a picture from a movie or an ad or article in a newspaper or just something you hear on the news. If you have been triggered by something, you can often find these so-called synchronicities or subtle signals everywhere. Uranus often shows us new opportunities to develop or gain new insights. If this does not suit us and we are not susceptible to this, Uranus often finds other ways to "force" us to understand the necessity of change. In these cases, anxiety can often be experienced as a symptom to show us that we simply do not want to change.

Then it's up to us how we look at change. I usually ask about your attitude. Do you mind changes, or are you content with everything in life? Are you more likely to be upset by change? Do you prefer that nothing should stop being as it is? Unfortunately, it's not the meaning of life to never have change. Opponents of change are probably those who experience the worst anxiety. Conservative people are particularly ultra-sensitive and vulnerable to change because they want to stick to the past and their routines. However, it contradicts the process of development and learning of life itself on a spiritual/karmic level.

Conversely, it is easy to note that open, conscious individuals often see the signals of change as potentially stimulating and exciting. In addition, empathetic feelers are more likely to accept life's changes than rigid "control freaks." By the way, perhaps "control freaks" are the worst, because the change is managed by life itself and not necessarily by the person (A crisis arises that the person has no control over).

Uranian people, however, are interesting and impressive in several ways. Here we find everyone from misunderstood geniuses to crazy extremists. They often live like restless Bohemians and are having difficulty with static relationships. Their families probably know these individuals as haywire and restless. However, they have gifts you should not underestimate. They can be extremely intuitive and sometimes even show mediumship or psychic abilities. I have encountered several with this strong energy. The musician Bob Dylan has this conjunction between the Moon and Uranus in Taurus. As a Gemini, he has channeled his political awareness into poetic and musical ways. I also know that he is extremely phobic and neurotic and

285

well aware of anxiety. Perhaps that was why he had a religious period in his career.

My own experience in anxiety

As for myself, I can give you several examples from my troublesome life. As Uranus was transitting my Moon in the late 70's, I was involved in a severe car accident; and on another occasion, I was run into in the back of my car by a taxi when I carelessly pulled out of a parking lot. The more severe of these accidents, I also suffered from acute panic attacks a few months later. The tricky thing was that the panic attack hit just after three months. I ended up in a psychotic state with hallucinations, noise cords, light effects in the eyes and periodic palpitations. Often I thought I would have myocardial infarction and fall down, whenever and anywhere. The fear escalated, and both the privacy and the work became a pain. I lived as a zombie both at home and at work and counted the anxiety attacks with minutes and seconds. My sex life was nonexistent (though, sex can be a common anxiety valve), and at work they wondered why I was always so quiet. This latent anxiety quickly became chronic, and my social life became a mere hell. The marriage collapsed because I both became aggressive and irritated by the least trifle. Aggressiveness is basically fear. This was obviously the death blow for my first attempt to live in a regular family, and we separated a few years after this event as life spiralled steeply downwards.

I would like to mention here, too, with respect for my former wife, that no shadow falls over her. The debt of this failed marriage is mine, and even though we got a couple of crazy but intense happy years and two lovely children, this sorrow is included in my own traumatic karma and no blame will be put on either her or any of my later female relationships.

At the same time, however, I took several important decisions (Uranian changes). In the death song of this particular anxiety, I decided that drinking should stop in all forms and that I also stop eating meat, as well as to try to clean myself up and reduce the poisoning of both the body and the soul. Comically, this also led me to deepen my interest in astrology, and after all I received a series of explanations for these events. Some explanations were hardly a surprise, for example, that I had a knack for alcoholism. (Compare with my bitter attitude towards alcohol today in the chapter **Drugs**). Just over two years later, I formed "Utopia," which became the symbolic start of my life's astrological call. This also became a Uranian effect, with my development accelerated.

Fear - the beginning

My first memories or experiences of anxiety did not come until the late 60's. At one point I ended up in the backseat of a car, completely unaware that the driver was drunk and was driving us to death at an insane speed. I just remember screaming and shouting that he should stop. The song *Happy Birthday Sweet Sixteen* is forever associated with this experience. Another event occurred in 1968 when I was not even twelve and had to visit Sahlgrenska Hospital where my father was in a complicated plaster cradle. He had slipped off a gangway and dropped nine meters down onto a stone dock. I even remember the headlines of the newspaper: "Sailor Dropped 9 Meters." That was my dad. What do you not do to get into the papers? Joke aside, this visit was probably a minor shock to me as a little guy. At junior high school, we were on a school trip to Oslo, and on the way home in the dark, the train slowed down and someone peered out and said we went towards red lanterns. Someone else joked and said that we would probably crash with another train, and in an instant the anxiety showed up. Just remember that I was terrified. Probably, therefore, I remember the event so clearly. Nothing happened of course.

However, the anxiety stayed away for longer periods. I had time to discover my sexuality, learned to smoke, drinking beer and trying out different drugs. When I grew up in Hisingen, a common suburb in Gothenburg, I was surrounded by people sniffing glue solution, drinking beer and smoking hash. Many of my peers ended up early in trouble with abuse and crime. Thankfully, my testing of drugs gave no kick, so I never stuck to it. However, I later discovered snuff (Swedish snus), which today is a faithful friend and my only "burden" in relation to poisons and drugs. In addition, I was lucky enough to meet a very good friend, Ronnie Krantz, (a Scorpio with Saturn conjunct Sun and his Moon in Gemini). He encouraged me to earn money on various projects and to start training instead of living like a juvenile. He took me to my first ice hockey and soccer games, and we joined the IFK Gothenburg boys section early. Later, he also got me to try judo in Masthugget. He even got me into Liseberg (Funfair) where we ended up in different jobs and where I later met one of my first loves, Ann-Sofi.

The anxiety stayed away for several years, which was both good and evil. My self-esteem grew, and girls and sex became more exciting than caring for my body and exercising. For the first time, in 1972 and aged 16, I came in contact with yoga. This also led to my introduction to astrology. Uranus passed in transit over my MC in Libra during 1972 (first meeting with astrology). Nevertheless, the anxiety remained almost gone until August of 1979, when the car crash became a destructive turning point. Uranus was at the time in Scorpio, but only at 17 degrees and in December made it to my Moon. Then panic attacks became acute. Between 1980 and until the move from Gothenburg in 1984, they came and went. I strangely did not contact any doctor or psychologist. Well, I probably thought insolently that "I'll figure this out on my own" (Scorpio Moon again). Also, I was quite phobic towards all medication, so I did not get stuck there in any addiction.

However, today I have to admit that it is neither the best nor the correct way to recommend. I know that pills and medication in various forms can be vital in order to even exist. Living normally is unthinkable for the one who lives with a chronic anxiety, and the one who has never had anxiety has no idea what I mean.

Another exciting experience I did occurred when the Moon passed my own Uranus in the chart. It was at that time that I met William Shaffer in 1997, and I found out all about my past, including my previous incarnations. To say the least, it was a frightening experience, but perhaps it was also one of the coolest adrenaline kicks I've had. A brief review of this "reading" can be found in the "**Medium**" section.

Living with anxiety

There are, after all, many people who are forced to live with a life-long disability in the form of latent or chronic anxiety. Many mental illnesses are unexpected effects of severe anxiety and worry, and medication can be a matter of life or death. Those who live with some form of schizophrenia, depression, manic-depression, borderline or obsessive compulsive disorder may be forced to take some form of medicine to even exist.

There are also many prejudices when it comes to most mental illnesses. On the other hand, if you have a broken leg and crutches, you can instead be treated with encouragement and empathy. However, the one who is "sick in the head" is, in my opinion, treated more often with suspicion or fear in an incomprehensible way.

Then we have a huge gray zone with people who "just" feel bad, are frustrated, unhappy or sometimes easily depressed. There are many who may never say openly that they are sad or down, but who will continually radiate fear like a perceptible scent in their auras. They also do not always take any kind of medicine but think it's normal to go through some tough periods of life without any kind of support. If I'd dare to say that most people I encountered radiate some kind of fear, you might be surprised. I quote the role figure *Pink* in Roger Waters' *Pink Floyd* (Moon in Scorpio) epic, *The Wall*: "I've got amazing powers of observation," (*Nobody Home*). All too often people seem to me to be both insecure and afraid, and I see badly hidden panic in peoples' body language or stare. This always makes me curious about WHAT they really are afraid of.

What to do?

How should you handle or live with your anxiety? First, I think you must have your own plan or strategy. One must absolutely dare to both feel and listen inwardly. "Why, why, why"? is vital to try to answer. If you are aware of that, you can probably come across a lot of reasons: I'm too ugly, fat or stupid, I fail in my career, I dare not be alone, I have to drink to be able to look happy, my guy/girl does not think I'm good enough in bed, my damn big sister always tells me I can not stay and take responsibility in my relationships, my mom is crazy about psycho drugs, my dad left when I was a child and did not even want to have any contact, I always buy cars that break, I always sleep badly, I console myself by eating candy when nobody sees, I'm probably abnormal sexually, I don't dare to "come out of the closet," I do not dare to say no to the buddies when they have a party but rather play along and often fall under group pressure, I never dare to say when I'm treated badly, I feel ashamed over my outbursts of anger, I feel shame about everything in my appearance. Yes, the list can be endless.

I just wanted to provoke the readers with some examples of why we can "feel bad." If you do not dare or cope with these "minor" problems, the risk is apparent that you instead build up an internal pressure in your psyche, which sooner or later explodes or breaks down your body and psyche.

Anxiety and medication

I am convinced that it is both possible to live with anxiety and to learn how to handle it, but it is important that you dare to acknowledge it and talk openly about the problems. Daring to be open about the fears is a big but important first step. Then doing an internal diagnosis, to try to find out if you can change it without medication can be a good continuation. You can not just end taking important medicines just because you want to. It can give an unexpectedly painful reaction. You must carefully process both the symptoms and the possible addiction to medication before making important decisions. Obviously, it is more difficult to deal with anxiety if you have already suffered from some medical dependency. It can be near impossible and take years before you can be considered completely free of anxiety attacks. I am thinking of many sober alcoholics who struggled for years being healthy and free from all side effects.

I do think there are solutions to most problems, but it is not possible to generally provide simple methods. The individual's anxiety is always unique and must be treated with care and patience. I have often tried to suggest small messages in my interpretations without the person even knowing it. But it must happen in different ways on a case-by-case basis.

Three possibilities to begin the healing

Some of you may know my view of my three basic factors: the body, the mind and the soul. Clearing the different aspects makes it easier to see where to insert action. This makes it easier to understand what is disturbing you or locate what is in imbalance. Often you can also see if it is temporary or long-term, which also facilitates my "impact" on the client. One can partly say that the meaning of one's karma may be to try to achieve a balance between these three basic factors in life.

I can definitely recommend focusing on the area you think is easiest to try and influence. If you are interested in your physical health, it pays to spend time and effort to keep yourself healthy and strong. Exercise is never unnecessary; and even if you think you already are strong or healthy, you can always improve your basic strength and hence your resilience. Some have gnawed over my advice about the importance of caring for their health, but it is impossible to deny that everything is connected. The Sun and its aspects are the basis of our physical well-being; and if the body is not well, it will affect both our thoughts (mind) and our feelings (soul) in the long run. If you feel bad in the mind with negative energy, pessimism, anger, envy, jealousy or bitterness, it affects both the body's mechanism and our feelings. If only the feelings are suffering, it is not easier. But by learning to take care of yourself a little more, you can fool the mind into being a bit more happy. I am also very aware that there are a lot of reasons why our feelings are not in balance.

Friends (that's what friends are for)

As we all differ, there are no ready-made recipes to use. But here I think our fellow people play an important role. Friends or professional therapists can give us support and encouragement when we need it the most. It is not easy even for our fellow-companions to be forced to take full responsibility for our recovery. We simply can't expect that love alone can save us from evil. Personally, my experience is that our "best friends" play a more important role, as this support does not have to be infected with sexual needs or joint conflict management. Take care of your friends, and they will take care of you. I usually say that you can more easily take a "scolding" from your best friends than from your partner.

What planets or combinations?

At first I hesitated to make a list or "cookbook" with all examples, but as I did not list all the planets in the text, I would like to do a brief summary, perhaps more to adjust your own concern than to reinforce it. It is important to note, however, that you cannot or should not literally interpret these individual effects without taking into account the overall picture and the surrounding aspects.

Sun and Moon

As for the planets, one must first look at the main basic factors, and then it's about the position and aspects of the Sun and Moon. In general, one can say that a balance or positive aspect between the Sun and Moon can be the basis of a balanced psyche. The conjunction, the sextile and the trine all mean that the individual has an inner balance between *yin* and *yang*, or their masculine and feminine parts. It is easier to relate to both sexes, and at the same time easier with recovery. People with a trine between the Sun and Moon seem to have easier dealing with crises, and also to achieve success in life in relation to both sexes. This is a common aspect in popular people's charts.

Imbalance or tension between the Sun (masculine) and the Moon (feminine) is unfairly labeled "the divorce aspect," which may not be so strange since they go in different directions. Often there is internal uncertainty and imbalance, and the individual can be both perplexed and uncertain about both decisions and what energy to use. I have often highlighted this as the "seesaw." You tend to commute back and forth in life between your"opposites," which can also be experienced as "what I do for my own sake and what I do for others." Or as a latent conflict between egoism and altruism. If you spend too much time or energy in one aspect and not in the other, then either power can come to a point where you start to doubt, feel guilty or just realize that you have gone too far. Then the pendulum can swing too far in the other direction and you begin to over-compensate or put power and time elsewhere. This results in the pendulum swinging back and forth between one extreme imbalance to the other, and this is very exhausting physically, mentally and emotionally.

These periods may vary in time. It can be everything from daily spontaneous fluctuations to year-long projects where you may neglect your own or others' needs for years. It can be like trying to walk on one leg. I discovered by chance that you can consciously compromise yourself simply by setting up a strategy for "commuting" between the two aspeacts. It is easy to decide in advance to devote a total of your own needs for a certain period of time and then to optimally focus on others according to their needs. In this way, you never risk losing into imbalance, feeling guilty, being accused of creating self-inflicted problems or, on the contrary, wasting yourself through sacrifices.

As I am born and have lived with a tension or imbalance (square) between my Sun and Moon, I think I can admit that I have repeatedly moved back and forth several times during my life with several home moves, career changes and new goals in life.

Now, if it turns out that you happen to have a tension between your Sun and Moon, do not despair. I heard during a lecture a Norwegian female astrologer tell us that these people often get deep insights and become empathetic and tolerant to others who othewise find this conflict difficult.

Sun

Although the connections of the Sun are mostly physical, they may sometimes have emotional effects. The Sun's contact with Mars can lead to a lot of energy; and unless released through physical activity, it can lead to internal tension and emotional fear.

The Sun's contact with Saturn is more common in longer conditions such as depression or long-term sickness.

However, the Sun and Uranus can have several effects, both physically and mentally. I have both undergone surgery and lived with some latent anxiety during similar "stressful" periods. Uranus often puts the Sun in the highest preparedness, which can lead to both bodily injury as well as a tendency to "flip out," purely emotionally. Of all the aspects, the conjunction may be the one that primarily contributes to these sudden feelings and emergency conditions.

The Sun's contact with Neptune is more connected to drug effects and long-term illnesses.

Likewise, Pluto's contact with the Sun is more on an unconscious level. However, it can lead to both a complete transformation of the psyche as well as a period of almost "aching skin," which may be very painful.

Moon

The instincts and reactions of the Moon are the closest to mental illnesses and acute anxiety states. It is actually about the feelings, and the Moon places great emphasis on the soul.

The Moon's contact with Mercury creates mostly a whimsical irritation in tension, as a conflict between the classical "sense versus emotion" can arise.

However, the Moon's contact with Venus can be a strong trigger factor. As Venus symbolizes balance and harmony, excitement here indicates both bodily and mental suffering in some form. A minor disagreement may be relevant, as well as physical nausea; but even more, anxiety may occur if the discomfort becomes too strong. Love or sadness may be a triggering factor. Tears are usually a common effect to channel this discomfort.

The Moon's contact with Mars can have a dramatic effect. A friendly soul can experience unheard of stress, which could lead to easier anxiety. On the other hand, an insensitive person can react with a violent outlet of emotion.

The Moon's contact with Jupiter has usually nothing to do with anxiety, unless one tries to eat or laugh themselves to death. I might point out that Jupiter can even enlarge other actual problems that arise.

The combination of the Moon and Saturn, however, is often a contributing factor to various milder degrees of anxiety. This effect is linked to the concept of time, and unnecessary or constant stress leads to a degree of anxiety. The reasons can be many, but the most common one is probably that the person tries to catch up with everything and never makes it or gets ready. Results can be a chronic bad conscience that can never be processed, due to lack of time.

The Moon's contact with Uranus is nevertheless the most contributing cause of many forms of anxiety and panic syndrome. Emotional tension and a feeling that everything goes too fast may be good for a Formula 1 driver, but not for common mortals. Either you drive to the fullest and never notice that you go through the wall, or "life happens" instead, and you end up in the hospital or in prison. The symbol here is actually "unexpected feelings," and that is not what you want to have.

There are actually some exceptions. People who are psychic or strongly intuitive often seem to have one of these contacts active, which I think is fascinating, as it is about a form of "emotionally elevated energy."

Neptune's influence, however, is very difficult to determine. Contacts between the Moon and Neptune often provide incredibly empathetic and good-hearted people, but they may have hidden concerns or disappointments within themselves. Addictions are usual; but if not, inspirations can be channeled through other creative activities like art or music. However, the influence has to be emphasized, and one must be aware of the risk of too easily ending in a spiritual suffering, by mistake, like in detoxification.

Pluto's aspects to the Moon usually appear on the subconscious level, but they are still extremely important. It may mean shock to the subconscious because of what can come up, but it can also give an ability to transform both physically and spiritually.

Mercury

As for the purely intellectual interpretation, it is true that the soul is in focus and thus also with the Moon. But the mental structure must also be taken into account. Mercury is not only called "The Winged Messenger," but it is also representing our language and our attitude towards others.

A good aspect between Mercury and the Moon makes it easier to ventilate both feelings and thoughts.

Mercury´s contact with Venus increases empathy and diplomacy, and these individuals may be more likely to discuss their concerns.

Mercury's contact with Mars is both good and bad. To the benefit, it is a tendency to speak before thinking (transparency) and perceived as honesty, spontaneity and forwardness. The disadvantages can be over-exaggerated comments or to become too keen and perceived as inconsistent or grievous.

Mercury's aspects to Jupiter give a positive attitude and at the same time increase your mental recovery through plans and hopes. This is good for all kinds of conversational therapy.

Mercury's contact with Saturn can, however, be complicated. Mercury is quick while Saturn can be a break pad. This can inhibit the thought process, and this is more common in depression and degrees of melancholy. Thus, this is not exactly anxiety but more of a discouragement with pessimism, suspicion and distrust. However, when focusing on the serious, good insights can be born and personally, I consider this contact extremely valuable. This is often found in both wise and serious people. I know that, for example, Albert Einstein had this conjunction. Through discipline, perseverance and conscious analysis, one can get a realistic clarity on all conditions. Also remember that the Swedish director Ingemar Bergman had this in Leo and was also perceived as extremely serious and pessimistic. He also suffered from recurring anxiety and depressions.

Mercury and Uranus aspects are perhaps the most difficult and most common during periods of anxiety, even though the Moon and Uranus are the more likely trigger. This is because Uranus is a higher octave of the intellect, where we find the intuition and the higher consciousness. Anxiety can be triggered simply because everything seems to go faster. The pulse, breathing and the body are on the rise, and this is one of the reasons for stress and long-term burn out. Here, too, there are advantages and disadvantages. People with this aspect can be both super-intelligent and witty in their comments (the movie *Rainman*) and are constantly in motion with "a thousand balloons in the air." Here we have the 90's social effects with the extended computerization. The disadvantages may not be so difficult, but the tendency to split mentally can lead to lunacy, and latent mental conditions may be exacerbated by "too many thoughts at once."

Mercury's contact with Neptune is also good and bad. The positive effects can lead to both a psychic ability and a more idealistic view of life, while the negative effects most often lead to temporary confusion. This, of course, is compounded if you are using drugs or medication at the same time. I often advise caution with drugs and medications during these periods in a prognosis. People who have this contact in their chart can be very sympathetic and loving, but at the same time can have problems with reality's requirements and conditions. Idealism can turn into being too starry-eyed as well as trigger major disappointments. This contact is very common in people who work with therapeutic methods as well as all aesthetic pursuits such as music, art or any creative expression. I don't personally think that this generates serious anxiety, but rather a state of absence more like zombieism than a psychotic person.

Mercury's contact with Pluto can even count as a complicated one. Here, there is a direct contact between our awakening (Mercury) and our subconscious (Pluto), and this connection can be used or experienced in several different ways. Curiosity can be strong, and an analytical intellect can penetrate deeply. However, restlessness can lead to mental blockages, and it can be difficult to get down to rooted problems. I have noticed a certain nervousness and anxiety in people with this aspect active, but they can also use suggestion and manipulation in their methods of influencing others, such as a hypnotist or skilled therapist. This aspect is not uncommon with a certain psychic talent, but they must learn to turn off their ambition to absolutely know everything.

Venus

Venus is not associated with anxiety or mental distress, but a disharmonious Venus can indicate a sloppy or nonchalant attitude towards serious things, which in the long term can lead to unnecessary frustration and thus regret and disappointment. This could be expressed as an indifference to or waste of money. As Venus controls the hormones, its sensitive placement is important not least for the balance of all kinds of relationships. A whimsical or tense Venus has difficulty both with faithfulness and permanent relationships, which in turn leads to conflicts. Hormonal disorders do not cause anxiety, but too much of life's good can easily lead to loathing and apathy, which may be a breeding ground for latent anxiety. Those of the most common contacts are Neptune and Uranus. Neptune can increase disappointment and crush illusions, and Uranus sometimes forces unwilling changes, especially in our relationships.

Mars

Energy wrongly used can lead to both bodily and mental suffering, and here we have several of Mars' effects. The physical aspects of this may not be directly anxiety-inducing, but rather of bodily suffering. All aggressiveness, anger and violence can have devastating consequences. Many accidents are often the result of spilled energies that are triggered suddenly and with violent power.

The psychological effects may vary. A Moon in action from Mars can give immense emotional outbursts (tennis player John McEnroe and also little singer Edith Piaf), which can destroy the best of relationships. The combination of physical stress and emotional stress often leads to purely hysterical conditions, which of course can be anxiety-inducing.

Mars' aspects to Pluto may sometimes exert extreme expressions of physical violence as well as mental discomfort and irrational fears.

Jupiter

Jupiter's effects are hardly ever experienced as anxiety symptoms, but of course, we may consider that any form of excess and exaggeration can be harmful. Jupiter sometimes lacks conscientious thinking and does not always realize its own shortcomings and limitations. This can lead to different states of discomfort, but not acute anxiety. However, in an acute state of stress, Jupiter can also trample on and enlarge the anxiety itself (rather tragicomically).

Saturn

"Satan´s Uranus," as I sometimes call Saturn, is probably the archetype for all forms of suffering, so therefore also anxiety. Why? Because it is most often associated with reality and the physical world we are forced to adapt to, including all duties, all responsibilities, all demands, all the resistance we meet and all our efforts. This aspect shows itself when we experience requirements and expectations from the outside world as well as our own inherent requirements and expectations.

An infected or delicate aspect of Saturn not only makes us miserable and tired, but it can also reduce or eliminate the joy of life. People in temporary crises or depression usually have one or another form of Saturn active in their chart. Individuals born with this can seek security in the material world by being extremely effective and productive. They are usually workaholics, but of course at the expense of the joy of life. Saturn's contact with the Sun can inhibit or reduce vitality, but it can also contribute to a disciplined attitude that leads to the person becoming more focused and serious. Much concrete work can be accomplished.

Saturn's contact with the Moon reduces all emotional flow, and the person can have trouble opening him/herself up for fear of attack. A lack of self-confidence must be dealt with unless the precautionary approach is to lead to a purely detached attitude. The most common causes of this effect are the increased pressure from the environment, increased demands and thus less freedom for the person. There is a lack of thought that can affect the energy, the time, the economy or a person's own sense of adequacy. Much support from the environment is needed.

In addition to the contact with Uranus, this aspect may be the one that usually leads to various anxiety symptoms. It is usually an anxiety that is the result of a long suffering or strain, and it is often preceded by some form of depression.

Uranus

This is the planet we most think about when talking about all forms of anxiety. Uranus speeds up life and often comes suddenly and unexpectedly, similar to a lightning strike. I should be able to give many examples, but it is enough with just a few completely different consequences. When you hear that your partner wants to break up, maybe it feels like when a mirror breaks, or when you hear of a fatality you have not counted on, or experiencing a car accident or caught in a tsunami. Perhaps someone has passed away too early by violence or suicide. It can be when you get a message that leads to shock or when you get fired or get a notice to leave your home. The most classic example is probably a sudden car accident that comes from nowhere, or as I said, when lightning strikes.

What's happening is just like an electric shock to the sensitive nervous system that puts both the body and the soul into the highest level of preparedness. Of course, one can react in different ways, but in addition to the most common reactions, anxiety or discomfort are the most common effects of acute fear.

Is it possible to completely avoid these effects? Hardly, but individually, we naturally have different forms of preparedness, even on the spiritual level. A person who already has a sensitive Moon will probably react more dramatically than one who may have the Moon in a more down-to-earth sign, or with cther beneficial energies that increase resilience. Thus, it also lessens the effects of anxiety more quickly.

You who viewed my chart can easily understand that my own consequences and reactions were not the easiest. My chart revealed minimal resilience, lousy self-esteem in youth, mild or hardly any physical strength, latent fear and lack of experience.

However, in tandem with my karma, I have learned to live with and manage these effects so that they do not have to destroy my entire life.

Neptune

However, the energy or planet that is always active in various diseases, both bodily and spiritual, is Neptune. It not only symbolizes bacteria, viruses, infections and bacilli, but it is linked to all physiological effects on the body as well as the effects of drugs on the psyche. Anxiety may not be the first thing you think about, but mental suffering can be experienced in many different ways. I think Neptune more has to do with the medical influence we face if we suffer from anxiety in any form. Additionally, you can also associate Neptune with the healing part of the process: recovery. This energy is also active when we undergo both therapy as well as bodily convalescence.

It is important to add, however, this involves all drugs. All the toxicity we come into contact with can have devastating consequences and of course lead to both psychoses and mental illnesses. Therefore, consider Neptune as a strong contributcry cause for many forms of anxiety states.

Pluto

This planet or energy seems to work mostly on a subconscious level and may be in focus in the case of more difficult anxieties. It may also have unexpected effects. Psychologically, it can indicate blockages and intrusive memories, including, perhaps, unpleasant experiences from very early in life. If these are then unexpectedly activated by other events, these can pop up to the surface and "mess things up." The revealing effect is common, and I usually recommend that you contact both a medium and a therapist if you are in a Pluto process in life. It might be a good time to look inside and find out things that you were not so aware of. Old relationships can be processed, or old wounds healed if needed. The consequence is that everything comes to the surface and is processed, much like a regression. Pluto is guaranteed at hand in the process of undergoing regression. Combinations between the Moon and Pluto are often interpreted as just a shock state and can mean both an inner revolution or a worst-case disaster.

From another more social perspective, Pluto is also linked to much that is dangerous or scary in life; and if exposed to risks and dangers, this could trigger some form of anxiety (For example, if a life danger arises). It is interesting to note that a majority of my clients often have this combination active in a forecast or transit when they contact me for the first time. Maybe I'm like a catalyst for this energy, emotional insights or disclosures.

In summary, we must note that crises belong to life, just like death, sickness and love. By looking at where you have your planets and see what aspects they have, you get a better opportunity not only to understand yourself, but also to better tackle the consequences you go through in life. My ambition is to give you a better understanding of how the different phenomena can be experienced in your own world through my examples.

Perhaps the best advice is otherwise to rely on the idea that nothing stops at any given moment. Any fear, discomfort, stress or anxiety you encounter is, and will always be, temporary, although it is most often perceived at the time that it will never be over.

Hell

"In a time of universal deceit,
telling the truth is a revolutionary act."
George Orwell (Sun + Moon in Cancer)

It is bad. Really very bad. The state of the Earth and Humanity is, at least, critical.

It may sound gloomy and scary, but I have to get these thoughts out of my head in contrast to everything beautiful and positive that spams social media. However, there is no *Dante's Inferno* or *Hell* after the end of life. At least not what you think or are afraid to end up in when you die (if you have been mean or evil). It's just scare propaganda from religious politicians and leaders to keep the masses in check.

Looking at the conditions of most people today, one can easily find that *Hell* is here and now on Earth today. (Geographically located in northern Norway, by the way): Poverty, famine, natural disasters, 9/11, tsunamis, *Estonia* and other ferry sinkings, oppression, dictatorships, war, violence, abuse of children, abuse of women, abuse of animals, smuggling, sex slaves, pedophiles, I.S. and beheadings on Youtube, HIV and AIDS, GMO-food, child prostitution, abductions (i.e., Josef Fritzl/Ariel Castro), racism, neo-nazism, animal experimentation to develop makeup, slaughtering dolphins and whales, China's rape on Tibet, North Korea's playing with missiles, I.S. hatred towards the entire Western hemispehre, Ku Klux Klan, terrorists and endless religious fanatics.

Man(Un)kind – Homo Sapiens

Looking from a historical perspective, one might wonder if it was "better in the old days."

If we look back to the "good old days," we can find: the Roman dictatorship threw Christians to the lions; permanent religious wars; permanent tribal wars in Africa; world dominators who only confiscated the countries they found; despots like Ghengis Khan, Alexander the Great, and in our time Stalin, who wiped out more Jews and dissidents than Hitler; punishment camps in Siberia; Hitler's Nazis who tried to eradicate not only Jews but also communists, socialists, mentally disabled, gays, Mormons and all non "pure-bred;" the fascists in Italy under Mussolini; "Cannibal-like" Ici Amin in Uganda; all military juntas in South and Central America; former eastern European states such as Poland, Hungary, Czechoslovakia, Bulgaria, Romania and East Germany; dictatorships in Iraq, Iran, Greece, Portugal, Algeria or Spain; the Spanish civil war in the 1930's; the fierce war in former Yugoslavia with hatred between Serbs, Croats, Christians and Muslims; the First and Second World Wars; the Korean War; Vietnam; Biafra; genocide of millions in Indonesia; the ever-ongoing conflict between Hindus and Muslims in India and Pakistan/Bangla Desh; Talibans in Afghanistan;

309

Chairman Mao's "Cultural Revolution;" the constant conflict in Northern Ireland between Catholics and Protestants and the eternal hatred in the Middle East between Jews and Arabs.

"Who threw the first stone?"

Everything almost started with Adam & Eve or Abel and Cain. Then we have the Inquisition and persecution of millions of heretics and unbelievers (mostly Jews) during the Dark Ages. Or how about the consistent genocide and extinction of North American indigenous Indians by "Europeans," the incomprehensible abuse and genocide of indigenous people in Central and South America by Spaniards and Portuguese or the abusive attitude of Norwegians and Swedes towards the northern Sami people.

I read somewhere that for 2,000 years of recorded world history, there are only four years of peace on earth. Mathematically, that makes war a "natural state." Dictatorships (one-party rule) are nothing new. Today we find them, for example, in: China, Syria, Azerbayan, Somalia, Sudan, Turkmenistan, Uzbekistan, Belarus, North Korea and Russia. Did I forget any other dictatorship country? We are also living today in the midst of a gigantic "religious World War III" where the militant Muslim I.S. (The Islamic State) simply want to eradicate all "unfaithful" in the western world. Today's warfare, though, is a bit more sophisticated. Anonymous terrorists train into pilots and fly into skyscrapers in New York, bombing in Thailand, Philippines, Madrid, London, Paris, Boston, Turkey, Egypt, Belgium and several African states. Even the confused Norweigan Anders Breivik "exterminated" "unclean" Norwegians (in total 77) in Oslo and Utöja.

The famous astrologer Michel Nostradamus suggested that the Moors (Muslims) should try to conquer the West. Does that suggest that all xenophobic refugee haters may be right?

You can't close your eyes and say that "it does not happen here." Sweden has long lived sheltered in a "duckpond," avoiding two World Wars, trying to act like the world conscience and making every effort to condemn everything and everyone. Former Prime Minister, Aquarius Olof Palme spewed courageously over Franco's dictatorship in Spain (called him "the devil's creature"), and Palme was more famous and respected abroad than in the duckpond here at home.

But even we have a hidden kind of hell, though it takes a different expression: concealed domestic violence, pedophilia, rape, bullying (including online bullying which is becoming more common), illegal smuggling of human beings, prostitution, killer gangs from former eastern states, criminal leagues laughing at the Swedish judiciary system, risk capitalists, professional politicians without a heart, addicts, neo-Nazis, homophobes and chicken and mink farmers.

There are also all the social injustices: the Social Security, Employment and Social Services act as police and harasses disabled and socially disabled and defenseless individuals. This reminds a little about the police state in the book *1984*. Geriatrics, schools and health care have been transformed into anonymous tiles in the risk capitalists' own monopoly game. In hospital, you are not a patient anymore, but a customer. Class society is clearer today than ever. The number of millionaires has never been as great as today. And there are market forces, commercialism and simple greed with parachutes, corrupt politicians and political "scandals" on a regular basis.

What about mental care and psychiatry today? The pharmaceutical industry today is governed almost exclusively by greed and profit interests. Cancer's 'riddle' has probably already been solved, but that is not profitable. The same with free energy threatens global corporations profiting on delivering energy (check Google on Nikola Tesla if you do not believe me). There are a wealth of intelligent people who invented alternative power sources and tools, but they are a threat to existing companies that want us to depend on electricity, oil, coal and nuclear power.

Is all this about fear? Does no one dare to speak their mind? Does no one dare to stand out, to go against the mainstream? Do all young people put up with this new society? Why do many people today put their heads in the sand and consoles, uninterested in GMOs, additives, colorants or cancerogens? Instead, they avoid and escape through weekend partying, taking "soothing" drugs, desperately losing weight, becoming consoling shopaholics, flying to warmer countries in the winter, turning the European Song Contest into a religion and daring not plan beyond their next status update on facebook.

Here is another denying avoidance: "Thank God for Netflix. Now I only have six seasons left of my favorite series. I hope the kids can handle their own I-pads so they can play games or watch their own series while I'm sleeping."

Long before the Internet, way back in 1969, John Lennon wrote, "Keep you doped with religion, sex and TV"(*Working Class Hero*).

I remember a scene from the movie *Eric the Viking* by the Monty Python gang. The world is about to go under. They sink slowly into the ocean, and they decide to appoint someone to investigate the matter. (Compared with climate conferences today). Blubb, blubb, blubb, and they sink slowly.

If the apocalypse is already here, or in any case on the right track, why do our politicians do nothing? The climate conferences are a bit pathetic and unfortunately remind you of the above-mentioned film scene. I just read that Trump does not "believe" in the climate threat and should also end paying US membership fees to the UN! Happy New Year!

Anyone remember December 21, 2012? This was when the world would supposedly go under. The planets would surely stand in a particular way with some mysterious point that would trigger the Earth axis magnetic poles to tip over, or what? I wrote a long article about the phenomenon on my website (still there) and faced a lot of unnecessary anxiety from close dear ones. I dared to say that the so-called *Apocalypse* is already here, NOW (2012). It is just so huge and fuzzy that we are not aware of it yet. Perhaps symbolically it started with the World Trade Center debacle on 9/11. It became a mega-psychosis all over the world. Islamic State was then born from the remains of the United States' widespread invasion of Iraq and Afghanistan, and today I.S. is more like a hydra monster: If you chop the head off, then two new ones grow back. "War is over," announced John Lennon.

"The power to keep despair away"

Yes, there are some positive powers and energies, people with love and generosity, but they do not always seem enough. Evil, greed and injustice dominate the scene today. The fact that many flee into drugs and escape reality (Saturn) is nothing strange or new.

But I absolutely believe you can choose a different way. One does not have to be religious and walk around and preach to the ignorant. Surfing online today offers a lot of positive alternatives. The first signals I discovered were the Environmental Movement in Sweden in the 70's. They warned about nuclear power, claimed there were poisons in the food we ate and dared question both politicians and big industry. This said by Hans Palmstierna and Björn Gillberg, two of my early heroes. Then I discovered Amnesty and Greenpeace. Many others sacrificed their lives in protest against oppression, like Buddhist monks who lit themselves on television. There were also the brave students at Tianmen Square in Bejing, China. There are still political prisoners and plenty of paranoid dictators yet today.

Historically, it is not only the religious prophets who tried to preach love. Who does not remember Mahatma Gandhi who brought the whole British Commonwealth on their knees with his non-violence philosophy. Nelson Mandela, who was imprisoned for 27 years, became president in apartheid´s South Africa.

Today we find different heroes. Computer freaks hacking and revealing power-makers and power conglomerates such as Wikileaks' Julian Assange, whistle blower Edward Snowden or network activist Aaron Swartz, who tragically killed himself after he received his sentence with millions in fines and imprisonment. Both Assange and Snowden have Moon in Scorpio, by the way.

Thanks to modern technology and the Internet, information is spread rapidly via social medias, and this benefits not least the grass roots or so-called protesters. The entire "Arab Spring" was followed via Youtube, Facebook, Twitter and SMS with a cellphone. The men of power can no longer hide in their armed castles. "*Power to the people*," as John sang, makes it easier today to change things for the better.

"Real" heroes today earn no money. Most are relatively invisible. But their influence and the influence of the mass are an unpleasant reality for our politicians today. They must listen and act or comment immediately, otherwise they will be questioned.

There are certainly people today who want to be well prepared to make an effort for those who have nothing or cannot. There are plenty of so-called NGO´s prepared to make an effort where needed to assist in collecting or supporting homeless people. But I also think of all hard-working nurses at stressed hospitals that do not earn the fraction of what sports stars, pop stars or movie stars do. These are good-hearted people who may stay for a few minutes more at a lonely pensioner's single bed. And there are firefighters who, with their lives at constant risk, save the lives of others. Certainly there are heroes, but not always in the spotlight.

I must admire organizations such as *Doctors Without Borders* or *Save the Children,* although many major organizations have fallen into stormy weather for irregularities and cheating. Yes, bad apples are everywhere. But if there were no non-profit organizations at all, a lot of relief efforts would collapse.

Looking at the ordinary hard-working person in his/her anonymous existence, I think there are more good-hearted ones than self-absorbed. Many struggle for bread and to make ends meet for their family and children. Think not least of all single parents, both mothers and dads, who may have to take care of themselves. Nevertheless, just being able to afford a smile or kind word, that's strength. Often you have to pretend it's not raining for the sake of the children.

I have no recipe for happiness but would like a little more honest and courageous politicians and spokesmen. Most politicians just think about their mandate and the time they get in the spotlight. Courageous politicians do not grow on trees. So, who will stand up for the weak? Many in the media and cultural workers have a big responsibility, including journalists, and not just the paparazzis who cover the nightly parties of high society and reveal when the King last farted. Brave journalists like Günther Wallraff (Google) has infiltrated many workplaces and revealed many embarrassments and prejudices. I think journalists like Wallraff do an heroic effort.

I believe it is a lot about responsibility and conscience (Saturn). We must dare to take responsibility for helping those in need and dare to follow our inner voice or conscience. We must dare to speak out and try to change what's wrong. Even so-called celebrities in film and music can take their responsibility. The Scorpio Leonardo di Caprio held a UN speech on climate change, and my own "guru" Roger Waters from Pink Floyd has a tough message with his concept in *The Wall*. There he dares to accuse both Jews and Arabs, as well as the multi-national companies and the war industry that indirectly governs the world today. Roger, of course, has his Moon in Scorpio. (also Google on *Zeitgeist* or *Thrive*).

The opposite of love is not hate, it is indifference. The one who is silent agrees? But there is a light on the horizon. For you, it may be important with your dreams and hopes, your longing for tranquility, staying healthy or just having a job. Ironically, I do not think money solves all problems, although it may be easier to cry in a Rolls-Royce than in an old tired VW. Money must be the greatest of all illusions today. Do you think billionaires can escape cancer, suicide or anxiety? Looking at alcoholism, it's actually more common among rich than poor people in society. That is a fact. Perhaps it is because they can afford to continue their addiction. The current "shots culture" that many young people watch on television, in movies and among the *beautiful people* (brats) at nightclubs today drink their skulls to pieces and party before they just drop and die.

One must be courageous to dare to refrain from drugs today. Dare to be sober and afraid, feel and dare to show feelings, longing, sorrow or loneliness. A person with a natural self-confidence does not have to take drugs to be happy or relaxed. "Do you want a drink? No thanks, I have confidence! "(From a sketch).

You must not escape the world's discouragement and misery just to appreciate life´s joy. Seek out more like-minded people and feel friendship or security in a group with the same goal. If you are vegan, you can hang out with other vegans. You can go to a party without drugs, or so I've heard...

Being a smoker in the 70's and 80's, I have no right to judge, but it seems deeply tragic to see young girls and guys who barely left puberty standing and sucking on cigarettes. Skinny, insecure and love-seeking, have they learned that you have to smoke to be tough or accepted? In my youth there was no one who said it was dangerous, even less for our totally ignorant parents. Smoking became glamorous in the 20th century, not least through the movie´s impact. I read that Martin Luther King was also a smoker, but he refused to be photographed with cigarettes because he would not be a bad example for younger people.

I am aware that much of my questioning can be perceived as moralizing; but nevertheless, I believe that you must follow your own instinct and inner conviction to live in balance with yourself. If you want to smoke, drink or take drugs, it's your free will and choice, but do not come and whine in 30-40 years time because you got cancer, have become overweight or depressed. I think it was the author Robert Green Ingersoll who wrote: "In nature there are neither rewards nor punishments - only consequences."

I strongly belive there are other ways to reduce your sadness, fear or lack of self-love. Some people often blame lack of time or money, and it may be ok sometimes; but what you do with your own time, you decide yourself. Certainly it's not so easy with the house full of kids to meditate or do yoga. But lack of money, I think, is a little pathetic. If you have a relatively wise budget and adjust your mouth to the food bag, you can still prioritize your expenses. It is an indirect lie that it would be more expensive to buy organic food. If you want to eat as healthy as possible, do it. It costs a little extra, but maybe you could cut expenses on other things, like travel, liquor, fun, or the latest computer model. Then it is up to everyone to decide what junk food they want to indulge in. If you want to give your kids millions of mixed candy with dyes and additives, fatty snacks, even fatter burgers and chips, you'll probably have to take the consequences of premature obesity, hyperactivity, sugar coma, early diabetes, allergic reactions or risk getting a diagnosis stamped on the forehead.

Life can still be both beautiful and wonderful

I love to wake up early mornings in September with birds singing, dew on the grass, light drizzle, the sun's first rays between tree branches. Go out barefoot and just listen and breathe. Feel both silence and nature's orchestra. I just love to walk in the woods all year round, mostly new roads. As the poet Tranströmer wrote: "To come to a glade in the forest where nobody has been in a hundred years." Feeling connected with everything that lives, the aura of the forest and positive energy fill both my soul and my mind. I need no company there. The residents of the forest see me and sneak away. I have encountered badger, hedgehog, copper snake, adder, hares, moose, deer, squirrels, cranes, Canadian geese and all crazy birds flocks cross and across.

Some people see my great passion for movies with light skepticism, but for me, movies are a multi-dimensional experience. I can cry and laugh at feel-good stuff like *Gilmore Girls* or movies like *Highlander* and *Love, Actually*. I feel grief, sadness and pain when I watch documentaries or feel intense emotions and passion with strong dramas. I sometimes choose an old epic saga like *Gone With the Wind* or *Spartacus* and see the story unfold to the end. If I just want to laugh or cry out laughing, I prefer an old silent movie with Buster Keaton, Chaplin or Harold Lloyd. The most beautiful and touching movies are actually black and white. The silent movie *Sunrise* is one of the best in the world, according to me. But film is a way for me to learn more, to hear other people's messages and insights, to share the lives of others and to get new experiences, to become more awake or conscious, but above all to understand that in contrast to many in the movies, my own life is pretty decent, actually. Everything is relative.

("*The Seven Sisters*" in Rondane National Park, Norway.)

When traveling, my soul lives, seeing new places and meeting new people, climbing mountain peaks like Krökla in Rondane, Norway, sit by strong rapids, feel small on earth but big in spirit. Photography is a wonderful art form. One can try to capture the magic moment and experience it again when you are back home. Filming is even more an enhancement and documentation of the experience. Still, I'm not thinking of shaky, clumsy, short little snatches posted on Facebook, taken by an Iphone.

Loneliness has never been any concern of mine. (*Loneliness* - Grand Funk Railroad). Even though I love people, like laughing or spreading joy, my periodical self-chosen loneliness never worries me. Rather, the opposite. Loneliness makes me strong and focused, relaxed and calm in both soul and body. I have never understood the concept of boredom. I have constantly planned more than I have time to and sometimes it seems almost unnecessary to go to sleep at night. All I need is a book for half an hour together with my guncatcher, my gray cat Paikea (name from the movie *Whale Rider* 2002), before I give in, put out the lights, make my affirmations, send light to them in my heart and pray my own homemade prayer. I think it's important to finish up every day and feel grateful for all I've got and experienced.

As a young boy, I lived for a long time as in *The Enigmatic People* as Olle Adolphson sang: strawberry straws, hay carts, thunderstorms and running nude in the pouring rain, mom's comforting arms, grandmother's always-tender eyes, solid, carefree days in the summer, ice cold feet in winter, on flushed ice, wobbling like *Bambi* on ice in wrong size skates. My childhood memories are more filled with bright than dark pictures. Still, today, I think that it's important to let children be children as long as possible. The agony of adulthood will come with seriousness and compulsion. Look and listen to your children. Suddenly they move away from home, and then it may be too late.

Rituals I have a little hard time with. I usually feel like an alien on a foreign planet. Same procedure every year. Because everyone else does them, you have to also. Christmas, New Years Eve, Easter, Midsummer, it never ends. Often, unconscious devotion to rituals can lead to silent compulsion for food orgies, intoxication, sugar shock or other ritual group behaviors. Failure to give Christmas presents is worse than forced group therapy. Maybe it's because I'd like to talk to one person at a time, but saloon-hunger and loud noise are not easy to overcome. Unfortunately, Christmas alone has become worse the older I become. It has become all sugar-sweet and commercial, all exploitation that only favors the trade, disappointed children who despite seventeen gifts still did not get what they wanted.

Love's power cannot be measured. It can scale mountains. You can give the gift of life for love. You can be prepared to give up everything for the one you love. In incarnation after incarnation, however, we seek love but only find new pain. Where is my "other half," we ask? "*If you can't be with the one you love, honey, love the one you're with"* (Stephen Stills). Love between two people can be the most wonderful thing to experience - if you are lucky. But love between parents and their children, or between siblings, or between best friends, are all probably even more important in the long run.

Love without sex or passion, manipulation, compulsion, complicated karma, guilt, loyalty based on need or consideration, or just because you want to save someone - these all lead to pain, not love.

In pain, however, there is a beautiful mourning. "*Certainly it hurts when buds burst.*" (Swedish poet Karin Boye). *Artistic depression*, said John Lennon. I don't know if I'm crazy, but the many forms of suffering can be very creative and inspiring. It can also lead you to insight. You may not always know exactly when you get together with someone, but definitely, almost on the hour, you know when it ends. Heartbreak has always existed and will always exist. No one gets away from it. Those you love, you must evenually lose, even if you meet on the other side. What we can possibly hope for is to make the best of the time we have together.

I must here and now acknowledge that I have been extremely lucky this time. When I asked William about my wife, he answered comically,

"Which one?" I've fallen in love at least ten times, possibly more, and there are people around me who never suffer from this madness. "*All lovers are deranged*" (David Gilmour). Isn't it weird? When you fall in love, you have found the right one and you do not have to search anymore. You're done. Eureka. Nevertheless, everything goes to hell when you wake up the day after, or ten years later. Surely it's strange?

I really loved my first infatuation with Ann-Sofie (photo below). We were both young, around fourteen or fifteen, relatively innocent, and we didn't know much about life or death. She was kind, a bit shy, thoughtful, responsive, humorous, enjoyed sex, laughed relentlessly and was absolutely tolerant of my mood swings. We were together a little over a year, then I broke up and moved on. My hunger for more was greater than her total devotion. What a fool I was. I describe this perhaps first true love with wonderful Ann-Sofie because I realize today that I perhaps did wrong. In addition, Ann-Sofie is not here with us anymore. She passed away a couple of years ago, probably due to severe alcohol abuse. However, I got the chance of a strange but fun phone call around 1998 when I had a sentimental trip back in time. When I heard her raspy hardened voice over the phone, I saw before me the young, shy, little giggly girl in front of me who said when I asked her on our first night out what her last name was, she replied, "Raunavaara, but I'm not Finnish." (She was afraid I would like her less if I thought she was from Finland). R.I.P my first teenage love, *Apti*.

The only photo of Ann-Sofie I have left, here with my best friend Ronnie, in the Southern Bishop's farm in 1971.

Since my other countless lovers are probably still alive, I do not mention them by name. Still, I want to pay tribute to all the women I loved, worshiped, cried with, laughed with, struggled with, who tried to save me, comforted me, put up with my whims and anxieties and put up with my being popular among other women. I have absolutely loved you all, short or long time, and you are many. Whether temporary or long-term does not matter. Love IS an optimum energy in which, at least, I've emptied all my energy and passion as much as I could. I have my Moon in Scorpio trine Mars in Pisces you know ...

From Darkness to Light

Hell is always very personal for each of us, and love may often be the culprit. Unrequited love is probably the worst thing that can happen. I have been lucky even in this phenomenon. I had a secret passion for

Elisabeth in high school, and she did not even know I existed. I adored her in secret and suffered from her absence. I do not know if I'm extra hard-headed, but I have never been really dumped or experienced unhappy love anytime seriously. If it means that love is not answered, I probably function as if my courtship is not answered, and I just move on. Getting stuck in low self-esteem or suicidal egoism was probably never for me. "Had you been twenty years younger, Jacob, so ..." is what they say instead today. (BIG SMILE).

Love is nevertheless the best and easiest way out of everyone's personal *hell*. If you do not have anyone that you can focus all your energy on, maybe you can focus on others who need you, for example, your parents, siblings, best friends, co-workers or teammates. If there is no one at all, you can always get a budgie, cat or dog. In the worst case, only *facebook* remains (the last resort!). There you will get as many friends as you like ("*facebook* saved my life"). Excuse my irony, but I hope you get the drift. In the world today (2017), there are 7.4 billion people, which means it should be statistically possible there is one for you as well.

We all want love, but it can't be the only meaning of life. I do believe that the meaning of life is a puzzle of needs and tasks. We want a lot of things, but do not always get everything we want. We try to avoid discomfort and accidents, yet we are forced to the dentist and the cemetery. Perhaps it's all about attitude. If you see life as only suffering, you might as well convert to Buddhism. However, if you think that dreams can come in and wonders happen, you can always strive to make it better for those you meet in life. Giving love or kindness costs nothing. Helpfulness and care should not be forced.

When the child cries, you comfort. When your neighbor is affected by an accident, you are at hand.

The last part of my own insight is perhaps a little hard to take in. The term *Healing* has today become a hazy phenomenon that many might associate with especially talented people, like Jesus, who could really heal. However, I am convinced that everyone has the power within themselves. But most are not aware of it. Or they dare not believe in what they are capable of. I think the heart chakra can both heal and help others. You do not even have to be in the same place. Time and space are just illusions. There is what is called distance healing today. Read Betty Shine or Sylvia Browne for more information if you want to know more. I think anyone who wants can get the power to heal. Maybe you won't cure cancer or take away all difficult mental symptoms; but perhaps you can relieve pain by filling the aura and the etheric body with your channelled healing energy.

The hard thing about this is that you have to dare to use all the love in your heart. It's not the easiest thing to do, and most people do not believe or dare not use this force. How could they do that, they wonder, when they can barely brush their teeth. Could I be able to do something for another? Yes, by using an open chakra, but it is not always easy. Let visualized light flow freely into and around the person you think of or have in front of you. I have read a lot of books describing the phenomenon but never claimed myself as able to do this. The times I try to send energy or light, the person is not always aware of it, but neither is it necessary.

Opening your heart chakra means absolute honesty, free from prejudices, fears or preconceived opinions about both yourself and the person you are sending light to. Some call this a kind of *Christ awareness,* and it is an appropriate description. Jesus himself had achieved such a high frequency in his personal vibration that he could easily manipulate matter or the physical body. He is himself a pure symbol for an all-encompassing love. Can we mortals really do what he did? Already, there is where doubt stops you. Perhaps it is best that most people live like zombies, completely unaware of their inner forces, because otherwise we would have to scrap most part of medical care apparatus and the church!

Surely there is a life after this one. But there is also a spiritual dimension all around where love, light, concern, empathy, solidarity and humanity rule. The problem may be that you can't make money on love. It just won't pay off.

If nothing else, you might sleep better if you tried to "pull your straw to the stack" in your own way. I myself can only focus on one person at a time. That's my strategy. I can always hope that I saw some positive seeds along the way among the over 2,300 clients I have worked with. Hopefully, with this book, maybe I reached some more.

Death

("Who are you?" - "I've walked a long time by your side. I'm Death.*")*

Many certainly recognize the quote from Ingmar Bergman's *The Seventh Seal*. Bergman processed and managed to understand his own agony through the film.

Everyone is affected by death, throughout life, in one way or another. It touches every life, either through movies, television, the web, books or other media, and everyone has their own relation to death, whether in a positive or negative (fearful) way. In addition, we all suffer sooner or later from family and friends' deaths in our own closeness, with funerals, sorrow and parting.

My curiosity and my great interest in death have probably always existed. However, I never realized the proximity of death until I was nearly nine years old. In the summer of 1965, my grandfather quickly became ill and died shortly after from stomach cancer. Uranus passed over my Mercury that summer (new thoughts and changes). That same spring, my twin sisters Anna and Kajza were born. Saturn passed through Pisces opposite my Mercury (siblings) and perhaps gave me a more serious mind. At the same time, my world image was diminishing because I was no longer the center of my mother's attention.

Death, this constantly taboo mystery, has followed me and prepared me for life and for the life after this. If you talk about life after this life, should there not have been a life before this one? This trip back in time can be found in another chapter.

Death surrounds us constantly. You can't turn on your television, read a newspaper or go online without meeting it in millions of forms. Celebrities die like flies, and it is always tragicomic how "surprised" most people become. Did they think they would live for 200 years? Yes, I know that many die too early through sickness, by accident or cancer, but constantly this astonished reaction?

If people abuse themselves and live in a self-destructive way, it may not be that strange that they die prematurely. I have also read several books that have raised the topic of dying "prematurely" in an in-depth manner; for example, Peter NcII's book describing his own process, knowing that he had an incurab e disease.

What then is the great fascination about death?

Personally, I think the most common fear may be because you do not know where you go, or because of the pain of losing your loved ones in this life.

Purely astrologically, there are several factors to analyze, even though the Scorpio's sign is most often associated with death. Scorpio is also usually linked to birth. I call this sign and the 8th House for the beginning and end of life: "From the Maternity Hospital to the Cemetery." We often associate death with both Pluto and Mars or also with Scorpio and the 8th House. When we meet new life at birth, we stand at the gateway between two worlds, right?

However, there are usually a series of aspects and combinations that tell you more about your own attitude and relationship with everything that concerns birth and death. For myself, I easily recognize my "obsession" on the subject having my Sun conjunct Pluto and my Moon and Saturn in Scorpio square the Sun. In addition, I have the Sun, Jupiter, Uranus and Pluto in the 8th House of Scorpio. The 8th House points also to Cancer, which can be interpreted as a strong emotional attitude about death, and the Moon's conjunction to Saturn in Scorpio implies a deeply serious attitude to everything concerning death. Add the Moon's square to death's own planet, Pluto, in the 8th House and then you might understand my interest better. Looking at it with a tiny bit of sick humor, you probably realize that I should have died several times already (many exits).

Although death is constantly present, you do not always talk about it. You can be forced to visit a funeral of tears, parting and sorrow. Personally, I didn't attend my first funeral until I was an adult. Nowadays the frequency has increased. It is like the pastor Daniel Björck said, "death times" sometimes. I worked one year as a verger and saw the funeral arrangement from the inside, though never inside the coffin.

Death can hit anyone at any time. Someone we know or know about is being murdered, dying or receiving any form of cancer. One can suffer from natural death within the family, as well as the curse of outlasting your own child. Everyone has known someone who died too early or participated in any collective mourning. I'm thinking in these times mainly about the I.S. and suicide bombers, the World Trade Center, the *Estonia* ferry disaster, the tsunami in 2004 or Breivik's massacre in Norway, 2011.

Who does not remember when John F. Kennedy or his brother Bobby or Martin Luther King was shot? Or when John Lennon was shot in 1980? I remember clearly when Lady Di died, but maybe I didn't feel the same sadness because I didn't know so much about her. In recent years, lots of famous faces have passed away, not always for natural reasons. Whitney Houston, Robin Williams or actor Paul Walker (in a car accident) to name a few. Every year the Oscars also have a beautiful memorial ceremony remembering all who passed in the industry the past year.

I also believe that the fear of death makes us both irrational and sometimes even self-destructive. We over-indulge and rush from one thing to another instead of staying in the moment and genuin ely enjoying our lives. Many save piles of money while constantly worrying about doing a bad deal. I can't help but wonder what these people will spend their money on when they are old, sick, tired and lonely?

Many feel that everything must be done now – at once. Tomorrow it may be too late. The fear of our own death probably makes us more likely towards gluttony in our instinctive habits, such as overeating, partying, sex abuse, etc. Many forms of addiction can probably be attributed to different degrees of the fear of death anxiety. We think this anxiety must be combated, attenuated or eliminated. Habits and routines (Moon) become important in order to experience safety in everyday life.

As one of my ex-wives said: "Do not fill life with years, but fill the years with life." On a daily basis I can frustratedly see many people fill their lives with, in my opinion, purely meaningless activities. In order not to be accused of pride, I am ashamed to admit that I have also "filled my life with years" for long periods of time. Death nevertheless gives me an increased reverence to life, and I can only hope that I'll get time enough to finish the fraction of my work here today before my own curtain goes down.

As most of you already know, I rarely or never talk much about death in my interpretations. If I have ever touched the subject, it has always been for a positive reason; for example, if the person is inclined towards a long life or if death may come suddenly or painlessly. Anyone who has Venus or Jupiter in Scorpio or in the 8th House can appreciate his or her luck.

I neither can nor will reveal the day of your death. I have never even wanted to know how to figure it out. My former colleague Roland Skogkvist (RIP) provoked people in the 80's by claiming "I can see your death day" (Google articles). It might have been just to scare the shit out of a journalist. I can, however, know how to speculate in this mysterious moment, but I still think that it is more visible in your loved one´s charts when *you* die because it indicates more strongly in *their* lives than yours.

I can remember an opportunity more than 25 years ago when I was contacted by a distressed client. Her husband was very ill, and she wanted to know a bit forward into the future to prepare herself. At the prognosis I made it looked very "bright" for her husband, but the more miserable for herself so I got a little split. After a few months she called back saying that her husband had passed away, but she was grateful for my honesty. Apparently, the analysis was correct for both of them.

On another occasion about 30 years ago, I was contacted by an elderly lady in Skåne who wanted a birthchart interpretation of her son. She and her husband had just one son, and he had been murdered in his 20s. Now they just wanted a more complete picture of the son they never got to see growing up. It gave me a strange feeling, but I did a complete analysis of the son that made them very grateful, but I did so without references to his death. They thought it was nice to know more about their beloved son.

How can you relate to death in life? I don't want to make a cookbook of all examples, but rather list the most common and clearest trends for those who are curious. Please note that you must NOT interpret these literally. Everything is included in larger patterns that can vary with both stronger and weaker trends.

The positions of your planets

If you have the Sun, Moon, Ascendent, MC or Mercury in Scorpio, you may have it easier to accept death in your vicinity. I read many years ago that if there is any zodiac sign that commits suicide out of pure curiosity, it would be Scorpio, just to find out what will happen!

Venus in Scorpio or in aspect to Pluto may have a soothing effect towards death, perhaps almost painless (maybe to die happy like Romeo & Juliet). At worst, with this aspect the person may become a victim of jealousy (Pluto).

Mars' effects, however, conversely can be a little more unpleasant. Death may be caused by an accident, violence or other bodily harm. Mars in Scorpio or with an aspect to Pluto often occurs in fighter´s charts. Mars also indicates damage to the head or face, like sharp or fiery hot things. Those with this aspect should perhaps try to avoid too many conflicts, and definitely avoid physical provocations.

Jupiter can have widely different effects. "Success" with death may indicate a painless death, or at least painlessly mitigating circumstances. Symbolically, death can occur during a long journey or abroad, far from where you were born. Jupiter's connection to both Scorpio and the 8th House also suggests a strong intuition and interest in death. This aspect is also positive for inheritance and will. Their death can also be noticed, for example through the media, if they were "famous."

Saturn in Scorpio can amplify a serious view of death but also show a death at old age. It may also mean that you work in this area, within the church or perhaps at a funeral office.

Uranus in Scorpio or in aspect to Pluto can mean a sudden or unexpected death, which may seem painless, but probably very unexpected. It might be you die for strange or weird reasons or to die in an unusual way.

Neptune in Scorpio or in aspect to Pluto could mean that death occurs from a drug influence, under the influence of medications or at a hospital. Neptune also symbolizes water and long journeys (Titanic), which suggests "stay home" instead. These contacts, however, are a bit fascinating. Spontaneous curiosity may mean a greater spiritual view of life and thus another view even on death. Strong religiosity is common. If so, death and the "other side" can be a comfort.

Pluto in Scorpio, which everyone has who is born approximately between 1984 and 1995, is indeed linked to death, but it appears to be on a more subconscious level. More interesting is in which house it is in and to what other planets it forms an aspect. Generally, a generation was born that can have a very intense and curious view of everything related to death and sexuality. In the negative aspect, there may be a stronger frequence in both abortion and rape.

The Ascendant in Scorpio may seem to have a crass view on death and even act a bit disrespectfully, like mafiosos or criminals. But it also shows a boldness and open attitude to the whole concept of death.

MC in Scorpio is similar to the Ascendent and may show a greater interest and perhaps "career" in areas linked to Death or the maternity ward. Equally occurring among murderers as midwives. The self-image, however, gives an intensity in all commitments and they are often very skilled in their passion.

Sexuality

The link to sexuality, such as abortion or rape, may depend on our ability to reproduce, i.e., propagate and "live on" through our offspring. In the case of death, abortion is a method of dying or killing.

Between January and November, 2016, around 38 million (!!!) abortions were made. On average, that is 90,000 a day. Perhaps it feels strange, but a strong sexuality can simply be a strong survival instinct on the subconscious level.

Orgasm is said to be an experience of temporary death or perhaps a temporary heavenly experience. Perhaps the sex addict suffers from pure death anxiety. Nymphomania may be a form of a hysterical need for confirmation, but it may also be caused by some diffuse underlying fear similar to unsound masturbation. I read that Swedish poet Gustaf Fröding suffered from obsessional masturbation. However, Fröding also suffered from alcoholism and diabetes and went in and out of the asylum.

I read that France has a legal term called "crime passionnel." It means that crimes committed during feelings of jealousy are often considered a little more mild than otherwise. Older laws gave someone the right to kill if the spouse was unfaithful. (*Hey Joe* - Jimi Hendrix).

Personally, it is a little hard for me to "mourn" when someone passes away. Perhaps this is due to my own view of life. In a little humble way I often say that "the person in question has been released" from this hard Earth life. Nevertheless, there is of course lamentation for the person, but that is probably just for my own sake. Why is it worse when one's pets die? Maybe it's' because you can not talk to them beforehand and explain how much you will miss them. I have cried blood when my pet dogs, cats and budgies died.

We must all end up dying sooner or later. As Gandalf says in *The Lord of the Rings*: "All you have to decide is what to do with the time that is given to you."

"*I have no fear of death*," Katharine Hepburn reportedly said at age 85. "*It must be wonderful, like a long sleep. But let's face it: it's how you live that really counts*." - actress Katherine Hepburn. (Died at age 96).

Suicide

Robin Williams himself said that "*suicide is a permanent solution to temporary problems*," but it's hard for those battling with mental illness to realize that fact on their own.

Unfortunately, this dismal phenomenon is meant to highlight a very common problem today. Actor Robin Williams is just one in the very long line of people who could not go on living. We have poet Karin Boye, director Tony Scott (jumped from the Golden Gate Bridge), Japan's artist Mishima (who commited *seppuku* or *hara-kiri* with a sword), Jim Jones (religious cult leader who ordered mass suicide from his followers), Hitler and Eva Braun, Hermann Göring, Heinrich Himmler, Ariel Castro (convicted of abduction in 2013), Kurt Cobain, Keith Emerson, Eric Harris and Dylan Klebold (Columbine School massacre), Ernest Hemingway, Ulrike Meinhof, Marilyn Monroe, Sylvia Plath (Scorpio), Ivar Krüger, author Wilhelm Moberg, George Sanders, Aaron Swartz (computer genious), Amanda Todd, Vincent van Gogh, director James Whale (*Frankenstein*), Virginia Wolfe, Philip Seymour Hoffman, L'Wren Scott, Whitney Houston, Amy Winehouse, Mikael Hutchence (INXS) and Christine Chubbuck (who in protest shot herself during a live broadcast TV).

I have not yet analyzed all of the charts from the above list, but their modes of suicide were either with drugs/pills, with rifles, by hanging or drowning. In most cases, too, the suicide is preceded from a long-term depression or other disturbances such as manic-depression or borderline depression. However, it is an act of desperation from most on the list and often caused as an effect of excessive self-abuse. Robin Williams also struggled for many years with alcoholism.

I read on a website that Sweden in 2012 was in 60th place in the world with "just" an average of 11 suicides per 100,000 inhabitants. However, it was with the ratio of 16 men and only 6 women. Worldwide so far through last year (as of November in 2016), there had been 976,000 suicides, which averages around 3,000 per day. What a wonderful world!

I don't want to undully moralize on this issue, but I must make it clear that many people do not feel good today. The reasons can be many. But not getting the help you need before it's too late is tragically typical in our modern society. Far too many do not care or dare not intervene. If you can't stand the pressure, the pace or the competition, then you´re done for.

Which planets, signs and aspects reveal how we make the final decision? Purely astrologically, there are several to look for. You just can't only point out sensitive Cancer or fragile Pisces. Many impulse-like fire signs such as Aries, Leo and Sagittarius can act recklessly and with exaggeration if they "snap" for unexplained reasons. Even the seemingly intelligent Gemini, Libra and Aquarius may face mental melt-down if their world becomes too overwhelming. Perhaps it is my personal prejudice, but I still believe that the earthly signs of Taurus,

Virgo and Capricorn are "best" at not being so often in the danger zone. Perhaps these signs posess the right mix of common sense and a penchant for the material.

In the horoscope there must probably also be an outline for the person to end up in this dead end. The Moon's position and its aspects, I think, are the most important to analyze because they control all emotional experiences as well as our personal safety. In addition, I strongly believe that different combinations with both Saturn (depression), Uranus (hysteria/anxiety), Neptune (drugs) and Pluto (fears) must be in the basic horoscope.

These can then be triggered or endangered at a later stage in life, and this can be traced through a forecast or by studying only the current transits (current situation).

This is where I think astrology could make a huge beneficial difference for the person or his/her family, both as support and explanation. If this issue turns out to be transient, the person can more easily tackle the situation. The difficulty with anxiety symptoms is that when they occur, one believes that it will never go away and will therefore have to live with it forever. By analyzing the birth chart, one can easily determine if it is long-term or temporary and can then take appropriate steps with the necessary measures. If the problem is of a more severe nature, it is advisable to consult both physicians and therapists to get a rational overview of the situation and help with a treatment plan. It may even be necessary to include some time with medication.

However, as an astrologer, I can never make decisions or advise anyone if my advice violates the person's own attitude or the doctor's. Nor can I assume responsibility for a person's recovery or medication. Astrological information works best as a timetable, i.e., how long a phenomenon or difficulty can sustain.

Certainly I have encountered many people in a difficult crisis, but I have never been told that someone killed him/herself afterwards. Probably on the contrary, according to many praise words, though sometimes I wouldn't hear about it until years afterwards. Throughout, I have to say thankfully that most experienced the analysis as a revealing catharsis or purification process. It is not easy to accept or realize one's shortcomings, but many explanations are still for the best. Either the problem is far back in time or is of temporary nature.

I made a mistake once at a lecture (in Nybro) when I referred to a visit to an astrologer as a spiritual filling of a tooth root canal, and that evening I received no orders. Perhaps that wasn't the smartest advertisement.

What I want to say is that I unfortunately realize that some people do not endure life any more. I find it just depressing that psychiatry or social security networks do not work better. There is no bed of roses to live today. Especially younger people are struggling with their existence and forced to humiliate themselves in pursuit of both work and housing. It is not uncommon for young people to move back home again, and of course, against their will. Employment, Insurance and care centers seem to act more like the police than support. If you were young in the 70's, these services were free, and there were cheap apartments and jobs everywhere. But it was a long time before all greedy directors in companies decided that outsourcing (moving production to less expensive countries) was more profitable and closed down factory after factory in Sweden. The list can be done any time. (Telecom Company Ericson in 2016).

If you develop cancer, experience high family mortality, come down with any other incurable disease or end up in a more severe depression, it is certainly not easy to get through hell on your own. I know from my own experience that a mix of existential anxiety and panic attacks can break the strongest psyche. "Been there - done that."

Here you have to balance with a lot of support. Unfortunately, I do not have much leftovers for either psychiatry or the usual medical care today. Doctors do not have time, nurses merely answer the phone and sighs, and in the psyciatric ward it's easier to prescribe drugs than to devote time wholeheartedly to the patient. I saw a short, somewhat cruel scene in Roy Andersson's *You, Living* movie from 2007, about a psychiatrist's confession. There were no beautiful words.

Purely astrologically, it is not just about Scorpio, Pluto and the 8th House. If you find yourself in a temporary or prolonged crisis, temporary medication may sometimes be necessary, but always combined with greater support and safety from the environment. Conversational therapy, CPT or hypnotherapy can be a good complement, depending on what suits you best. Rest homes and spa resorts were more common way back in time. Where are they today? No outcast or homeless person can afford to make a reservation in a sanatorium today.

I still have to end this with my own personal perception of death. In my view, after reading a lot of books, there is no real death. Everything is a big trickery inventory invented by the church and the men of power to threaten us with reprisals in the afterlife if we do not take care. It is only the physical body that dies. In my view, many people think that death is only the beginning of life between lives. There's also no hell in the sense you're brainwashed to believe. Yes, there is a hell, but not after life. It is here and now, in this we call life. That is my absolute conviction. Read more in the chapter on "Mediums" and Michael Newton and his hypnosis regression research, if you doubt.

"I´m so much happier now that I´m dead."
(Amy in the movie *Gone Girl*, 2014)

Nils Ferlin: "*The stars doesn´t care if someone is born or dies.*"

" *Melancholy Man*"

(from The Moody Blues album – *A question of Balance* 1970)

I´m a melancholy man, that´s what I am
All the world surrounds me, and my feet are on the ground

I´m a very lonely man, doing what I can
All the world astounds me and I think I understand
That we´re going to keep growing, wait and see

When all the stars are falling down
Into the sea and on the ground
And angry voices carry on the wind
A beam of light will fill your head
And you´ll remember what´s been said
By all the good men this world´s ever known

Another man is what you´ll see
Who looks like you and looks like me
And yet somehow, he will not feel the same
His life caught up in misery, he doesn´t think like you and me
cause he can´t see what you and I can see

God

This is a sensitive but important subject, regardless of your own attitude. I want to say that it is an embarrassment that those who do not consider themselves believing in God at the same time look down and have a slight contempt for all who call themselves religious. The majority of the people of the world believe in a God of different names, or a higher power; and if you have no money or power and are in a vulnerable situation, it might not be strange to rely on some kind of higher power. Personally, I have a light rainbow-colored attitude that I have come across after many years of searching for an opinion. Today, I not only accept the attitude of religious people, but I can also admire them for their courage to stand up for their convictions. Nor should you despise the beliefs of others and "believe" that you know better or more than anyone else. This is discussed in a special way in the film *Contact* (1997) with Jodie Foster. (SPOILER ALERT) When they ask her if she believes in God, she can't answer "Yes" and thus is not approved for the mission.

Many times I have been asked, "Do you *believe* in astrology?" I have then answered, "No, but I know it's working".

Previously, astrology may have been seen as a kind of religion, such as to worship Gods in the sky in the form of different zodiac signs. Today, however, astrology is neither a religion nor a pure science. I would like to more closely summarize astrology as an approach to the world and life, to consider life on the basis of cycles and consequences. Astrology is not fateful as many believe, because we always have a choice, and we live with the consequences of our own decisions, whether "good" or "bad."

How many times have you heard someone say, "Oh, my God!" when fear or shock strikes and you think you're going to die? It's not the Prime Minister or your budge you're calling for, but rather that mythological figure that is often the last resort. How many times have you not seen and heard in movies where characters in their agony call on the Lord or God if they could just get off?

I heard in one of Woody Allen's movies a funny story. It was the Jew who came to heaven when he died, and when he met Saint Peter, he had to ask, "Was it really that we Jews were the Chosen People?" Whereupon Saint Peter answered, "Of course." Then the Jew asks again, "Ok, but can you choose someone else the next time around?" It's obviously not that easy to be "chosen."

In the critically acclaimed television series *West Wing* they already raise the problem of the Old Testament view of condemnation of people when the president himself comes in and berates a religious fanatic whose view is completely bizarre.

God's fault?

A common criticism of all concepts of God is to look at everything negatively that happens with war, disasters and human suffering. Look at all the wars that took place in the name of God, as if God Himself participated. This is obviously pathetic, because it is humans who start wars, not God. Natural disasters are not the fabrications of God, but perhaps more of a consequence of the Earth's own way of reacting with "growing pains." The continental plates are constantly moving and causing earthquakes, volcanic eruptions and storms. Hurricanes and other weather phenomena today may be related to, among other things, climate change. To blame God is nevertheless to overdo it. Or is blaming God a way of doing nothing about anything at all? If "He She" saved everyone who suffers or has difficulties, then all karma would disappear too. The very concept of God that is in the majority perceived is also nothing for feminists, as God is referred to as "He." Today maybe God should rather be gender neutral (Swedish *Hen*).

In the case of war, of course, there have been conflicts and massacres in the name of the Lord. Look at the Inquisition or the cruel Crusades. Today, we have I.S. (the Islamic State), which is a time-typical phenomenon where Muslim fanatics are promised a place in heaven if they act as suicide bombers. The pilots who flew into the World Trade Center Towers were fanatic Muslims. And look at the Christian Right Movement and Ku Klux Klan in the United States. You can be afraid of the dark for less.

Also that comes to mind is the inhuman rape of Tibet in 1959, when the Dalai Lama fled Tibet and the Chinese slaughtered monks and nuns. Mao called all religions "poison." If I had chosen my religion, I would probably have chosen to be reborn as a Tibetan Buddhist monk. The Dalai Lama, still living in exile, preaches like Gandhi, with non-violence. It is better support Tibet and protest against China's oppression and assault.

What signs are associated with God or religion?

Of course, it is first and foremost the planet Neptune or the sign Pisces when looking at religion or God as well as certain special features in our own chart. But also the Sagittarian influence is important. Sagittarius represents our moral view of man and is the basis for all of our legal communities on which today's legal and moral acts are based. You do not say "sin," but rather punish people who violate the law. Murderers are executed or have a lifetime sentence, depending on where they live. Sagittarius symbolizes both our higher consciousness and our philosophical ruminations and thoughts about existence. Here we find convinced religious people, but also, ironically, agnostics and atheists. Many with their Sun, Moon or Ascendant in Sagittarius seem to want to follow their vision and share it with others (the arrow is knowledge conveyed outwardly into the world). Therefore, usually they are drawn to work as a journalist, teacher, writer or within the church as well as almost everything in the field of online trading and the spreading of information.

Pisceans, however, strive a bit further away than that. They look beyond the horizon and dream about the other side, or life after this. They take more often than others their refuge in God or into their own dreams and take more care of others from a more pure empathy or human love. You can think about your own attitude if you are looking at the importance of Sagittarius and Pisces in your own life. I must say that it is very common with people who do not have a clue on the concept of God or even think religious thoughts, that they often "miss" Neptune or Jupiter in their chart. That is, they have no clear or strong contacts with these planets or signs. This is, of course, contrary to the more self-convinced spiritual persons. However, Neptune is mostly influenced by all kinds of spirituality.

Jesus

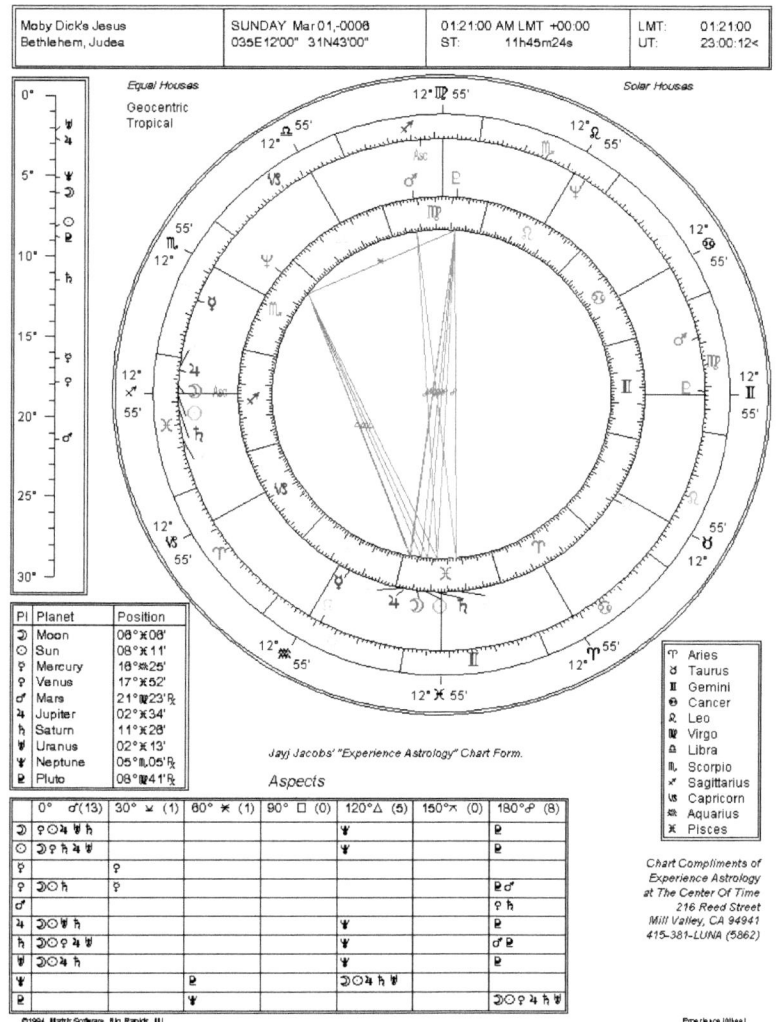

Moby Dick's Jesus Bethlehem, Judea	SUNDAY Mar 01,-0006 035E12'00" 31N43'00"	01:21:00 AM LMT +00:00 ST: 11h45m24s	LMT: 01:21:00 UT: 23:00:12<

Equal Houses
Geocentric
Tropical

Solar Houses

Pl	Planet	Position
☽	Moon	08°✕08'
☉	Sun	08°✕11'
☿	Mercury	18°✕25'
♀	Venus	17°✕52'
♂	Mars	21°♍23'℞
♃	Jupiter	02°✕34'
♄	Saturn	11°✕28'
♅	Uranus	02°✕13'
♆	Neptune	05°♏05'℞
♇	Pluto	08°♍41'℞

♈	Aries
♉	Taurus
♊	Gemini
♋	Cancer
♌	Leo
♍	Virgo
♎	Libra
♏	Scorpio
♐	Sagittarius
♑	Capricorn
♒	Aquarius
♓	Pisces

Jayj Jacobs' "Experience Astrology" Chart Form.

Aspects

	0° ♂(13)	30° ⚺ (1)	60° ✶ (1)	90° □ (0)	120°△ (5)	150°⚻ (0)	180°♂ (8)
☽	♀☉♃♅♄				♆		♇
☉	☽♀♃♅♄				♆		♇
☿		♀					
♀	☽☉♄	♀					♇♂
♂							♀♄
♃	☽☉♅♄				♆		♇
♄	☽☉♀♃♅				♆		♂♇
♅	☽☉♃♄				♆		♇
♆			♇		☽☉♃♄♅		
♇			♆				☽☉♀♃♄♅

Chart Compliments of
Experience Astrology
at The Center Of Time
216 Reed Street
Mill Valley, CA 94941
415-381-LUNA (5862)

Experience Wheel

(Pictured representation of Jesus "materialized" by Sai Baba. From the book *Follow Jesus*, 1982. Sai Publications, London)

For example, we can take the phenomeron of Jesus, which according to the astrological tradition, is the archetype of the sign of Pisces. There are many who think that he was not born on Christmas Day, the 25th of December, but in February-March when the Sun was in Pisces. I have seen many different examples of charts where he would be born not only in Pisces, but also in 7 BC (i.e., 7 years before the year 0).

This thesis is based on the fact that the three magi (wise men), the word actually means "those who look at the stars" (astrologers), observed a powerful and unusual conjunction in the sky that was in the Pisces sign between the largest planets Jupiter and Saturn. This conjunction was at its strongest in year 7 before Christ and not the year 0. In addition, historically, Palestine was associated with the very sign of Pisces. That's why the astrologers/magi went there. The Bible told that a king would be born in David's house. Everything culminates with several other planets jostling in Pisces around these days, so it is astrologically more likely that the person who was called Jesus was really born during Piscean springtime.

Google "Don Jacobs - Moby Dick's chart of Jesus." It is incredibly fascinating to study that person's chart who was actually born the night of March 1, 7 BC. "Joshua bar Joseph ish Nazareth" may even have the Ascendant in Sagittarius if he was born at night.

"Someone" must have been born "then" and "there" in Palestine. If so, then this person was born with his Sun, Moon, Venus, Jupiter, Saturn and Uranus all in Pisces. Simply put, this is an extremely psychically, hazy, kind-hearted person with great responsibility and an extremely strong emotional life. This Moon-Uranus aspect is common among psychics, and the Moon conjunct the Sun is the absolute synthesis between his masculine and feminine energies. To all of these, except Venus, Neptune is at the beginning of Scorpio in a powerful trine. Talk about water, Pisces, emotions and spiritual inspiration!

Neptune in your map

Purely astrologically, Neptune enables you to utilize both the attitude and ability to use these psychic/emotional energies. Without generalizing, it can be noted that so-called Neptunian people are more loving, empathic and gentler in mind than most who lack a clear or strong Neptune. It does not have to mean that the person in question is religious, but rather more likely that their interest is in the beautiful arts, music or other creativity.

Without showing any statistics, I can add that not only Pisces and Sagittarius seem to have spiritual needs. Even Capricorn and Taurus can have spiritual needs. Yes! They do! They might have their Moon in Pisces or Sagittarius! My experience with Pisces and Sagittarius nevertheless makes them experience life a bit harder with "this bad reality" we all have to live in. Some escape through drugs. Others take their refuge in meditation or privacy. But they all show a significantly higher level of human understanding as well as higher ethics and morals.

Here are some simple statements about the Sun and Moon's contact with Neptune. Do not read literally without regard to other planets and aspects involved. With just your birth year, you can see in what sign Neptune was located.

Generally, Neptune was in Cancer at the beginning of the last century (1901-1915), then in Leo (1915-1929), Virgo (1928-1943), Libra (1942-1957), Scorpio (1956-1970), Sagittarius (1970-1985), Capricorn (1984-1998), Aquarius (1998-2012) and now Pisces (2011-2026). On March 30, 2025, Neptune enters for the first time into Aries.

Years overlap due to retrograde motion. It has thus not passed through Aries, Taurus or Gemini since the 19th century. You can see in what year you were born where your Neptune is. Keep in mind that it may overlap two signs some years. Then you have to ask me.

Sun and Neptune

All the Sun's aspects of Neptune provide a flow of inspiration that you can interpret as "divine inspiration." However, these people seem to lack a little realism and have difficulty in manifesting their own will while showing more responsiveness to the needs and feelings of others. The transition to abstract dimensions is common and strong regardless of aspects.

Moon and Neptune

All the Moon's contacts/aspects with Neptune are multi-faceted, depending on which sign it ends up in. The Moon is perhaps strongest in Pisces or Sagittarius, but other signs as well show how emotional needs are expressed. Since the late 19th century, Neptune has only passed through a little more than half the Zodiac, so people living today can only have this combination from Leo up to Pisces.

Moon-Neptune in Libra (people who were born between 1942-1957) are the peace-loving diplomats. They are those who see conversation and cooperation as ways to harmony and balance. The negative tendency can be an inability to collaborate because of a too-quick disappointment in other people.

Moon-Neptune in Scorpio (1956-1970), however, is very different. Here we can see intensive devotion may exist, but also a hidden fear of everything mysterious or incomprehensible. There can be both religious fanatics or people who sacrifice everything to others. On the negative side, there is a suspicion of "hazy" or religious people, and a pure fear of the unknown is common.

Moon-Neptune in Sagittarius (1970-1985) people are perceived as visionaries, for good or bad. The positive ones have a high human morality and amazing visions, while others can easily be disappointed in all that is worldly and carefree. An example of this is "The Good Mother" who takes care of everything and everyone. Those on the negative side tend towards blind devotion to everything mysterious and occult so that they ignore the sheer reality.

Moon-Neptune in Capricorn (1984-1998) people can be very sensible and emotionally committed at the same time and take great responsibility for others in a very educational and positive authoritarian way. Will these leaders save the world? Those caught in the negative aspect tend to be insecure before authorities and have a fear of excessive responsibility.

Moon-Neptune in Aquarius (1998-2012) gives us a new humanistic generation. Neptune empathy and Aquarius humanism can lead to unsuspected worldly involvement and a natural participation in a collective conscience. The negative tendency is to feel emotional exclusion and thus experience self-sufficient isolation.

Moon-Neptune in Pisces (2011-2026) is "at home" for good or bad. These little *angels* despise everything hard, violent and painful for all living beings. Vulnerability is their major disadvantage, and they will avoid conflicts rather than challenges. Religiosity or human involvement can be fruitful, but it can often be a very inspiring creativity that needs a positive outlet. The negative tendency is a certain difficulty in handling everything practical and adapting to the difficult requirements of reality.

Moon-Neptune in Aries will be children born between 2025-2039. What may become of these "enthusiasts?" Will they become religious hot spurs or fighting for the weak? Maybe I will do a child's chart when I am 70?

Of course, there can also be religiousity and spiritual inspiration among the other planets, but the position and aspects of the Sun and Moon are the strongest.

Personally, I have a relatively neutral Neptune. There is only a wide sextile to the Sun and a wide trine to my Venus, so I probably use mostly my semi-square to Mercury, and this in a more practical way. Perhaps this aspect also illustrates a more intellectual view on mysticism and the concept of religion.

However, there can be a strong fascination for the strong power of a conviction. How many Jews did not survive their anxiety of faith in another world or that God would save them? This despite the indescribable suffering they went through. Likewise, I have to respect millions of people who have their faith as the only line of justice, such as people in poverty, those who are vulnerable, lonely, addicts or at the edge of society. For many millions, their faith is the only thing that keeps them alive.

I have recently read two books by Paolo Coelho (Virgo with Moon in Sagittarius) where he addresses the great subjects of life, God and mystery. In one of his first million-copy sellers, *Pilgrimage*, he walks along the "Santiago de Compostela" (translated as *Jacobs Road of Stars*) and connects with a master to learn different rituals and trials in the art of becoming human. The book is absolutely magical. His other work, *Brida*, is about a 22-year old woman searching for both a master and magic knowledge because she knows she has the "gift." This novel is a fascinating depiction of modern witches today.

Who does not remember Beatle George Harrison's megahit, *My Sweet Lord,* which was not only loved by ordinary Christians and the Hare Krishna, but it also got many people curious about God. George, along with the other Beatles, visited Maharishi in India and learned to meditate from him. George was a Pisces with his Moon in Scorpio. Later he had to live with an infamous reputation ("Oh no, here he comes again with his God").

I don't think that religion in a genuine human way hurts anyone, so long as it does not manifest as extreme radicalism as we see from Islamic State. I also do see the United States as a deterrent example of religious extremism with its ultra-right wing Christians, in which the Ku Klux Klan is also on this extreme edge.

I actually realized just over 10 years ago that I had not read the Bible, and I read it during a six month period from start to finish. You can't intellectualize or reason about it if you do not know what it says. Bit by bit it is extremely tedious, boring and literally repetitive, (begot, begot, begot, begot, begot on several pages), but there were sections of both beautiful poetry, wise thoughts and well-meaning moral cakes and mindset. What I found very interesting was actually the most famous sections of the Book of Revelations, which contains the Apocalypse and the question of "the world´s destruction." It was both amusing and pathetic and actually relieved rather than worsened my already non-existent fear of "hell" or the afterlife. It was, of course, written for a time and a world thousands of years ago and can't really be applied to our time. In all times civilizations and cultures have feared their demise, and all major dominions and cultures have finally fallen, not just Atlantis. Everyone is blessed by his or her faith, but no one should sit on their "high horses" and condemn others. The English comedian Dave Allen always used to end his television show with the lovely quote, "*May your God be with you.*"

Finally, a couple of revolutionary thoughts from the "immortal" Libran with his Moon in Aquarius or Capricorn, John Lennon, from 1970. This is from the same record where *Working Class Hero* is included:

God

God is a concept by which we measure our pain
I´ll say it again
God is a concept by which we measure our pain

I don´t believe in magic, I don´t believe in I-Ching
I don´t believe in Bible, I don´t believe in Tarot
I don´t believe in Hitler, I don´t believe in Jesus
I don´t believe in Kennedy, I don´t believe in Buddha
I don´t believe in Mantra, I don´t believe in Gita
I don´t believe in Yoga, I don´t believe in Kings
I don´t believe in Elvis, I don´t believe in Zimmerman (Bob Dylan)
I don´t believe in Beatles

I just believe in me, Yoko and me, and that´s reality
The dream is over   *What can I say?*
The dream is over   *Yesterday*
I was the Dreamweaver   *But now I´m reborn*
I was the walrus   *But now I´m John*
And so, dear friends   *You´ll just have to carry on*
The dream is over

The Future - Globally

"Astrology bestows joy through the expectation at the same time as it strengthens people against evil" (Lucian of Samogata, 121-181 AD)

I have read Nostradamus' prophecies, and much is fascinating. But the interpretations are difficult because he wrote them in riddles so nothing would be too evident (to avoid persecution by the Catholic Church).

When we come to this topic, I have to admit that here I have mixed feelings, partly due to the actual consequence of global development and partly my own intuition. However, the astrological image can be interpreted in several ways with several likely scenarios. We can also have a positive or negative attitude towards reality as we choose to see today, with lots of scared people and panic, or we can choose to attune to new signals of awareness that can help at least change the reaction to occurrences that seem inevitable.

My own view is that there is always a choice. However, my trust in humanity is unfortunately not as strong. I can even commute between the powerlessness of human stupidity (read politicians) and an anger over all the stupidities and banalities that prioritize real change for the better. There is food to feed all people, so why do the majority starve? Why does it pay to lie, cheat and promote fear at the expense of others? Corporate executives and economic power owners own most of the major companies today, living in a sheltered bubble, bathing in their money, like Scrooge McDuck. Why does the abuse of innocent animals continue just so vain people can continue their private illusion? We eat dead animals, take drugs to avoid seeing reality and avoid dealing with our personal fears and shortcomings. We are voting for lying politicians like dumb sheep and love to point out the flaws of others' ideologies. We believe in a God who punishes or rewards, while we are hypocritical and ignore our neighbors and their personal problem. We spend time working with meaningless tasks without empathy just to fill our bank accounts, and we use that money to deceive our fear of where it all leads. Work today has become a project for the few, and those who have work dare not to jump off the spinning wheel for fear of losing their safety.

What then does the future look like? Well, I can see several options. The most pessimistic can look at, for example, Islamic State and point out that even Nostradamus suggested that radical Muslims would try to conquer Europe. Islam is also the strongest growing religion today, which is not that strange because it attracts millions of poor people from the world's most vulnerable continents. If only "dad,"The United States, and the other world policemen would bomb Islamic State before they grow too strong, then there's possibly less danger. We'll probably make time to see another season on Netflix before it's all over.

Is there anyone who remembers the debates about climate change a decade ago? Al Gore, who almost became president, worked wholeheartedly with this issue, and several films were made about the issue, including *An Inconvenient Truth*. This film came out in 2006, and that is over 10 years ago. Just take this film as an example. Should global warming escalate and get out of control, then it's already too late to do something about it. We will get used to more natural disasters and extreme weather changes, and in the long run we will witness our shores and lowlands under water when the polar ice caps have completely melted. Forget about London, the Netherlands, Denmark and all the stunning South Sea islands in the Pacific Ocean where you have been on holiday. A few meters of risen sea level will definitely have indescribable effects for life. I can continue to point out other changes that in one way or another are the result of human stupidity, but the primary causes are our passive cowardice and paralyzed politicians who can not resist economic power. Those who own real power today are not just politicians but mainly big finance, and it's not just me whining that says so but also social scientists. As long as money rules, it's hardly profitable to save people.

What are, then, the positive signals? I had long hoped that future generations and maybe even those born in the 90s would realize the new threats and distance themselves from much of idiocy of today. The number of young people who become vegetarians and vegans is increasing, and young people seem to have an idealistic view of the human role in the world. They engage in PETA, organizations for animals, join protest movements that are quickly activated thanks to facebook groups and twitter and seem at least a little more braver than my own generation. If they can just avoid getting stuck in their selfies and their narcissistic navel-contemplations, there may be hope.

The cellphone has many advantages but also alarming disadvantages. Many seem to suffer from acute panic attacks if they lose their cellphone, and they start hyperventilating if they do not change their status on facebook in more than 12 hours. I think we have a whole new public disease on our hands.

The future as I see it can become pure science fiction or give us a better world to live in, but it will require a lot of those who own something today. All types of petrol-driven vehicles are fast becoming an extinct phenomenon, and today the smart businessmen are investing in electric cars. But as long as, for example, China is expanding economically, everyone wants to live as over-grown Americans. Of the Earth's 7.4 billion people, approximately 1.6 billion are classified as "overweight" (source WHO). Of these, around 650 million are counted as "obese" (health-risk fat). And where are 1 billion Chinese to dump their waste? Sending it to the moon may become their only option.

There are already both electric cars and alternative fuel engines, but politicians have to push for more benefits and improvements for those who are going to utilize these choices and maybe want to change their living habits. I also think that the issue of food will soon be an even more urgent issue. It is unsustainable to feed millions of animals just to be slaughtered because even more millions of humans want to eat burgers with fatty chips and slimy brownish carbonated drinks. (I refuse to write the names of specific fast-food chains here because they might sue me). Obesity, diabetes and hypertension are growing public diseases, and not only in the United States. I also read that it's better for the climate and the environment to eat healthier food, including more vegetables. That, I already knew back in the 70's; but thanks for new data. Back in the 1960s the environmental critic and Professor Georg Borgström wrote the book *Food for Billions*, recognizing the upcoming population explosion and that the future's food must come from, among other things, the great oceans. Today, giant fishing fleets have been fishing out many areas, and many fish species do not catch up with their biological growth. Even here it is money that governs. Do I have to comment on the massacre of dolphins in Japan every year? Please see the filthy movie *The Cove* that was released in 2009 and addresses this shameful subject.

One of our few heroes today, Morgan Spurlock (a Scorpio, of course), made a radical documentary about what happens if you only live on food purchased at a special restaurant. It was called *Super Size Me* and came out in 2004. In any event, it led to the fact that restaurants now also serve vegetarian options and more vegetables, so he did something good.

Even the cartoon series *The Simpsons* has featured several contemporary environmental and economic issues, and little Lisa Simpson became a vegetarian in an episode. This was something that helped positively affect my own daughter. I remember that Richard Gere was in the episode, and I know he is a Buddhist. If he is a vegetarian, I do not know.

As I said, for those who think or believe that everything is just peace and happiness today, it will probably be for them a veritable nightmare. We can't continue like the ostrich with the head in the sand

and pretend everything is alright. It's not alright. It's actually quite bad. Both politicians and ordinary people must take radical action, and the big finance companies must realize that they could make money on other things than just meaningless production for consumption alone.

We need to have a positive view of the future. I still believe in future generations and do not think they will be just as passive and cowardly as my own generation's politicians. Since I'm convinced that the frequency increase of human awareness is already beginning, it's only a matter of time before even politicians understand what's right and wrong. The Internet is both good and bad, of course, but joins people faster today. This, in turn, indirectly leads to increased awareness of new events even of a positive nature. Only politicians avoid to restrict the privacy of the citizens. Watch the movies *Citizenfour* and *Snowden* if you want to know what's actually going on today.

In order to round off my pessimism, for example, I do not think clean drinking water will be for free in the near future. Today, 650 million people do not have access to clean drinking water and nothing points to any improvement. Rather, deterioration continues, given the population explosion. The one who has his own well will probably be looked upon with envy by the townspeople. Politicians will probably invent a new water tax. Agriculture will have to return to small scale and locally produced farming, with more choosing organic, poison-free and locally produced food. Then you can hope that future generations will fight for a more democratic and fair society. Today you can choose between hospitals, kindergartens and schools based on your economic standing, but this will only increase the segregation and the gaps in society.

There are also many positive signs regarding health care today. Cancer is no longer a mystery. You can google or search on Youtube for the pioneers Charlotte Gerson and her father Max Gerson to listen and read for yourself. Most people eat unhealthilly, think fearfully, feel badly and live in an imbalanced way, completely contrary to the laws of nature. This must and will begin to finally change.

Young people today are braver and are not afraid to live more consistently in harmony with nature, animals and the environment. Personally, I think the planetary frequercy increases will cause more and more people to learn that they can actually heal both themselves and others; and by living more naturally, they can also avoid to end up in the traditional medical circus. The more people understand why diseases arise, the fewer will need medical care. It is not more difficult than that, and I hope that new generations will realize this.

Money does not mean automatic happiness, nor must work automatically mean slavery or serfdom. The banking system is likely to collapse when people exchange services and goods instead. The economic hierarchy today will use all kinds of frightening propaganda to dupe us, but there are more and more people now who realize and speak up. Through the Internet and today's faster communication, more and more people will dare to act with greater resistance to those who are in power, so some kind of global revolution is probably inevitable in the near future.

Today there is both technology and resources to feed the world's starving, but the economic imbalance and its ensuing chaos must be overturned before this global awareness can begin to work. After all, I believe in human intrinsic goodness and its ability to always make the most of any situation. The worse the scenario, the stronger becomes humanitiy's will to jointly control changes in the right direction. These scenarios may include floods, natural disasters, genocidal dictatorships, environmental disasters due to climate changes and chemicals in the water and the atmosphere. It's strange how all of us agree in the worst times when everything is about to collapse. Look at the tsunami in 2004 and how everyone helped to care for each other and rebuild everything destroyed. In the worst moments, mankind finally realizes what is important.

I hope anyone reading this realizes that we are all equally important. Changes do not start just *around* you. They start initially *inside* of you. You are important! Tomorrow is the very first day of the beginning of the rest of your life. Even a journey of a thousand miles begins with a single small step. Take it today. Or tomorrow at least…

The Future - Astrologically

The future is perhaps the one issue that most attracts people when they contact an astrologer. It's a little sad, though, that most people would rather look forward than back. Long before the understanding of how to work with astrology at the time of Atlantis, I realized that it was most interesting to try to analyze WHY you became the one you are, or HOW you are who you are today. For many years my *Basic Interpretation* was called "From the Cradle until Today," which clearly reflects this process. It was also easier to get "answers" and confirmation of the analysis from the client. In a Prediction, you work more with abstract energies or potential events, and you would not know HOW or WHAT until some time had passed. It could take several years before I received answers or confirmations on my thoughts.

However, there are many who are not at all interested in the future, and maybe even hesitate to come in contact with it, just because they do not want to hear about what lies ahead. Then there are those who just want to hear about what's coming, and are barely interested in the past or their basic chart. So   have to compromise.

I stressed very early on that I did not make any forecasts without first having a birth interpretation. It felt strange to talk about the future with someone you never have had a dialogue with or did not know at all. In addition, I was careful to require some important conditions before any forecast. These included what the person's history looked like, if something bad had happened recently or why one wanted to look forward. Often, I had to combine the analysis, which of course took a bit longer. At the same time, I have to admit that it was a bit shattering to tell both the past and the future in the same process. I usually tried to divide the work into two different phases because I work differently with the various processes.

I still argue that the most important and fruitful way is to analyze backwards in time: to reflect on how you become who you are, to see how you were shaped and characterized by parents and to understand the circumstances and events that led up to today. That's when you can try to learn lessons from past mistakes and disappointments and thereby look at options for the future.

Prognosis

For your curiosity, I will nevertheless try to describe the process we call Forecast. This will be through a series of examples of what you could experience in different situations.

Looking forward you can use several different techniques. The most common is perhaps the Sun Progress or the Solar Progression, where you see the progressive movements for each year. There is also something called Solar Return, where you simply make a new chart for each year at the exact time the Sun returns to its original location. For example, leap years will cause the Solar Return to sometimes be the day before the birthday, which several of you found out when I pointed this out by my congratulating you a day ahead.

Another useful technique is the so-called Secondary Progression, where every day after birth represents a year. I often use this in parallel with the transits. However, the transits are the most important, partly because they are activated more often and partly because they also describe a current event now. The transits represent the exact movements of the planets in relation to the birth chart in real time, i.e., right now.

One can say that I prioritize the transits and complement primarily with the Sun and Secondary Progression. Ironically enough, the same energies often show in all three analyses, which, of course, emphasize the exact transit activitites. In the following review, I will mainly use examples of transits and supplement with important times, even for the Sun and Secondary. I will both give examples of my own experiences as well as of people I know or read about.

You can actually study your chart yourself and see when different periods of your life may have stronger relevance. In the Solar Progression, the Sun, Moon and planets move about 1 degree per year. If you have any planet in front of the Sun, just count it forward to that next degree. Note that everything goes *counter-clockwise*. If you have access to the Ephemeris or House Tables, you can figure out where the planets are in transit and when they tangent any point in your chart. There are currently minute online tables that show accurate planet positions. I have the actual positions on the website https://www.astro.com/astro-databank/Main_Page as the starting page on my computer. Figuring this out via this "lazy-bones" method with the planet symbols will make it easier.

In the case of examples, there are countless combinations, but we will only analyze the conjunctions in transit, i.e., when they are in exactly the same location or cross a point in your chart. There are, of course, lots of points that you can take into consideration, but it would be too tight and take too much space if you would like to add all aspects.

The Transits of the Sun

Sun transit Ascendant: I'm calling this the *Little Birthday* because an important event may occur. Birth or Start of a new Year Cycle. New outgoing active period begins.

Sun transit MC: Successful task. Know what you want. Insight into ambition or a new way. Better conditions in the profession. Career advancement. Focus on responsibility. Reward or achievement.

Sun transit Sun: Same as Solar Return.

Sun transit Moon: In progression, this can only happen once in a lifetime while for some, never, depending on location. During a transit once a year. Highlights often an important event or milestone in progression, and transit often indicates strong activation of all feelings. Can indicate a new cycle that starts or important routing selection. Can also mean that an important relationship begins.

Sun transit Mercury: Good day for conversation and planning or studies and new skills.

Sun transit Venus: Activates social needs and makes us more emotional. Good day to start a relationship or to start a new project. One of the best days of the year.

Sun transit Mars: Strong physical ability is activated, but can be experienced as stressful if you are not used to physical activity. May experience both your own and others' anger. Impatient if hindered. Pay attention to unplanned impulses. Easily unfortunate if there are other negative energies. Headache. If your efforts are focused, great success can be achieved.

Sun transit Jupiter: Great enthusiasm and optimism. A little more luck than otherwise. Hard things comes easier. Good day to bet or risk, but watch out for blind optimism. Excessiveness may occur.

Sun transit Saturn: Good day for hard work but mistakes can occur. Great fatigue if not used to physical work. Better with routines than improvisation. May experience resistance or environmental demands. Lousy day for love or resting. Stress may occur due to shortage of time.

Sun transit Uranus: A day that breaks both patterns and routines. May indicate a whole new meeting or new period. Watch out for unexpected events. Not a good day for peace and quiet. Will suddenly change your routines and habits. Brilliant solutions if realistic.

Sun transit Neptune: An either inspiring or tiring day. For aesthetics, inspiration is on top. For realists and practical people, a tendency to confusion and ambiguity. Risk of infection or bacilli. Misunderstandings or fraud may occur. Take special care with medicines or drugs.

Sun transit Pluto: May encounter the unknown. Something unexpected can come by. May experience danger or discomfort. Introspective analysis better than social needs. Give a hundred per cent, but risk to tighten the bow too hard.

Transits of the Moon

The Moon's transits belong to the clearest and strongest, but they are also the shortest in time. These transits may be effective in half an hour at their strongest. When the Moon crosses some point, this usually triggers other transits, planets or progressions in the chart. The Moon can pass all points in a full circle over a 28-day period. It compares with the menstruation cycle.

Moon transit ASC: This occasion may feel like being released (such as a hospital or prison) from a certain time of isolation (12th House). The feelings are quickly expressed. Meeting with women and children quite probable. Brand new cycle begins. Perhaps a short trip. Publicity.

Moon transit MC: Symbolically an emotional "eureka moment." To arrive or succeed in performance. Emotional involvement in the work. Possible connection to a child's birth. Meeting a woman at work or in her career.

Moon transit Sun: The synthesis between Yin and Yang. Different effect for men and women. For men a memorable sense of perfection or the feeling of success. Women can change their minds and feel a certain fatigue. At best, an intense or important meeting for both sexes.

Moon transit Moon: Full circle in life. Return to something earlier. Cycle completes or starts. All instincts are activated and intensified. Contact with children or women. Good for planning new habits.

Moon transit Mercury: There is a need to communicate and express feelings. Reason and feelings in balance. Good opportunity to speak out or plan short-term.

Moon transit Venus: Social needs. Loving. Good contacts. More fun than serious. Lucky day.

Moon transit Mars: May be perceived as a conflict. Temporary physical stress. Strong need to release emotions. Urgency can lead to minor incidents or injuries.

Moon transit Jupiter: A long journey may begin, possibly with family. Success with social activities. Good for business or speculation. Lady Fortune can smile. Beware of exaggeration and nonchalance.

Moon transit Saturn: Sudden fatigue or miscalculation. Failure may occur, as well as lack of time and increased stress. May end up in embarrassing or unpleasant situations. Not a good time for emotions or social activities. Better for disciplined or hard body work.

Moon transit Uranus: You may experience something unexpected. Emotional tension such as a scary funfair attraction. If simultaneous frustration period, this can activate strong but transient stress. You might become a whole new person or meet one. Be prepared for the unexpected news.

Moon transit Neptune: Possibility of surreal new experiences. Dreamy or sleepy state. Suitable for artistic activity or meditation. Tendency towards disappointment or fatigue if other negative energies are active at the same time.

Moon transit Pluto: Daily routine or life structure are interrupted by obstacles or emotional agitation. Something intervenes or is missing. "Stick in the wheel." Often seen as bad luck. In severe cases an emotional shock that can have deep consequences. Horrible time for romance.

Other typical transits

The transits of the Sun and Moon are both the strongest and most important, but I want to give some more examples of typical effects through the transitions of the other planets.

Mars transit ASC: This occurs when Mars is on or crossing your Ascendant. It is usuallly experienced over a period of two days. This combination is a classic. In a birth chart, this can occur in the charts of a butcher, a surgeon or a knife killer. Symbolically, they all use the knife as a tool. The difference lies in how the other energies work, and not in the least is the issue of morality. The actor and Cancerian James Cagney had this conjunction in Virgo and in addition the Moon in Scorpio. Cagney was very famous for his impulsive fists. Mars, which symbolizes different energies, often activates the planet it passes. In general, you can interpret in many different ways, but the most common is that you feel physically tense, stressed or impatient. You can also experience the surroundings and other people as provocative or inconvenient. This is one of the few combinations that can actually indicate physical injury or an easy accident. This transit usually occurs every two to three years, depending on possible retrogrades. This transit is not a good day to be exposed to unfamiliar situations or strangers. However, it can be effective if you use your body for your own efforts, such as for athletes.

Mars transit Mercury: This may be a day of intensive communication, as in the case of other negative energies or from a quarrel that can easily arise. Try not to speak before you are done thinking.

Mars transit Venus: This transit creates a very good day for both love and sex as well as creative inspiration and efficient productivity.

Mars transit Jupiter: This is one of the best transits for success of all kinds, though perhaps primarily for athletes. Perfect for physical stress, e.g., childbirth.

Jupiter transit ASC: This symbolizes both luck and healing. This transit also covers recovery after a longer period of illness, the start of a long or successful trip and success in the public light. This transit is good for long-term investments. Everyone will experience this process, but only around every 12 years, so it is important to be effective. Often a memorable experience during this time that may last several weeks and sometimes repeated twice, depending on the retrograde effect.

Jupiter transit MC: This transit is similar to the effect of the Ascendant but with more emphasis on social status and career. This reveals the crown with longer-term goals to win or achieve a goal in life. "You hit the jackpot." It's a good period to get both paid and rewards, as well as to sow new seeds with companies or relationships.

Saturn transit ASC: Here a person enters a new phase with more focus on him/herself, rather than socializing with others. With hardly any extreme effort, people can succeed in learning about themselves through studying the environment and its mirroring of weather to human emotions and consciousness Long-term illness may occur or a period of introverted isolation. In the worst case, this indicates more difficult separations and terminations in life, such as someone´s death or if you are forced to leave a job. We all experience this transit process, but only a few times in life, about every 28th to 29th year. So maybe a maximum of three times in life.

Saturn transit MC: This transit is a bit milder than the Ascendant transit. It focuses on your own career, helping you to achieve your long-term goals because Saturn enjoys and symbolically rules over the MC in the 10th House. This transit can symbolise a promotion or a setback. If this is negative in the birth chart, you may be fired or dismissed. Something is terminated or prevented in the profession.

Uranus transit ASC: This can be a very intense and messy period of life that only occurs once in your lifetime and may last for several months. It can indicate jumping between different projects that never end. Many new interests or new people may appear. You may want to change your physical appearance and/or move. This transit is common with a change of residence, even often several times over a longer period of time. I had this myself between 1982 to 1984 before I finally settled in Småland.

Uranus transit MC: Suddenly there may be changes in career or new goals. This can also entail completely new interests and a quest for new goals to achieve. Unstable work can lead to cancellation or termination. It can become difficult to adhere to routines. Uranus wants to release and break free, so it's common for persons to choose to go their own way. Indirectly, there can be a danger to relationships if any tension already exists.

Neptune's transits can last for a year over three different periods in your life. I will just mention the transits over the Ascendant and MC.

Neptune transit ASC: There can be unusually complicated periods of time depending on how you work. If you are realistic or practical, this time can be characterized by constant recurrent periods of fatigue and at worst indicate a period of fatigue or disease that often takes a long time to cure or get rid of. There tends to be an experiencing of more disappointment from people, and dreams tend to be crushed. It becomes easier than usual to unconsciously take stimulants, which only exacerbates the experience. A religious crisis may occur. If you are an idealist, more imaginative or artistic, this period can be extremely creative and inspiring. This period of time is great for devoting more attention to personal interests, and there may also be a need for greater privacy and loneliness. Conversely, it's harder to stick to routines and handle the needs of others.

Neptune transit MC: This transit is similar to the ASC but with emphasis on your employment or your goals in life. You may experience ambiguities, disappointments from co-workers or executives and a sense of meaninglessness from work may occur. It becomes difficult to live up to others' requirements, especially the bosses. This may lead to a kind of defection or aimlessness and not knowing where to go. The positive side is that aesthetists or artistic people often make use of this time to become absorbed by their creativity and their dreams. It can become better to wholeheartedly devote oneself to one's idealism and dreams rather than to labor meaninglessly with ordinary wage labor without freedom if only one can take the consequences or can afford this "time out."

Pluto's transits are even longer and can come back in a two-year period due to Pluto's yearly retrograde experience. Since these are not so physical or concrete, they feel more like a subconscious phenomenon. This can most likely be experienced in dreams and can indicate both fears and one's own phobias. Usually, however, you come into larger collective experiences, such as a rock concert or a cinema visit. Pluto's energies are often experienced with many people.

Q & A

Here are some exciting questions I have received and my answers to them. These are now, of course, without regard to other aspects or planetary combinations.

When do we get children? This is one of the most common questions I've had in all the years I've worked with astrology. Unfortunately, there are no simple answers to this important question, and you must analyze both parents' birth charts and the eventual time you hope to have children. There are clear indications of people who are more fruitful than others, and some who have a significantly harder time to become pregnant. In general, one can say that if both parents fulfill a couple of criteria, then you can start looking for the best time. This can be triggered by both progressions and transits. Often it is a mix of both. The planets most often in focus are Saturn (more responsibility), Uranus (changes), and Pluto (birth and revolution). The birth of a child is also very different between men and women. The woman's experience is strongly characterized by Saturn (weight, resistance, struggle, physical pain), while the man often experiences a stronger Uranus (physical anxiety, revolution). Pluto, the planet that symbolizes birth occurs in different forms of aspects for both parents. In addition, the births often differ widely from time to time (i.e., the birth of siblings). Over the years, I have worked with several couples who adopted, and there has often been a strong Uranus, or the influence of Aquarius has been clear. Both children and parents with their Moon in Aquarius can symbolize adoption, foster family or "other children."

When will I or will I ever get married? Even this fun but important issue is on my top list. It's not always easy to find the best moments that will harmoniously coincide for two people. But if you have patience, there are some clear indications. The progression of the Sun or the Moon to Venus is most common; but since these do not occur so often, one should look for other positive alternatives, preferably with Jupiter or Mars involved.

When will I fall in love? This question can be a little easier to speculate. Of course, one must have a certain disposition, but periods or occasions return on a regular basis. A sudden love or infatuation can be short-lived and must not involve a deeper relationship, so it's not easy to see if just love leads to a permanent relationship. However, the more permanent relationship occurs most commonly when Venus and Uranus are in contact. This may occur up to eight to ten times per year through transits. The strongest trends are found in conjunctions or oppositions (therefore, at least two times a year for everyone).

When will I change my job? This important issue is also a common one. It is, though, difficult to decide. Many factors must be included in such an important process, with both a tendency to end a cycle and an ability to change or restart. I would recommend a combination between Jupiter, Uranus and MC, but it is very individual as to what is most beneficial.

When should we move or buy a house? This is reasonably easy to find out. There is often a strong and obvious effect, preferably involving both the Sun and the Moon. Contacts with the Ascendant or MC often indicate important decisions and new goals in life. But yes, you can either choose a terrible or beneficial moment.

Can I and will I start my own business? This is both easy and difficult to give important advice on. Many factors must coincide, and I often place high counter-claims on the person asking in terms of knowledge, economics, practical ability or social conditions. Working with these qualities, one can look for symbolic milestones when a new process is due or at the end of an old process. Consideration must also always be taken to the world's own chart; for example, which periods are favorable for starting long-term cycles. You may avoid an overly negative Saturn or if several important planets happen to be retrograde. Otherwise, it's only a matter of finding the person's positive periods and looking for a good opportunity.

Can I take a bank loan? This is also most importantly a question of the World Horoscope and the person's prerequisites. It is often about a longer investment or risk taking and can be difficult to find a suitable time. But you can. A positive Pluto is favorable.

When will I become ill? When will I be healthy? This is a very sensitive but important issue as both questions. I try as a barometer to measure the positive and negative cycles of the individual, but I often have to know both the time and the cause of the disease or vice versa if there is a danger of disease. Here are many factors to analyze, and it can be difficult to "promise" recovery. However, it is easy to see periods when the tendency is to ease or improvement occurs, as in the example of

Jupiter on the Ascendant. It is significantly easier and more thankful to prevent warnings about future periods of fatigue, physical weakness or increased sensitivity. These can be of both physical and psychological nature. However, the periods are relatively easy to predict and thus prevent. You may not want to go on a tiresome Round-the-Globe journey if you happen to have Saturn around the Ascendant or Uranus passing over your Moon.

When will I or any relative die? Of course, you will never get a response from me, but I can tell you about possible future times of sadness and worries, as it may be for a close relative who is very ill or very old. In this way, we can be better mentally prepared and prepared in good time. I have consciously not taught myself these codes. I usually say that your own death is quiet visible in your loved one's chart. Here it is not only a matter of Scorpio and the 8th House, but there are considerably more factors to take into account.

Will I inherit? This is linked to the previous question, but the potential is in your chart. For example, with Jupiter in Scorpio or the 8th house. However, in my opinion, the eventual time should not be speculated.

When can I start to study? This is a simple and smart question that should be asked by anyone who wants to study for a longer or shorter period of time. Our mental capacity with its ebb and flow goes in cycles, and here you can more easily see periods of mental focus, as well as periods when frustration or fatigue may hinder studying. There needs to be a good flow from Jupiter, primarily to Mercury, which can provide greater ease. Saturn, meanwhile, can also contribute to being objective in analysis during a long time, preferably with the 9th House in focus.

Yes, there are questions about all areas of life. The astrologer either can or should answer all your questions. He or she is no oracle, but one can play with the idea of trying to exploit one's talents during positive periods, relying on your intuition, at the same time as one can try to avoid more difficult projects in times of worry or negative energies. In fact, it can be a treat to make the interpretations harmless and fun. For example, one should sow seeds at the right time, depending on whether it is vegetables or flowers you want.

"The wise learns to master his stars while the foolish is ruled by them." (unknown author)

Some reviews about Jacob

Here are two samples of thankful letters from clients I worked with. Please note that both have given their consent to the publication of their letters.

The first is from the crazy TV star of the series *Ullared*, Gitte Svensson, after a birth horoscope and a forecast in 2014. Gitte was born in 1966 and is a Cancerian with the Moon in Scorpio.

Hi Jacob!

I have listened twice now to your analysis! The first time I cried through the entire recording because everything was right on the dot! And emotional, I am.

The second time I only smiled!! You are a genius and have really opened up my interest in astrology.

You should also know (open, straightforward and honest as I am) that "you have saved my life!" For now, I understand it all the way I'm in today!

As you said, I'm impulsive (like hell) and cohabitation is not my thing! I've been living together three times earlier in life and it did not work! Still, I was over-impulsive and thought I'd make it now that I am older! My guy needed to hire a cheaper house and it ended with my idea to buy one together!

You do not know Jacob ... After moving in November, I've been feeling so bad. The stress first led to pneumonia and now a prolonged gastric cataract with cruel reflux problems. I will soon have a gastroscopy ... my God how it scares me. I think they'll find cancer!!! Fears of serious illness and death have persecuted me always!

I do not feel at home in the house and the troubles between me and my guy are many. He blames me because of my compulsion, fears and my edgy mood! He is, by the way, born in Scorpio and has no signs (more than kindness) on this! He is more Cancer than I am, you told me! My feelings freeze when I'm angry and for some time now I do not even know if I love him. We have only known each other for 1½ years, so it was impulsive to suddenly buy a house!

What I mean by you "saving my life" is that I now know what to do! Namely, sell the house and split up, which will surely run into the sand later. We have now decided to do that, because the whole situation has lowered my immune system! I have been crazy then after the move. I have said earlier that "this house will be my death" if I stay!! I want so much more in life! I want to meet friends and laugh often. I have a constant hunger after things to happen! In the house I only sit by the TV or sleep away time.

My guy, on the other hand, is still in love with me and he is just pleased by my company in this house, where I feel locked up! In addition, he has a 13-year-old son (living part-time with us) who feels bad (stays home from school and gets no bounderies at home). My guy is too lenient with the kid and I can't stand it! I can't figure out how lenient he is against the child! His son needs help. He'll drop out of society elsewhere in a few years. His 21-year-old sister sits today at treatment homes, thanks to me and my ability to act!!

But when I tell my guy that he raises the son incorrectly, he gets pissed off! And I become a real "bitch" because I'm right !!!

Well. I feel fine by the decision to move on (when the house is sold) but my guy is feeling bad and blames me! So when you talked about the fact that my time is moving fast and exciting, I realized what leg to stand on!! And I suspect I will be accepted to my education, which is a project that the state pays! I'm going to take a truck card, a long-lasting dream I had. And you're right: when I entered the adult education program with the headmaster, I made a strong impression! Between the lines he said that we will meet again soon. I knew in advance that my charisma and personality would get him "on my case!" That's how it's always been when I'm really looking for something with my driving force! I always win in the wishes I have!

Here you have proof that I was hysterically happy by your analysis and I will think carefully now before everything I do, even if it goes too fast ... both in my head and in action.

I would like to talk to you too, so I will call you someday when I can speak undisturbed!!

Thank you very much Jacob !!!

See ya!

Hug

The second letter is from a wonderful woman who started as a course participant more than 27 years ago and still keeps in touch, my good friend "Taurus with Moon in Capricorn from Växjö," who wants to be kept anonymous. She was born in 1962.

"I wanted you to hear from me and tell you now everything has evolved for me and how amazing you are (but you know that). You may not remember, but when you made my forecast in the spring of 2014 you said I should finish everything that was unfinished before the end of 2014, since I would "neither be able nor get time to" until 2017. I was worried that I would become ill again or get a stroke, but you said that: "no, it's only positive things." I am a psychiatric patient because of severe fatigue depression between 2001 and 2006 and have chronic fatigue syndrome and deep sleepiness and depression after that. So in May 2014, I was able to try Lithium medication (usually for

bipolar disorder) and it calmed down the dips significantly, which allowed me to do much extra work in 2014 and felt super!

I "finished" as much as I had time to do, ordered my will (for safety), gained a few kilos from the medicine (as you predicted) and waited for what would happen. In January 2015, I gained increased responsibility at work (which was planned in autumn 2014) and was net dating a couple of months. Network dating takes MUCH time, I discovered. After some "mistakes" I met a younger man. It was just a strong physical attraction and nothing else and we had a short and intense love affair (as you had predicted). Much later, I discovered that Mars had crossed my "birth-Mars" the day I met him. (Sexuality, Jacob's note).

Since spring 2014, I was in a queue for investigation of ADHD (I had suspected it for a few years because it has been established in recent years that there is a connection between ADHD and fatigue depression), and in June of this year I was examined and diagnosed - there was no doubt.

After 15 years, being able to change my attitude from "having a depression disease" to "the one who has too many fun ideas in my head and far too little time" felt perfectly right because I felt that it was more like how I always have been before I got sick in 2001! I ended taking Lithium in August. I have realized that the dips are because I constantly over-strain my enthusiasm and instead of fighting what I have thought every time was the beginning of a new dip, I will instead rest for a few days, and it has worked out good so far.

(I tested ADHD medicine (Concerta) for a short period but could not stand the side effects). I have begun courses in Mindfulness and an ADHD group this autumn, and I've joined a small book club at work (I have not read with any discipline in 15 years!). I have also started painting for the first time in 20 years and listen to lots of good music, (Moneybrother and Muse around the clock). So my schedule is really full.

I also realize that during the 15 years I've thought that concentration and memory problems have been due to injuries after the difficult periods of the *early 2000s, I have found plenty of good strategies that makes everyday and my job work great.*

I fully enjoy feeling that I am more myself than in MANY years (although the fatigue syndrome is chronic and I may continue to have a half-pension), but realize that this good thing can not last for ever - joy and sadness pre-supposes each other in life, which I am always aware of.

As I said, I would only like to tell you how correct you (of course) were in your forecast and I hope you are feeling good and are doing well.

A GREAT THANK YOU, Jacob, because you are there and want to share your gift !!

GREAT HUG from Xxx "

Thank You

This was hard to write. How do you thank everyone without forgetting someone? In addition, I needed to avoid listing the most important people in my life in a certain order. I recalled that the simplest way was to do it in chronological order and in the order I met and got to know each of you.

First of all, I must give a great "thank you very much" to my parents, Gull-Maj Margaretha and Åke Ewert, who, with silent respect and positive encouragement, have always supported my strange career choices and never questioned my out-of-the-ordinary choices and decisions privately.

Also heart-filled thanks to my grandmother Margit, grandfather Gunbert, grandmother Tekla and grandfather Gerhard, who were outstanding people in their own ways, even if I only got to know my grandmother Margit, who was my steady rock throughout my childhood.

I also want to thank all my partners for everything they taught me and for the children we were blessed with (my three marriages and even more lovers). I must admit that love has been generous to me, even though my restlessness has continually pushed me on. (*Changes* - Black Sabbath).

Of course, all my children have an important place in my heart, perhaps for my inability to live with them, (but also for their forgiveness with my mistakes and shortcomings). I harbor a silent hope that I did not hurt them too much through my periodical absences.

Generous thanks also to my sisters Anna and Kajza, who have always been there through all my ups and downs. I have never been particularly spoiled with friends, but Leif Ahlm (Capricorn) and Ronnie Krantz (Scorpio) were my best friends early on and became very important. I have many cousins, but Simon (Virgo) was perhaps the closest.

My first "guru" or spiritual teacher became my yoga teacher, Bert Yogson, who opened lots of new doors in my life in 1972. He may be the one I have the most to thank for today. During a shorter time at adult school in Gothenburg before moving to Småland in 1984, I met wonderful Lise-Lotte (Taurus with Moon in Capricorn), Johnny (Aquarius with Moon in Taurus) and Bitte (Sagittarius with Moon in Capricorn), who became important people in my life. Eventually, I met Eva Hallor (Aquarius with Moon in Pisces) in Uppsala and several astrologers important for my development, such as Derek Seagrief, Ivan Wilhelm, Roland Skogkvist (RIP) and Roger Algehov, who helped me a lot with many practical things, such as charts, prints and computer programs.

In 1990, I got to know both "psychic Britta" in Nybro, (Double Scorpio) and her daughter Ewa (Leo), both of whom gave me many new insights. In addition, many of my friends today started out as participants in my astrology courses, such as Cancerian Iréne Eriksson, Taurean Eva in Växjö, Ulrik the Leo and many more.

Now the 90's were here, and the *frequency increase* started seriously. I met several mediums, such as Leo Pia Palm, Scorpio Terry Evans, Geminian William Shaffer and the medium Carina Jeppson in Skåne, all of whom gave me a dose of new awareness. I made several new friends for life that I'm grateful for: Kerstin Lilja, Malin Mellstam, Tina Lundberg, Helen "Funne" Furness, Carina Svensson, Ann-Marie Söderberg, Pia Stengard and Carl-Arne, Mikael and Nina Mathis, the water healer Bibi Arud, my regular customer and sponsor Jemmy, my neighbor Ing-Marie, my constant support Cancerian Maggan in Simrishamn and Heidi in Santa Monica, California, who donated music, books and paint gadgets to my daughter Amanda as a thank you for a prognosis in addition to a generous fee.

I really hope I did not forget anyone important. I can't count all the thousands of wonderful people who helped me by sharing their lives during all these years. I pondered for a moment on a list with just the forenamnes, but 2,300 were too many.

Finally, a deep gratitude to those of you who no longer wander among us.

R.I.P: Kent Svensson, my maybe best friend and comrade since the 70's, a Geminian with his Moon in Cancer; Scorpio Maria Linder; Cancerian Zia from Iraq; Geminian lumberjack Bengt, my father-in-law, Aquarian Cyril; the uncles, Sagittarian Ola, Libran Finn, Geminian Leif and Taurean Hans. Thank you also "Nicke" and all the rest of you. "*We'll Meet Again.*"

Among all of them "up there," there are also a lot of people who have been important in my life, such as departed writers, directors, actors, musicians, artists, etc. (*See more in Appendix Book List and Movies*.) Therefore, I feel a lot of gratitude to many I have never even met.

I would also like to thank all my animals that passed and kept my faithful company over the years, all my dogs, cats and birds. They gave unconditional love and have been both comforting and healing with their constant love. My sorrow is almost harder when my animals pass away than humans, perhaps for my own sake. However, some of them I can still feel present, particularly the cats *Little My* and *Pricken* and our wonderful Golden Retriever *Honey* who rests here at home in the garden.

Finally, a generous thanks for the help of Jan-Erik and Gunvor who lit the sparkle in 2013, and to Leo Pia and Arian Tina for all the invaluable help with the book.

(Astrologer in his favourite position – resting in his hammock. Photo by Pia Stengard, July 2016)

PART 5 APPENDIX
Wordlist – Astrology

ACC – the Acceleration. Calculated on the interval 9.86 seconds/hour

Aquarius – the 11th sign (element: Air)

Aries – the 1st sign (element: Fire)

ASC - Abbreviation for the Ascendant - The rising sign in the sky to the east. Also called the rising sign. Same as the beginning of the first house

Aspect - Angular distance between two points in the chart

Astrology - The Doctrine of the Stars. Star Knowledge:. *Astron* = Star, *Logos* = Knowledge, from the ancient Greek language

Astropsychology - Another modern name for astrology

Biquintile - 144 degree aspect

Cancer – the 4th sign (element: Water)

Capricorn – the 10th sign (element: Earth)

Chart - Horoscope / Birth chart / map

DESC - Abbreviation for the Descendant - The descending sign in the tip of the west and beginning of the seventh house

Directly - Marked with a "D" when the planet "turns" forward after a retrograde motion

Ephemeris - Star tables of the movements of the planets

Equator - 0 degrees latitude towards north or south

G.M.T - Greenwich Mean Time 0, degrees longitude

Gemini – the 3rd sign (element: Air)

Semi-square - 45 degree aspect

Semi-quintile - 36 degree aspect

Semi-sextile - 30 degree aspect

Holistic astrology - Holistic means total view. You see everything as linked to the earth and the universe. All astrology is actually holistic

Horoscope - means "see the hour" in Greek

House - Living area

House cusp - Grade in the sign where the house begins

House table - Table of places longitude and latitude on the earth

Imum Coeli - IC. The lowest point in the north. Fourth House cusp or beginning

Interpolation - Formula to calculate the exact position of the planet during a day

Intervals - Time difference between birthplace and Greenwich in England

Jungian astrology - Interpreted from a psychological perspective based on analyst Carl G. Jung

Cardinal signs - Aries, Cancer, Libra, Capricorn

Karmic astrology - interpreted from a reincarnational perspective

Conjunction - Two points within the same degree within a certain orb, synthesis of two or more energies

Cosmopolitan Psychology - Other astrology words

Cosmology – Ebertin school of astrology

Square - 90 degree aspect

Quintile - 72 degree aspect

Latitude - Latitudes North or South from the equator

Leo – the 5th sign (element: Fire)

Libra – the 7th sign (element: Air)

Longitude - Longitude East or West of Greenwich

Longitude equivalent - The actual t me of birth

M. C. - Medium Coeli - Highest point of the sky in the south and the Tenth House beginning

Mundane Astrology - Worldly astrology. Horoscope on countries, cities, different projects, invitations, etc.

Moon's northern node - The point where the Moon in its orbit crosses the Ecliptic. Also known as the Dragon's Head. This has to do with associations and relatives

Moon's southern node - Corresponding point on the other side (crossing up or down). Also called the Dragon's tail. Indicated as our weak point or "Achilles heel"

Opposition - 180 degree aspect

Orb (Orbis) - Deviation from the exact degree

Pisces – the 12th sign (element: Water)

Progression - Calculation of future forecasts

Quincunx - 150 degree aspect

Radix - Birth chart/map. Really means "root"

Relationship Horoscope - Comparison between two persons' charts

Retrograde - Apparent movement "backward" in the chart. Not in reality

Sagittarius – the 9th sign (element: Fire)

Scorpio – the 8th sign (element: Water)

Sextile - 60 degree aspect

Sidereal time - Abbreviated SID. Starting time for the day of the year

Stellium - 5 or more planets in the same sign or house. Typically characterizes a great talent or specialization

Synastry - Comparison between two horoscopes

Taurus – the 2nd sign (element: Earth)

Transit - Comparison between the birth chart and the current or selected moment. The relationship between the person and the present. A transit can be interpreted for any moment

Trine - 120 degree aspect

Tri-square - 135 degree aspect

Virgo – the 6th sign (element: Earth)

Zodiac - The 12 signs in the Zodiac Circle

Books – Astrology

Here are only some of the numerous books I have read. Many are gone or sold, and therefore much information is missing, e.g., the publisher and ISBN numbers. I hope, though, that I have remembered most of my absolute favorite writers. I'm very happy to share this "Jacob´s list."

Arroyo, Stephen - *Astrology, Karma & Transformation*, 1978. Deep and fascinating.

Arroyo, Stephen - *The Practice and Profession of Astrology*, 1984. Interestingly written for professional astrologers.

Arroyo, Stephen & Green, Liz - *The Jupiter-Saturn Conference Lectures*, 1984. Covering the seminar after the great conjunction between Jupiter and Saturn in 1981.

Aster Wig, Rigmor Elisabeth - *Between Us and the Stars*, 1973. Fantastic and complete for beginners. In Swedish. One of my first.

Bailey, Alice A. - *Esoteric Astrology*, 1951. Not for beginners, and not traditional astrology.

Bradley, Donald - *Stock Market Prediction*, 1950. For stock market speculators.

Carter, Charles E. O. - *The Principles of Astrology*, 1925. English. Basic facts.

Clark, Brian - *The Sibling Constellation*, 1999. About sibling relationships.

Cunningham, Donna – *An Astrological Guide to Self-awareness*, 1978. One of the better.

Ebertin, Reinhold – *Cosmopsychology*, 1973. Pioneer in astrological research. Classic.

Ebertin, Reinhold - *The Combination of Stellar Influences* (KdG), 1940.

Ebertin, Reinhold – *Transits*, 1971. Complete review in English of all transits. "The small orange-colored."

Gauquelin, Michel - *The Spheres of Destiny*, 1980. Started as a skeptic but collected data in favor of astrology.

Greene, Liz - *Saturn: a New Look at an Old Devil*, 1976. Perhaps the best of books about the hardest of planets, Saturn.

Greene, Liz - *The Outer Planets & Their Cycles*, 1983. In-depth insight into the outer planets: Uranus, Neptune and Pluto.

Hand, Robert - *Planets in Transit*, 1976. ' Cookbook" and review of all transits. He's written many more.

Hodgson, Joan - *Astrology & Healing: Four Parts About the Elements*, 1982. In-depth analysis of the four elements with emphasis on the healing process.

Jones, Marc Edmund - *The Basics of Astrology*, 1976. Good textbook for beginners.

Lieber, A.L. & Agel, Jerome – *The Moon Effect*, 1982. Statistical research.

Marks, Tracy - *Turning Oppositions into Conjunctions*, 1980.

Parker, Derek & Julia - *Astrological Handbook*, 1973. Complete for beginners. Revised edition in 1991. My first.

Paul, Helen & O'Toole, Mary Bridget - *Interpreting the Houses*, 1976. A deeper analysis of the houses.

Robertson, Mark - *Critical Ages in Adult Life: the Transit of Saturn*, 1976. Deeper analysis of Saturn.

Robertson, Mark - *The 8th House: Sex, Death & Money*, 1976. Focus on Scorpio and the 8th House.

Rodden, Lois M. - *The American Book of Charts*, 1980. Today online for free in 2017. https://www.astro.com/astro-databank/Main_Page. Collection with hundreds of charts to study.

Skogkvist, Roland - *Scandinavian Tables of Houses*, 1982. First Swedish book with complete tables of houses for Swedish latitudes and longitudes.

Miscellaneous Litterature

Even here, some information, such as the publisher and ISBN numbers are missing, primarily because I do not have them any more.

Adrienne, Carol – *The Purpose of Your Life*, 1998. Co-worker of James Redfield.

Adrienne, Carol - *When Life Changes*, 2002.

Altea, Rosemary – *Proud Spirit*, 1997. Shamanism.

Bays, Brandon – *The Journey*, 1999.About curing cancer.

The Bible - Various Writers. Tiresome but a bit wise and sometimes fascinating.

Borgström, Georg - *Limits for Our Existence*, 1964. Early fighter for global justice. He has written several books.

Busch, Oscar - *How People Are intertwined: Millennial Memories from Four Earthly Lives*, 1984. Channelled book.

Chopra, Deepak - *Choosing the Joy*, 2003. One of several positive books by Chopra.

Clarke, Arthur C. - *2001: A Space Odyssey*, 1973. Based on the movie's script with the same name. One of my first "mind-blowers" in the cinema. Takes up the origin of man and into the future "and beyond."

Cleese, John - *So, Anyway*, 2014. Biography to laugh at very seriously.

Cleese, John & Skinner, Robyn – *Families, and How to Survive Them*, 1983. Humor-genius with comic explanations of difficult problems.

Cleese, John & Skinner, Robyn - *Life, and How to Survive It*, 1993. Wisdom and humor.

Cockell, Jenny - *Across Time and Death (A Mother's Search for Her past-life Children)*, 1993. Fantastic book on hypnotherapy recommended by author Brian Weiss.

Coelho, Paolo – *The Alchemist*, 1988. One of many by Coelho.

Coelho, Paolo – *Pilgrimage*, 1987. About the walk *Santiago de Compostela*.

Coelho, Paolo – Manuscrito encontrado em Accra (Port), 2012.

Cook, Grace, medium - *Sir Arthur Conan Doyle* [Sherlock Holmes] *Comes Back*, White Eagle. 1963. Channelled book. A gift from Sannmarie.

Fontana, Dr. David - *Meditation Manual*, 1992.

Freeman, Arthur & DeWolf, Rose - *The Ten Dumbest Mistakes Clever People Do and How to Avoid Them*, 1992. Cognitive psychology.

Fromm, Erich – *The Art of Loving*, 1956. Jewish psychoanalyst on the biology of love. Advocated humanistic socialism. Best book on love's different terms.

Govinda, Anagarika - *The Way of the White Clouds*, 1966. About Buddhist monks.

Grant, Joan & Kelsey, Denys - *All My Lives*, 1975. One of several they wrote about hypnosis regression.

Gray, John – *Mars and Venus in the Bedroom*, 1995. Relationships and sex.

Hadfield, Chris - *An Astronaut's Guide to Life on Earth*, 2013. Fascinating and universal about human conditions today.

Haley, Alex – *Roots,* 1977. Family history and slavery.

Hay, Lois L. - *You Can Heal Your Life*, 1987.

Hendrix, Harville - *Instead of Divorce - from Power Struggle to Cooperation*, 1988. Excellent for family counselors and therapists.

Hesse, Hermann – *Siddharta*, 1922. One of my absolute favorite authors on the meaning of life.

Hesse, Hermann – *Steppenwolf*, 1927. Favorite author.

Hultgren, Gunilla - *Road of Life - A Book of the Hopi Indians*, 1977.

Ingstad, Helge – *Trapper's Life*, 1952. Amazing book on survival in the wilderness of Canada in the 1920's. The author was born in 1899 and died in 2001, aged 101.

Jampolsky, Gerald - *LOVE Is Letting Go of Fear*, 1979. Based on *A Course in Miracles.*

Kharitidi, Olga - *The Master of Lucid Dreams*, 2001. Shamanism.

Kharitidi, Olga – *Entering the Circle*, 1996. Shamanism.

Korczak, Janusz - *The Child's Right to Respect*, 1929. Child psychology.

Krishnamurti, Jiddu – *Freedom from the Known*, 1974. My first spiritual discovery.

Lama, Dalai & Cutler, Howard C. – *The Art of Happiness! A Tutorial in the Art of Living*, 1998.

Larkin, Molly & Heart, Bear - *The Wind Is My Mother*, 1996. Wisdom of the shaman.

Larzon, Ann-Christin - *Love Gift*, 1989. Loving and informative about living with a child with Down's Syndrome.

Liedholm, Nils - *Football, Stars and Wine*, 1984. About soccer and astrology.

Lindahl, Hillevi - *The Girl from Atlantis*, 1990. Memories from the Atlantean culture.

Lindbohm, Dénis – *Fire of the Ego*, 1971. Reincarnation case.

MacLaine, Shirley - *Out on a Limb*, 1983. One of many spiritual adventures with Shirley about UFOs and meeting with Ambres (Sture Johansson) in Sweden. Also available as a movie with an authentic seance.

Macrae, Janet - *Therapeutic Touch, a Practical Guide*, 1988. Healing.

Martinus, Rolf - *Book of Life, Third Testament*, etc., 1975. Danish mystic. Recommended by Bert Yogson, Roger Algehov, et al. Fantastic books about Good and Evil.

Marx, Groucho - *Groucho and Me* (Biography). 1959. Wonderful spiritual medicine for the most part.

Mathis, Ranerås Michael - *The Time of Ascension*, 1995. Frequency increase in the New Age. About Marina Munk. One of many.

May, Rollo - *Love and Will*, 1972. Humanist psychologist.

McGraw, Dr. Phil - *Family First*, 2004.

McGraw, Dr. Phil – *Relationships*, 2000.

Missildine, W. Hugh, MD - *Your Inner Child of the Past*, 1963. Regression hypnosis.

Monroe, Robert A. - *Ultimate Journey*, 1994. UKU. Out of the body experiences.

Moody, Harry R & Carroll, David - *The Five Stages of the Soul*, 1997.

Munk, Marina, Mathis, Nina & Mikael - *The Great Mission: Conversation with Marina Munk about Earth's High Conscience (The Great Mission)*, 1994.

Munthe, Axel - *The Book about San Michele*, 1930. Fantastic book by Doctor Munthe. A must among your classics.

Newton, Michael - *Journey of Souls*, 1994. His first. Regression hypnosis.

Newton, Michael - *Life Between Lives Hypnotherapy - Michael Newton's Therapists Trained in LBL Hypnotherapy*, 2004.

Newton, Michael - *Memories of the Afterlife - Case Studies by Members* of *TNI* (The Newton Institute), 2009.

Newton, Michael - Memories of Life Between Lives. 2009. His third book.

Noll, Peter - *The Elapsed Time*, 1984. Living with the insight that one knows when to die.

Orwell, George – *1984*. 1949. He was right. Equally scary today. Also filmed classic from 1984.

Redfield, James - *The Celestine Prophesy*, 1994. First of many.

Rohn, Jim and Widener, Chris - Twelve Pillars, 2005. Synchronism.

Roman, Sanya - *Personal Power Through Awareness*, 1986. Channel for "Orin."

Rowling, Joan K. - Harry Potter (the whole series). Fictional fantasy but amazing experience and insight into exclusion and friendship. The books are a completely different experience from the movies.

Sandweiss, Samuel H. - Sai Baba the Holy Man and the Psychiatrist, 1975.

Sathya, Sai Baba - *Conversation with Jesus*,1982. One of many about Sai Baba.

Shelley, Mary – *Frankenstein,* 1818. Original classic book about the ultimate outcast. A fantastic book.

Shine, Betty – *Free Your Mind*, 1999. A medium, this was her last book. One of my favorites which I highly recommend.

Shine, Betty - *My Life As a Medium*, 1996. Fantastic book.

Shine, Betty – *Mind Waves*, 1993. Wonderful medium.

Stoltenberg, Inge - *The New Kingdom, Prophets of the Nordic Region*, 1984.

Sutphen, Dick - *Past Lives, Future Loves*, 1978. Regression hypnosis.

Sutphen, Dick - *Predestined Love*, 1988. Regression hypnosis.

Sutphen, Dick - *You Were Born Again to Be Together*, 1976. Regression.

Sörman, Py - *Saint Tomas More*, 1983. About the author of the book *Utopia*.

Tipping, Colin C. - *Radical Forgiveness*, 1997. (Gift from Heike in Los Angeles).

Tolkien, J.R.R. - *The Lord of the Rings*, 1954-1955. The original trilogy series. Indescribable journey.

Tolle, Eckhart - *The Power of Now - Your Way to Spiritual Wake Up*, 1997.

Tranströmer, Tomas - *The Truth Barrier*, 1978. Nobel Prize-winning poet.

Tuiavii from Tiavea - *Papalagi (The White Man)*, 1920. Naturalists in the South Sea. To live in harmony.

Twyman, James F. – *Emissary of Light*, 1996. Exciting spiritual journey into the unknown in Croatia and Bosnia. A gift from Ninni.

Waerland, Are - *In the Witch Chapel of the Disease*, 1934. About the importance of food. One of many amazing health books.

Walsh, Neale Donald - *Conversations with God*, several books from 1995 onwards.

White Eagle - *The Road of the Soul - Esoteric Astrology*, 1959. Swedish White Eagle Lodge.

Yogananda Paramahansa - *Autobiography of a Yogi*, 1946. One of my first spiritual "kicks." Hard but unbeatable.

Yogson, Bert - *Life Force, Meditation & Modern Yoga*, 1998. Practical life vision.

Yogson, Bert - *Reincarnation, Sexualism, Life Sense*, 1989. In-depth wisdom.

Yogson, Bert - *Yoga, Meditation, Reincarnation*, 1973. One of my first and most important books written by my first teacher in Life Art.

Zukav, Gary - *The Seat of the Soul*, 1989. Trust your intuition.

Films

I have deliberately omitted many of my major favorites and many more other famous movies, otherwise the list would flood the entire book.

The movies below are just a selection that are a bit odd (but in my opinion important movies), and I have tried to comment on what they are about. Film is an important medium to tell and enrich others about their experiences. Much pleasure!

Amour (2012) Tender French film about aging.

An Inconvenient Truth (2006) with Al Gore about the climate threat.

Before the Flood (2016) Leonardo di Caprio on climate change.

Bigger Than Life (1956) About the complications of the first experiments with Cortison. James Mason.

Blackfish (2013) Awesome film about killer whales in captivity.

Bowling for Columbine (2002) Oscar-awarded documentary by Michael Moore about the high school shootings.

Brother, Can You Spare a Dime? (1975) Documentary about the great depression in the 30's.

Capitalism: a Love Story (2009) Michael Moore on the world economy.

Christiane F. - Wir kinder vom Bahnhof Zoo (We Are Children from the Bahnhof Zoo) (1981) Authentic and touching about a young girl in 70's Berlin drawn down into the drugswamp. With music by David Bowie. Many consider this the best "drug film."

Citizenfour (2014) Documentary about whistle-blower Edward Snowden.

Conversations with God (2006) based on the book by Neale Donald Walsch.

Days of Wine and Roses (1962) Drama on alcoholism with Jack Lemmon.

Disconnect (2012) Unpleasant film about the impact of the Internet.

What Dreams May Come (1998) Unpleasant but fascinating drama about death, suicide and life after this. With Robin Williams and Max von Sydow.

Earthlings (2005) Terribly unpleasant and scary documentary about how man treats animals and cattle for food production and profit. WARNING! Not for the very sensitive!

Fahrenheit 451 (1966) Dystopic sci-fi about the future where books are forbidden.

Fahrenheit 9/11 (2004) Michael Moore about speculation around the WTC.

Food, Inc. (2008) Documentary about the food industry in the United States and what it actually contains (About GMO).

The Birthday (2000) Unbelievable film by Richard Hobert with an anonymous astrologer as an extra. The final chapter of the seven deadly sins.

Gaby: A True Story (1987) Distinct depiction of a severely handicapped girl and her struggle for her education. With Liv Ullman as the mother.

I Am Sam (2001) Oscar-nominated film about an easy-minded father who fight for his rights as a parent. With Sean Penn.

I, Claudius (1976) One of my favorites in the jungle of television shows today. Still in place 40 on Imdb list with 9.0 out of 10 points. About the ancient, royal Roman family history and the limping, stuttering Claudius.

Jesus of Nazareth (1977) Fantastic series with lots of famous stars.

Koyaanisqatsi (1982) Godfrey Reggio's epic description of humanity. Music by Philip Glass. No dialogue, just picture and music.

Lost Weekend (1945) One of the first films on alcoholism that won four Oscars, among them, Best Picture and Best Actor, Ray Milland.

Mary & Max (2009) Awesome animated adult film that deals with exclusion and Asperger's syndrome, which lies on TOP-250 on Imdb.

Mommie Dearest (1981) Revealing about the movie star Joan Crawford's life and morbid behavior against her children.

My Name is Khan (2010) Strongly speaking out on the debate about being a Muslim in the United States today and at the same time struggeling with Asperger's syndrome.

Nineteen Eighty-Four (1984) Filmed version of George Orwell's book with Richard Burton and John Hurt. Wonderful dystopic and still scary today.

*Oceans (*2009) Extremely beautiful and important documentary about life and our own existence.

Patch Adams (1998) Astonishing feel-good film with Robin Williams, based on a true person who changed the entire care debate in the United States through his positive and humorous way of caring for his patients.

Persepolis (2007) Artistic animated adult film about Iran's political history.

Pink Floyd The Wall (1982) Epic musical film about exclusion, racism and drug abuse. Music by Roger Waters & Pink Floyd. Bit-wise animation.

Powaqqatsi (1988) The continuation by Godfrey Reggio with emphasis on different cultures on earth.

Racing Extinction (2015) Oscar-nominated documentary about endangered species.

Requiem for a Dream (2000) Well-made and unpleasant film by Darren Aronofsky about both drugs and drug abuse, with Jared Leto, Jennifer Connelly and Ellen Burstyn.

Shine (1996) Oscar-winning drama about the real concert pianist David Helfgott who also married an astrologer. Wonderful Oscar-winning Geoffrey Rush.

Sicko (2007) Michael Moore's post on health care.

Super Size Me (2004) Morgan Spurlock's film about living exclusively on McDonald's food.

The Cove (2009) Oscar-rewarded documentary about dolphin slaughtering in Japan.

The Miracle Worker (1962) Reality-based drama about Helen Keller who lived as blind and deaf and learned to read and speak.

The Story of Film: An Odyssey (2011) Absolutely fantastic movie history in 15 parts.

Thrive (2011) Strong movement with revealing secrets, both globally and politically, and suggestions for options for our survival. Available on Youtube. Well worth every minute.

Triumph des Willens (1935) Scary documentary about Nazism by German director Leni Riefenstahl.

Tuesdays with Morrie (1999) Fantastic low-key, reality-based drama that addresses the diseases Lou Gehrig or ALS. With Jack Lemmon and Hank Azaria.

Zeitgeist (2007) Revealing documentary about society's invisible structures and how we are manipulated by a few super rich.

"Outside The Wall"

All alone, or in twos

The ones who really love you

Walk up and down outside the wall

Some hand in hand

Some gathering together in bands

The bleeding hearts and the artists

Make their stand

And when they've given you their all

Some stagger and fall after all it's not easy

banging your heart against some mad buggers

Wall

(from album *The Wall* – Pink Floyd – 1979)

FEEL FREE TO TAKE PART IN

HEALING
THE ASTROLOGER´S
WORLD

*(*July 2016.Astrologer with blueberries in his hand. Photo Pia Stengard)

THE
END?